PERFUMERY AND KINDRED ARTS

PERFUMERY AND KINDRED ARTS

A COMPREHENSIVE TREATISE ON PERFUMERY

CONTAINING

A HISTORY OF PERFUMES,

A COMPLETE DETAILED DESCRIPTION OF THE RAW MATERIALS AND APPARATUS USED IN THE PERFUMER'S ART

R. S. CRISTIANI

GYAN

Published by

Gyan Publishing House
5, Ansari Road
Daryaganj, New Delhi-110002
Phone: 011-47034999, 9811692060
E-mail: books@gyanbooks.com

Distribution Network
gyanbooks.com
India, USA, Canada, UK, Australia, France

ISBN : 978-81-212-9454-6 (PB)
First Published, 1877

2nd Impression 2023

Printed at: Gyan Press, Delhi.

PERFUMERY AND KINDRED ARTS
Author: R. S. CRISTIANI

PERFUMERY AND KINDRED ARTS.

A COMPREHENSIVE

TREATISE ON PERFUMERY

CONTAINING

A HISTORY OF PERFUMES,

A COMPLETE DETAILED DESCRIPTION OF THE RAW MATERIALS AND APPARATUS USED IN THE PERFUMER'S ART;

WITH

THOROUGH PRACTICAL INSTRUCTIONS, CAREFUL FORMULÆ, AND ADVICE AS TO THE FABRICATION OF ALL THE BEST PREPARATIONS OF THE DAY:

INCLUDING

ESSENCES, TINCTURES, EXTRACTS, SPIRITS, WATERS, VINEGARS, POMADES, POWDERS, PAINTS, OILS, EMULSIONS, COSMETICS, INFUSIONS, PASTILS, TOOTH POWDERS AND WASHES, CACHOUS, HAIR DYES, SACHETS, ESSENTIAL OILS, FLAVORING EXTRACTS, ETC.,

AND FULL DETAILS FOR MAKING AND MANIPULATING FANCY TOILET SOAPS, SHAVING CREAMS, ETC., BY NEW AND IMPROVED METHODS.

WITH AN APPENDIX,

GIVING

DIRECTIONS FOR MAKING DOMESTIC WINES, CORDIALS, LIQUORS, CANDIES, JELLIES, SYRUPS, ETC., AND FOR PERFUMING AND FLAVORING SEGARS, SNUFF, AND TOBACCO, AND MISCELLANEOUS RECIPES FOR VARIOUS USEFUL ANALOGOUS ARTICLES.

BY

R. S. CRISTIANI,

CONSULTING CHEMIST AND PERFUMER, PHILADELPHIA.

PHILADELPHIA:
HENRY CAREY BAIRD & CO.,
INDUSTRIAL PUBLISHERS, BOOKSELLERS, AND IMPORTERS,
810 WALNUT STREET.
LONDON:
SAMPSON LOW, MARSTON, SEARLE & RIVINGTON,
CROWN BUILDINGS, 188 FLEET STREET.
1877.

PREFACE.

In giving to the trade and the public generally the result of his experience of thirty years in the manufacture and sale of articles appertaining to the perfumer's art, the author does not claim to have originated every preparation here enumerated. He does, however, claim that, with this experience, combined with a knowledge of chemistry, both theoretical and practical, he is enabled properly to judge of the materials of which these articles are composed, as well as of the most simple and the right mode of compounding them. Accordingly, he has adopted an original and simplified system in the arrangement of the subjects and in the preparation of the various compounds, which will enable any one of ordinary intelligence readily soon to fit himself to produce every valuable variety of perfume, soap, and cosmetic at present known.

The recipes and formulas given have been carefully revised, and are generally devoid of all substances which can be at all injurious; and will be found to be the most pleasant and the most useful for their various purposes possible. While a large body of them are entirely original, the author has for obvious reasons refrained from adding his name to any but a few. In the Appendix will be found many recipes of a kindred nature, which, while useful, either did not come under any of his special classifications, or were not deemed of sufficient importance to be placed in the body of the book.

Most of the existing works on perfumery belong to one of two classes: the first filled with old and obsolete, or impossible recipes of no use whatever at the present time; the second written in an ambiguous style and intended to direct attention to the virtues of particular preparations made and sold by the authors of these books, but with no intention whatever that the reader shall be informed how such preparations are actually made. In this connection, the present author would state that he has no secrets of this character which he has attempted or desired to withhold from his readers.

The climate of the United States is so diversified, and in many parts so well adapted to the cultivation of numerous plants which are useful to the perfumer, that the author hopes by this treatise to awaken attention to the practicability of establishing flower farms and orange groves, as well as to the utilization of many indigenous plants now neglected, but with odors peculiarly adapted to the uses of this art.

In a national point of view the industries of perfumery and toilet soaps are of great importance; and with us, while giving increased employment to labor, their development will add increased wealth to the country, and enable us to become daily more and more independent of the supplies we now receive from abroad; and finally, in time, ourselves to become large exporters of such products, for which there is a great and growing market throughout the world.

PHILADELPHIA, Sept. 15, 1877.

CONTENTS.

CHAPTER I.
INTRODUCTORY.

CHAPTER II.
HISTORY OF PERFUMES.

CHAPTER III.
THE CULTURE OF FLOWERS, ETC., FOR PERFUMES.

CHAPTER IV.
MATERIALS USED IN PERFUMERY.

CHAPTER V.
THE LABORATORY AND ITS REQUIREMENTS.

CHAPTER VI.

Tinctures.

CHAPTER VII.

Extracts and Bouquets.

CHAPTER VIII.

Aromatic and Toilet Waters.

CHAPTER IX.

Sachet Powders, Etc.

CHAPTER X.

Preparations for the Skin.

ROUGES AND PAINTS FOR THE FACE.

CHAPTER XI.

Pomades and Cosmetics.

CHAPTER XII.

Hair Oils and Hair Tonics.

CHAPTER XIII.

Hair Dyes and Depilatories.

CHAPTER XIV.

The Teeth, the Gums, and the Breath.

CHAPTER XV.

Essential Oils and their Tests.

CHAPTER XVI.

Distilled Waters and Essences.

CHAPTER XVII.

Flavoring Extracts and Fruit Flavors.

CHAPTER XVIII.

TOILET SOAPS. IMPLEMENTS AND INGREDIENTS.

CHAPTER XIX.

TOILET SOAPS. MANIPULATION.

CHAPTER XX.

TOILET SOAPS BY THE COLD PROCESS.

CHAPTER XXI.

CASTILE SOAP FROM COTTON-SEED OIL.

CHAPTER XXII.

COMPOUNDING TOILET SOAPS.

CHAPTER XXIII.

MISCELLANEOUS SOAPS.

CHAPTER XXIV.

MILLING AND MOULDING TOILET SOAPS.

APPENDIX.

SECTION I.

SYRUPS, JELLIES, CANDIES—THEIR FLAVORS AND COLORS.

SECTION II.

LIQUORS, CORDIALS, DOMESTIC WINES, ETC.

LIQUORS AND CORDIALS.

SECTION III.

FLAVORS AND PERFUMES FOR SEGARS AND TOBACCO.

SECTION IV.

WEIGHTS AND MEASURES.

SECTION V.

MISCELLANEOUS FORMULAS.

PERFUMERY AND KINDRED ARTS.

CHAPTER I.

INTRODUCTORY.

SOLOMON remarks, "Ointments and perfumes rejoice the heart." Of all the five senses the faculty of smelling affords the most exquisite pleasure. Although to many it is the least valued, to the refined and cultivated it is the most esteemed; for those who neglect to develop this pleasant faculty fail to appreciate—

> "Nature's swift and silent working hand.
> The garden grows, and fills the
> Liberal air with sweetest odors,"

and are often led to breathe vitiated air. Thus poison and malaria enter the system by neglecting the warning given by the nose, that outpost of the animal citadel. All persons using and appreciating perfumes become most sensitive to the presence of bad air.

If refinement consists in the knowledge of the best mode of enjoying the higher faculties we possess, we must learn to distinguish the melody of perfumes, as well as the harmony of color, form, and sound, and enjoy sweet odors equally with all other pleasures so liberally bestowed to gratify our senses.

In a sanitary point of view, the use of perfumes is

in the highest degree valuable. For although we cannot claim great curative properties for them, yet at the same time we hold that their moderate use is more beneficial than otherwise, and their refreshing properties have often been known to assist in restoring the invalid to health.

Many think the use of perfumes and cosmetics prejudicial to health, but in refutation it is only necessary to say, that when the cholera prevailed in Paris and London, all those persons who worked in the laboratories of the perfumers escaped its ravages; and as further evidence, when the Dutch on the island of Ternate destroyed the clove tree the colony suffered from epidemics and diseases unknown before.

The large and increasing consumption of perfumery throughout the civilized world has made it one of the most important of the arts, and as we, in this country, increase in wealth and refinement, the use of perfumery keeps pace with other luxuries. The constantly increasing value of perfumery as an article of commerce, has led to the enrichment of many parts of the world. Several districts of France, Italy, India, and Turkey, where the flowers and materials are cultivated exclusively for the purpose, give employment to large and prosperous populations.

It may be in vain to expect that the United States will at this time devote much capital and labor to the cultivation of the raw materials of perfumery, yet it cannot be long before we shall see the importance of it. With our varied climate and soil, and our usual enterprise, we may soon hope to rival the old world in its present monopoly.

The writer, after an experience of thirty years in the manufacture and sale of perfumery and fancy soaps, is led to think that he can usefully apply his knowledge and experience as a guide to the manufacturer and dealer, to the proper formulæ for preparing the various articles now in use, and as a chemist and pharmacist in cautioning the purchaser against deleterious and improper compositions.

From this long experience he is impelled to the preparation of this treatise by a knowledge of the many errors of judgment committed by those who have no proper understanding of the harmony of perfumes, and who, from a want of this knowledge, often use improper odors, or such as are useless and wasted for the purposes intended, and who may, by his assistance, be led to the use of those which are appropriate to their several manufactures. For, singular as it may appear to the uninitiated, each article made seems to require a perfume properly adapted to its nature or to the use to which it is to be applied.

Until quite recently, those who followed the art of perfumery endeavored to surround it by a mysterious secrecy. Now, however, all may learn the secrets of the craft; for although a chemical art, and a knowledge of the elements of that science, and a study of the properties of the materials, will greatly facilitate an operator in it, such are by no means absolutely essential to skill and success with a person of ordinary intelligence.

The author has also a desire that his treatise may impart to the people of the United States the fact of the adaptability of their country to the cultivation of much of the material used by the perfumer. Hitherto our attention has been more particularly devoted to the more useful arts, and we have and still do import from foreign countries nearly all the finer goods and the most important materials used. Yet there are so many parts of our country which possess the proper climate for the growth and maturity of the flowers now used in perfumery, and which doubtless have native plants from which new and pleasant odors may be extracted, that attention may properly be called to the importance of this subject; so that the plants may be cultivated for its use, and new discoveries made which will promote it, and thus add to our wealth and our refinement and pleasure.

To France we must yield the palm of being in the first rank in the art of perfumery; to it we have to look for the finest material used in its fabrication. England, by virtue of her moist climate, has attained superiority in the growth of a few plants, whose odors are much prized. India and Turkey also devote much attention to the culture of many fine and indispensable articles. To our own country we look for but few articles now used by the perfumer.

In my history of perfumes I shall try to interest my readers with a view of the progress of perfumery from the earliest times to the present; how the ancients used it in all their sacred rites; and how it was gradually adapted to private uses; how it was studied and cherished by all the various nations which held in turn the sceptre of intelligence and civilization; how it was transmitted from Persia to Egypt, to the Jews, to the Assyrians, the Greeks, the Romans, and the Arabs, and finally to modern nations. I shall try to trace its course through all these different phases and record its progress down to the present period.

Who has not experienced that indescribable emo

tion that invades the whole being, the soul melting in rapture, when nature awakes from her slumbers in the spring and shakes off the trammels of hoary winter, and with her richest perfumes fills the balmy air with refreshing fragrance? Does it not silently fill each and every one of us with homage and gratitude to the Creator of the great blessings bestowed upon us, and as Thomson sings—

> "Soft roll your incense, herbs, and fruits, and flowers,
> In mingled clouds to Him whose sun exalts,
> Whose breath perfumes you, and whose pencil paints."
>
> * * * * * * * *
>
> "Fair-handed Spring unbosoms every grace.
> Throws out the snowdrop and the crocus first;
> The daisy, primrose, violet darkly blue,
> And polyanthus of unnumbered dyes;
> The yellow wall-flower, stained with iron brown,
> And lavish stock that scents the garden round."

Besides these emotions excited by pleasant odors, they have other and charming influences on the mind. They are associated with our most pleasant enjoyments, and have also the property of refreshing the memory, recalling scenes in which they held a prominent part, or in which entered for pleasure or sorrow—

> "The smell of violets hidden in the green,
> Pours back into my empty soul and frame,
> The time when I remembered to have been
> Joyful and free from blame."

Some delicate people may be affected painfully by certain odors, but it is generally imaginary. While to some a musky scent would give a headache, the odors of the citron would afford relief. Dr. Capelli relates the story of a lady who could not bear the smell of the rose, and fainted on receiving a visit from a friend who carried one, and yet the fatal flower was only artificial, showing that the bad effects attributed to perfumes by some persons are more or less the result of imagination, or come from mental action through association of previous ideas as to the effects.

Desiring to write a practical treatise, I have endeavored to keep in view the capabilities and facilities which the American perfumer may possess for procuring the principal materials he needs in his art, and my experience has caused me to adopt a system of manipulation and terms most easily understood by him. The various terms and numerous systems of the European books result in much confusion to the American perfumer, and while there may appear a certain monotony there will be found in experience a great variety in effect. And let me here remark that much attention should be bestowed upon the cleanliness and neatness, if not elegance, of putting up the different articles, the additional trouble and expense always being repaid in the enhanced price or increased sale of the article. In the articles of glassware this country now rivals Europe in its products, and is constantly improving. So also in the porcelain jars and earthen-ware a great advance has been made, but for many of the finest goods we still go to Europe.

In my chapters on soaps, I have also kept to the most practical instructions, for, though a chemical art, it is most easily understood when plain terms and results are given. Having all the different materials at hand, or made ready for our use, there should be no difficulty to a person of average intelligence in conducting the different branches and processes of the art. I have given my formulæ and manipulations, based upon practice, and have commented on new substances to produce new articles, or to improve the methods formerly in use.

The American mind, open to all improvements, taking a lively interest in all that is new and meritorious, is constantly alive to new methods and the latest results. Let this desire continue, for it is this interest and this desire for improvement that stimulate the manufacturer to devote attention to the production of novelties, and an endeavor to outstrip his rivals in making something that will excel them, and from this rivalry, the people are benefited in having goods constantly improving in style, elegance, and quality.

CHAPTER II.

HISTORY OF PERFUMES.

THE origin of perfumery, like most of the ancient arts, is shrouded in obscurity. Arabia has long enjoyed, and still retains the name of the land of perfumes. The first mention of perfumes is of their use as incense, as man, in first discovering their nature, in his first emotions of pleasure and gratitude, offered up their fragrance in worship to his deity; hence the derivation of the word, per (through) fumum (smoke), clearly indicating that perfumery was first recognized by burning aromatic woods, spices, and gums.

Perfumes seem to have been first imported from Persia, and were very important articles of commerce between that country and Egypt. The caravans that traversed the great deserts carried great quantities of gums and spices, as the Egyptians, the most civilized and cultivated of ancient nations, used them in great profusion, both in their sacred rites and for private purposes.

From the Egyptians the use of perfumes was transmitted to the Jews, thence to the Assyrians, the Greeks, the Romans, the Arabs, and the Turks. The Holy Scriptures furnish us with abundant details of the use of perfumes, as Moses was commanded to speak to the Children of Israel that their offerings to the temples should be spices and gums and anointing oils.

In those ancient days, the priests alone seem to have possessed the art and mystery of compounding perfumes for private uses as well as for incense for their altars, and their use became very great, and some that have been excavated with the mummies retain their odor after the lapse of nearly four thousand years.

At festivals, public or private, perfumes and flowers were used in great profusion, and incense was burned, and music charmed the ear; showing the great luxuriance and refinement of that period. To the Egyptians is due the invention of the system of baths that was handed down to all Eastern nations, and imitated by Greeks and Romans, as also the custom of embalming the dead, which was also pactised by the Jews, as the Gospel mentions that Nicodemus "brought a mixture of myrrh and aloes about an hundred weight, then took they the body of Jesus and wound it in linen cloths with the spices, as the manner of the Jews is to bury."[1]

[1] The Balm of Gilead, so often mentioned in Scripture, was from a ridge of mountains running southward from Mount Lebanon, east of the Holy Land, which was covered with the shrub that yields the gum, and many fields in Palestine were full of these balsam trees.

The Asiatics acquired the use of perfumes and practised it in great profusion, and flowers were extensively cultivated, as we read of Nineveh and Babylon among the wonders of the world, and descriptions of their gardens, their altars on high places. And, according to Herodotus, the consumption of perfumes was so great, that besides the production of their own country, they received from Arabia a thousand talents of frankincense, and he tells us of the great consumption of aromatics and perfumes, and of the great cost of many of these scents, and of their universal use.

All these nations paid great attention to the hair and beard, which were usually lavishly perfumed and curled. Many wore wigs instead of their natural hair as a protection against the heat of the sun. The custom of anointing the whole body with oil after bathing was due, no doubt, to the same cause, as this custom is yet practised by the natives of Africa as a protection against the extreme heat of the climate.

The Greeks, whose deities were as numerous as the stars, almost always associated perfumes with the presence of the gods and goddesses, and attributed skill in the compounding of perfumes to the marvellous, and gave the name of magicians to those who prepared them. Venus is described as sprinkled with perfumes, and Pallas, the goddess of wisdom, anointed with oil when practising the exercises of the *palastra*, and to their use is attributed the great beauty of Helen of Troy.

Perfumes were generally supposed to possess great medicinal virtues, so much so as to cause the recipes for many of the most celebrated essences and cosmetics to be inscribed on marble tablets in some of their temples. The rose in those days was considered no less beneficial than beautiful, and formed the basis of many remedies.

The Romans as they advanced in civilization adopted the luxuries and habits of the nations they conquered, and used perfumes in the same profusion as the Greeks, from whom they seem to have acquired the use, as they were of the same general nature. They used them at public festivals, and for private and religious purposes, and after burning their dead mixed perfumes with the ashes in the funeral vase.

So great and universal was this use of perfumes that their generals when going upon a military campaign carried essences and cosmetics to adorn their persons, and among the spoils in the camp of Darius, Alexander found quantities of these substances with all the luxurious appliances of the toilet.

In the ruins of Pompeii have been discovered handsome bottles with perfumes and ointments, and all the appurtenances of the toilet and bath which tend to show the refinement of the ancient Romans.

The Roman perfumers called Unguentari occupied a certain part of the city in the Velabrum, and in Capua, a city noted for its luxury, they occupied a whole street of the town called Seplasia, and some of their products are described as exceedingly costly.

The custom of using flowers and perfumes at their feasts was very common, and no banquet was considered complete without them, and the decoration with flowers is described as very profuse, and even their drinking cups were adorned with flowers.

Distillation is said to have been discovered by an Arabian doctor named Avecinna, who was also the first to apply the principles of chemistry so imperfectly known to earlier nations. To him also is ascribed the invention of rose-water, which was considered a great discovery, and was at the same time used as a remedy for nearly all diseases, as well as a perfume and cosmetic. It was customary to use this perfume to sprinkle the floors of apartments, and bottles were formed for the purpose, which were also used to sprinkle guests when they arrived at a feast.

Mahomet encouraged the use of perfumes among his followers, and makes frequent mention of them as a part of the many attractions of his paradise, and musk is often named by him. This perfume, so much admired by all orientals, is the strongest and most lasting, and it seems singular that the warmer the climate the greater is the love of strong perfumes, for we read of a mosque with the mortar of which this perfume was mixed, which gave out its perfume whenever the sun shone upon it.

The oriental ladies use great quantities of costly perfumes and cosmetics, and the duties of the toilet are their most important occupation, no doubt tending to preserve their personal charms. Living in an atmosphere of fragrance, they are kept in a state of dreamy languor, which to them may be the nearest approach to happiness. They are noted for their skill in retaining their charms by these various means.

Lady Mary Wortley Montague, who lived many years in eastern lands, gives us many interesting details of the habits and customs of the orientals, of their costumes and mode of dressing the hair, and the uses of cosmetics and perfumes.

In India perfumes are used in the form of incense in sacrifices offered in their temples and upon their altars, and the private use of unguents and perfumes is very great among the wealthy and their priests color their faces with an ointment of saffron, and when the suttee was in vogue, widows perished on piles of burning aromatic wood. To that country we are indebted for much of the celebrated otto of rose, as at Ghazepore, situated on the Ganges, near Benares, the flower is cultivated for the manufacture of this universally admired perfume.

Among the celestials perfumes have been in use from the earliest times, and if it be true as they claim that their history extends to thousands of years before our own, they may have been in use for countless ages. Joss-sticks and tinsel paper are burned as incense to their gods, and the consumption is very great, as Canton alone is said to have ten thousand manufactories. Morning and evening they burn them before their idols. Noted for their many ceremonies, they are also celebrated for their profuse use of perfumes in nearly all their observances of a public or private nature.

The Chinese have an alkaline earth called "Keen," which they use as a substitute for soap, of which they make but little; but they use various cosmetics, and shave their heads except a tuft on the top, giving occupation to a great many barbers, who also combine bleeding and other surgical operations with their calling.

In Japan the customs are similar to those of China, and their perfumes are much the same, although, being a more progressive country, they are gradually adopting the products, as well as the manners of foreign countries, and now import from Europe many articles of perfumery and cosmetic. The exhibit they made at our Centennial attracted great attention, and helped to demonstrate to our countrymen the great advance which they have made in arts and manufactures.

The use of perfumes became almost obsolete in Europe after the fall of the Roman empire, but only for a brief space of time, for after the Crusades it again revived and soon became in general use. The gallant knights brought home to their lady-loves the far-famed perfumes of the East, and specimens of the wonderful cosmetics by means of which the beauties of the harems were enabled to preserve their charms.

Perfumers came into prominent notice in the twelfth century in France when Philip Augustus granted them a charter which continued in force for several centuries, and was renewed and enlarged by Louis XIV. in 1658, and the craft became a very important one, and we read of the use of their products in vast quantities.

The Arabs, when they conquered Spain, introduced their numerous perfumes, and also the general use of their celebrated system of baths.

Alcoholic perfumes and essences do not appear to have been known before the fourteenth century, when Elizabeth, Queen of Hungary, invented the celebrated Hungary water, and is said to have by its use retained her beauty until she was past seventy years of age.

In Italy, with the revival of the fine arts in the fifteenth century, luxuries were common among the merchant princes, and perfumes were largely consumed, and were adopted by all people of fashion, and the first book on the subject was written at this time, which contained many curious recipes. Catherine de Medicis brought with her to France a Florentine named René, who established the first perfumery shop in Paris, which was a great resort for the beaux and belles of that period.

During the reign of Henry III., the use and abuse of perfumes was denounced by the satirists of the day, and a book published at that time gives many curious recipes for perfuming gloves and various cosmetics, with recipes for a specific perfume against the plague, and a marvellous water warranted to make the ladies who used it beautiful forever.

Perfumes in England were not in general use before the reign of Queen Elizabeth, when they seem to have been brought from Italy, and soon became fashionable. During the plague perfumes were extensively used as a preventive, and the prophylactic property of scents cannot be doubted, for when the cholera prevailed in Paris and London those who worked in the perfumery laboratories were exempt from its ravages; nor has it been very long since medical practitioners used to carry on the tops of their canes cassolettes filled with aromatics, which they held to their noses when visiting contagious cases.

Perfumes were in great favor in the reign of Charles II., "the merry monarch;" and the fashion of wearing patches on the face was common among the ladies, as it was supposed to give piquancy to the features; and the use of hair powder was first introduced about this time, and continued for over two hundred years.

Louis XIV. is said to have had a strong dislike to all perfumes; but it may be doubted, for, by some, he is called the sweet-smelling monarch, and they were extensively used by his family and by all his courtiers. In the reign of his successor, Louis XV., they were used in great extravagance, as fashion ordained their use in ever-varying routine, each day having its particular odors, the apartment of the palace being one day perfumed with tuberose, and the next with musk and saffron; nor were they confined to the fair sex, for the gallants gloried in all the favorite scents of their mistresses, and thus were often recognized by smelling of the favorite perfumes of the fair ones who enslaved them.

Italy, in those days, excelled in the fineness of its products, and supplied the rest of Europe with the best perfumes then in use; and we read of large sums being expended for Italian perfumery and cosmetics by the Court of France.

During the sanguinary days of the French Revolution, the use of perfumes was very much interrupted, but revived with other luxuries with the advent of Napoleon; and the Empress Josephine is said to have been passionately fond of them. About this time the venders of perfumery also sold various sorts of medicines and cure-alls, and were usually strolling charlatans, in gorgeous apparel, in elegant equipages, who addressed a gaping multitude extolling the virtues of their nostrums; but when they became obnoxious they were suppressed. The calling has since assumed greater consequence and importance, until, at present, it is in point of respectability excelled by none.

The use of perfumes is not confined to civilized and refined countries, but is extensively practised among barbarous and savage nations; though of perfumes of sweet scent they may know but little, yet to them a rancid smell may be the most pleasant.

The African chief anoints his hair and whole body with oil, often perfumed with herbs; though this practice may be intended as a protection against the rays of a scorching sun, and his well-polished skin may be with him as fashionable as our shining boots.

Dr. Livingstone and other African explorers give very interesting accounts of the manners and customs of that country, and often speak of the use of cosmetics and the fantastical modes of dressing the hair or wool, to which they seem to devote much care and attention.

The natives of Australia, though they have many and rare perfumes and flowers, seem to prefer a bad smell to any perfume, which is also said to be the case with the Esquimaux. The custom of tattooing, which may be called a permanent cosmetic, is practised by the natives of New Zealand and by the Polynesians, who pride themselves upon the elegant arabesques that decorate their persons.

The Tahitian women, who are generally handsome, devote much care and attention to their hair, which is usually long and beautiful, and use cocoa-nut oil, with various scents, in dressing it. The South American Indians also decorate their heads and hair with flowers and ribbons, and cut it straight off in front, something like the custom now prevalent among the votaries of fashion.

In our country the Indians use a great variety of paints, that may be called cosmetics; and the various colors have a certain symbolism, as red denotes joy, while black signifies grief. The chief gives much time and trouble to this ornamentation, and endeavors to make himself frightful to his enemies or lovely in the eyes of his squaw.

Of the fashions and perfumery of our own time it were needless to write, as they are fresh in the memory of all; nor can we venture to give an opinion of their merits, as ladies alone are the best judges of what is fashionable and becoming, as well as to what is in good taste as a perfume.

At the present day perfumes have become a necessity to all civilized nations, and the art of perfumery has, with the aid of chemistry, attained a leading rank, and the constantly increasing demand for fine odors testifies to their usefulness and efficiency.

CHAPTER III.

THE CULTURE OF FLOWERS, ETC., FOR PERFUMES.

OUR readers have seen how we have endeavored to trace the history of perfumery from the earliest times up to the present period. We will now try to portray its present standing, uses, values, and great importance to commerce and to the world.

Flowers, from whatever point of view we regard them, are replete with interest, and are a source of gratification and pleasure to all mankind. There is no heart, savage or civilized, that does not feel their influence in some degree; they gratify the painter's eye, they charm the poet's fancy, and science finds engrossing interest in studying their structure and qualities.

That man was not created for toil alone is evident, and among the many pleasures given him for his enjoyment, flowers are not the least important; they delight him in childhood, they interest him in manhood, and they accompany him to the grave.

How important then is the art of extracting their fragrance; for while flowers please and gratify the senses while fresh, they soon wither and fade. Shakspeare says:—

> "But flowers distilled, though with winter meet,
> Lose but their show, their substance still lives sweet."

Science teaches us the properties of perfumes, and art gives us the manner of their preparation; for flowers grow and yield their fragrance in all climates, but those that grow in warm latitudes are most prolific in odor, while those of colder climes are generally the sweetest. They owe their fragrance to molecules that require many different modes of extraction, which we shall describe anon.

Though from the East we still obtain many valuable and indispensable perfumes, the south of Europe is now the only reliable source of supply, Cannes, Grasse and Nice being the principal seats of flower culture for commerce; though we receive many odorous substances from India, Algeria, Turkey, Italy, and Spain, in fact wherever the plants and flowers grow the most abundantly, and the extraction of their odor is the most convenient and profitable.

From the geographical position of the south of France and of Italy, this district possesses the most favorable climate peculiarly fitted for bringing to perfection the most odoriferous of flowers, such as the rose, jasmine, orange, etc.

Thus they are cultivated on the largest scale, and there are hundreds of houses engaged in their production and sale, which give employment to many thousands of people and riches to the State.

In these countries each plant seems to have its alloted place, as Cannes excels in the culture of the rose, cassie, jasmine, and tuberose; Nismes of rosemary and lavender, so Nice is celebrated for its violet and mignonette, while to Sicily we look for the citron and the orange.

To Italy we are chiefly indebted for the citric odors, as lemon, bergamot, cedrat, and limette, with neroli, petit-grain, etc.; from Turkey we receive the indispensable otto of rose. Algeria also is now making some progress in this manufacture, while Spain and Portugal furnish some odors, but not in the quantity that we should look for from their floral wealth. British India gives us cinnamon, cloves, patchouly, santal, ylang-ylang, and many odoriferous gums and spices. China yields musk, civet, and ambergris, which, though not pleasant in themselves, yet blended with other odors give them piquancy, strength, and durability.

England excels in two important perfuming ingredients, viz., lavender and peppermint, for which its moist climate seems peculiarly adapted, as the plants have a mildness of fragrance unknown in other countries.

The United States has but two or three perfumes that as yet have commercial value, though we may hope that our extensive country and varied climate will soon produce many valuable materials and novelties for the perfumer's use.

The odors of plants exist in different parts of them: sometimes in the wood, as in cedar and santal; sometimes in the leaves, as in patchouly and thyme; in the seeds, as in caraway and tonquin; in the bark, as in cinnamon and cascarilla; and again in the roots, as in orris and vitivert. Some plants yield more than one odor; the orange, for instance, has three—one from the flowers called neroli, one from the leaves called petit-grain, another from the rind of the fruit called portugal or orange; and on this account is perhaps the most valuable plant cultivated for the use of the perfumer.

The fragrance of plants is almost always due to a volatile oil contained in small vessels in the petals of the flowers and in the leaves, and is extracted by distillation with water or by absorption with grease or oil. By means of incisions in the tree we procure many gums, such as benzoin and olibanum, and the balsams, which are not only valuable to the perfumer, but form an ingredient in many medicinal preparations. In extracting the odors of plants and flowers, four processes are now employed, namely, absorption, expression, maceration, and distillation. This latter mode, though thought by many to be the only method employed, is in reality the least so, for we distil plants, barks, and woods, but very few flowers.

In distilling flowers, plants, etc., they are now put into a sort of wire basket or perforated kettle suspended in the still, allowing the steam to pass through the material and carry with it the odor of the plant and be condensed with it in the receiver or worm, when the fragrant molecules are collected either on the surface of the water or at the bottom, as they may be lighter or heavier. By this simple improvement all fear of burning the material is avoided. This water, which is often distilled several times with fresh material, is sometimes of value, as is the case with rose and orange-flower waters.

The process of expression to obtain essences or oils is confined to those of the citron family, as the lemon, orange, bergamot, etc., and has heretofore been performed in a very primitive manner, generally by grating the rind and collecting the product with a sponge. But, at the present time, improved machinery for the purpose is made, which produces a greater quantity of purer essence. These rinds may be distilled, but the result is not of so pleasant an odor.

Maceration and absorption, which are the most interesting processes, are both founded upon the affinity the odorous molecules have for fats and oils, being readily absorbed by them when brought in contact. The finest flowers yield their aroma to greases, called pomades, and to oils, which is afterwards extracted by alcohol, which latter material, if placed directly with the flowers, would not extract it from them.

There are two modes adopted for extracting these odors, and making the scented pomades and oils. Maceration is used for flowers of strong odor, such as the rose, orange flower, cassie, jonquil, and violet, and is conducted in this manner: A certain quantity of grease is put in a pan, which is placed in a larger one filled with water in which is dissolved a portion of salt, called a marine bath, and, when liquefied, a certain quantity of flowers are thrown in and left to digest for a stated number of hours, being frequently stirred and the temperature regulated, after which the contents are taken out and passed through horsehair bags; which process is repeated until the fatty body is sufficiently impregnated with the fragrance of the flowers. Oil is treated in just the same manner, but naturally requires less heat than the more solid grease.

By absorption, called in France *enfleurage*, is meant the contact of the flowers with the grease and oil, but without heat, which would injure the delicate odor of such flowers as the jasmin, tuberose, etc. To conduct this process a number of squares of glass framed with wood are provided, the glass being removable; the grease is spread upon the glass in a thin layer in which ridges are cut, and covered with fresh flowers and placed one frame upon another; the next day these flowers are removed, and fresh ones substituted until sufficient odor is absorbed. The operation continues as long as the flowers are in bloom. When the grease has acquired a sufficiently strong odor, it is scraped off the glass, melted with a gentle heat, and strained. Oil is treated in the same manner, except that instead of the glass the frames have a wire bottom, on which are laid thick cotton cloths saturated with olive or benne oil, which, when they are sufficiently impregnated with odor, are submitted to heavy pressure to extract the perfumed oil. These frames are so constructed as to fit closely upon each other, and covered so as to exclude the air and insects.

Many new modes of enfleurage have lately been devised, having in view the saving of labor and time, which, though ingenious, have not yet received any practical application. M. Millan, a French chemist, has invented a means of extracting the aroma of flowers, in the form of a concrete substance, but it is exceedingly costly, too much so to be used with economy; it has, however, served to interest us and show the imponderability of odorous molecules, for, although at first sight it appears as a solid principle of scent, yet if treated several times with alcohol it loses its perfume, but is found not to have lost an atom of weight.

The three towns, Grasse, Cannes, and Nice, all in the south of France, are the places where the processes of maceration and absorption are principally carried on. The latter is the most admirably situated for procuring the flowers for the purpose; and its violets are superior to any others. By the following statistics it will be seen what is the quantity of flowers consumed in this locality; the quantities given are approximate, as are also their values:—

Orange flowers,	3,000,000 lbs.	. .	Value	about	$300,000.
Rose "	1,000,000 "	. .	"	"	75,000.
Jasmine "	250,000 "	. .	"	"	50,000.
Violet "	100,000 "	. .	"	"	35,000.
Cassie "	150,000 "	. .	"	"	50,000.
Tuberose "	50,000 "	. .	"	"	25,000.

From this annual product are manufactured one million pounds of scented oils and greases, besides quantities of orange-flower and rose water, and about a thousand pounds of oil of neroli. There are also distilled in these towns, oils of lavender, rosemary, thyme, geranium, etc. To those who have looked upon flowers as simply ornamental, these figures may give some idea of their commercial importance.

The famous otto or attar of rose is not made in these countries, but from Turkey and India is procured nearly all used in commerce. Very extensive rose farms exist in Adrianople (Turkey in Europe), and at Uslak (Turkey in Asia), and at Ghazipoor in India, where this perfume, so valuable to the perfumer, is extensively made by means of distillation of the fresh leaves in copper stills, and repeating with fresh leaves a number of times, collecting the distillate in cool receivers; 500 pounds of leaves yielding about an ounce of the otto.

Perfumes may be divided into classes. Linnæus, the most learned of modern botanists, divided them into seven; three of which were pleasant odors, viz., the aromatic, the fragrant, and the ambrosial; but the division is very arbitrary, as the theories differ with every writer. For, I think, only an expert in the art of perfumery is properly able to give a just classification of the odors used in his business, as he might classify the geranium and sweetbrier with the rose, lilies with jasmine, jonquil with tuberose or hyacinth, mignonette and cassie with violet, etc. etc. To enumerate all the odors that could be classified, would occupy too much space.

Paris may be called the head-quarters of the perfumery manufacture, which branch of the art is an important item of the trade of that city; and a large amount of capital is invested in it. These manufactures consist of scents for the handkerchief, toilet soaps, and innumerable cosmetics, and are exported to all parts of the world. London may be ranked next in importance as a centre of the art; and many of their manufactures are of a superior class, especially in the item of scented soaps, which are largely exported to all countries. There are many manufacturers of perfumery in Germany, Spain, Italy, Russia, and the United States; but the industry has never reached the importance of those of the two cities named. In this country we are accused of making our business in this line by copying and counterfeiting the articles of celebrity of Paris and London, in which accusation I am afraid there is too much truth; but there have been and still exist a number of legitimate manufacturers who do not imitate the goods of others, but are content to stand on their own merits, and their manufactures rival the best products of Paris and London.

To Paris, however, we must yield the palm of being the great centre of the art, for it is said to have a hundred and fifty houses engaged in the business, employing, directly and indirectly, five thousand men and women, and a capital estimated at fifty millions of francs, with a product valued at seventy millions of francs, and an export of forty millions, which is sent principally to their neighbors in Europe, and to the United States and South America.

London, the next in importance in the trade, exports about one hundred and fifty thousand pounds sterling of its products, principally to India, China, and Australia; but the products of its manufacture can be found in nearly all parts of the civilized world or wherever her commerce extends.

Eau de Cologne is perhaps next to Hungary water the most ancient of spirituous perfumes, and is still in vogue throughout the civilized world. It was invented about the middle of the last century, and is supposed to be best made at the place of its birth, the city of Cologne. It can, however, be made anywhere, as its ingredients are mostly extracted from the leaves, flowers, and fruits of the citron species, which are procured from the south of France, Sicily, and Italy, blended together in certain proportions.

Perfumes or extracts and bouquets for the handkerchief are made in various ways, principally by infusing the scented pomades or oils obtained by the processes already described in alcohol, to which they yield their odors, and the product is the pure aroma of the flowers. As, however, the number of flowers cultivated for their odors is few, the skilled perfumer can imitate nearly all others by a judicious combination of the six or seven he possesses, and in this consists an important branch of the perfumer's art, and may truly be called artistic, for it is done by studying the affinities, and blending the scents as a painter does the shades of color he uses.

Toilet soaps, which are so important a branch of the perfumer's art, are made in great quantities in Paris, London, and the United States, and in fact more or less in many other countries. But to England must be given the first place for the quality of its soaps, as there they take especial care to have the materials pure and devote a great deal of labor to their proper manipulation. All soaps are improved the more they are worked, and to perfect a soap for toilet use, it should be frequently melted and ground in a mill, and the oftener this is done the better is the product.

French soaps may be said to rank next, and are of a more costly character, as the finest are made of the flower pomades and oils, which in other countries is seldom done. German soaps are seldom of good quality, for it is customary there to use a great deal of cocoa-nut oil in their manufacture, which gives them a fetid odor, which no amount of perfume effectually disguises. They are also very deceptive, as they have the property of retaining more alkali and water than other soaps, which causes them to melt away in a very short time when in use.

The United States is constantly gaining the proper knowledge of the art of making fine toilet soaps, and some of our products will compete favorably with any made abroad. We must, however, admit that we have been sorely imposed upon by tallow chandlers and others mixing bone-fat and candle grease with an impure alkali, perfumed with cheap essential oils and called toilet soap, while it is not even fit for use in the laundry.

Cosmetics, pomatums, washes, dentifrices, and the many requisites of the toilet are made in large quantities, but are so numerous that to describe them at length or descant on their respective merits would alone fill our volume. Preparations for the hair are also very numerous, and vary according to the taste or necessity of the consumer; for while one may need an oil, another may require a pomade, whilst some should use a wash or lotion. So in the selection of a perfume it is impossible to say which is best, for it is a matter of taste, and you might as well dictate what others may eat or drink as to advise them as to the choice of a perfume. But as this choice indicates in some degree the taste and refinement of the user, so the vulgar will surely betray themselves by the choice of a common perfume.

The volatilization of perfumes by passing a current of steam through a concentrated essence, and by that means spreading it rapidly through the atmosphere of the apartment, promises to be of great utility, as a theatre or drawing-room may by this means be perfumed in a few minutes, and it tends to purify the air. This process could be usefully employed in hospitals and other public institutions.

Glycerine, an article of comparatively recent discovery, is one of the most useful articles ever discovered for the purposes of the toilet, and its merits are now being fully recognized. And perfumers have not failed to avail themselves of its useful emollient properties, and to combine it with soaps and other cosmetics with the happiest results.

A word of caution may here be said of the many lotions for the complexion which are often carelessly prepared by ignorant persons who have no proper ideas as to the deleterious substances found in the numerous formulæ, for eruptions of the skin, which latter are usually the effects of diseases or constitutional conditions, and in their treatment should have a skilled physician.

Paints for the face should also be carefully selected, as unprincipled quacks offer many pernicious articles that they laud to the skies as beautifying and rejuvenating. Let them be avoided as far as possible. Rouge when made of carmine or safflower is inocuous, and white paint, when made of a proper material, is harmless. The theatrical profession require the use of these cosmetics. To them we advise the utmost care; to all others we would say,

"Nature paiuts the best color."

CHAPTER IV.

MATERIALS USED IN PERFUMERY.

HAVING briefly sketched the history of perfumes, both ancient and modern, we will now proceed to the more practical part of our treatise by describing the principal materials used in the perfumer's art. These materials are drawn from all parts of the world, from the frozen regions of the pole, the milder regions of the temperate zone, to the burning sands of Arabia.

To give every article used by the modern profession would require a very large space in our volume. Yet in writing a practical work we must endeavor to make the perfumer acquainted with the most important ingredients used in his art, and which are indispensable to it.

Allspice or pimento. Eugenia pimenta.—The essential oil of this useful spice is procured by distillation from the unripe fruit, and is of very pleasant odor, and can be usefully employed for scenting toilet soaps in combination with other perfumes. Its odor resembles cloves, and it is a native of the West Indies and South America.

Almonds. Amygdalus amara.—The bitter almond is a native of Egypt, and is grown in Algeria and Italy for its fruit, the kernels of which form a very useful material for the perfumer. The oil expressed from the kernels is very bland, and enters into many cosmetics. The essential oil distilled from the cake or residuum is much used in essences, soaps, creams, etc.

Ambergris. Secretion of the Physeter macrocephalus or sperm whale.—This peculiar substance is found floating on the sea on the coasts of China, Japan, Greenland, and other places, and was long used before its source was determined, and was thought to be of the nature of yellow amber (a fossil), hence its name (amber-gris) gray amber. It is the result of a diseased state of the animal Ambergris is not of an agreeable odor in itself, but in combination with other perfumes it imparts a fragrance and a permanence very remarkable.

Aniseed. Pimpinella anisum.—The seed pod, from which the essential oil is procured by distillation, has a very strong and pleasant odor which can be used for toilet soaps, etc., but it is chiefly used in flavoring liquors, cordials, etc.

Star aniseed. Illicium anisatum.—The fruit of an evergreen tree growing in China and Tartary, the essential oil of which is distilled from the fruit, which is formed like a star, and is like the other aniseed but with a more pleasant flavor, and is used for the same purposes.

Ambrette, see Musk-seed.

Balm. Lemon; Milissa officinalis.—It is a fragrant oil obtained by distilling the plant; it is frequently mentioned in formulæ, but is at present old, and seldom used, and yet we think it might be, should it be cultivated in sufficient quantities to be made economically, which at present is not the case.

Balsam of Peru. Myroxylon Peruiferus.—Is a native of the western pàrt of South America, and is procured from incisions made in the tree, or by boiling the leaves and branches in water. It has a strong vanilla-like odor, and is much employed in the form of tincture mixed with other perfumes.

Balsam of Tolu. Toluiferum balsamum.—Is also a native of South America, and is procured in the same manner as the preceding one, and its uses are the same, but its odor is more pleasant. It has the consistency of resin, or when warm of treacle, is very soluble in alcohol, and, like all other balsams, gives permanency to extracts and bouquets.

Bay. Laurus nobilis.—An evergreen tree, a native of the East, but growing in Southern Europe and in the West Indies, where a pleasant perfume is made of the leaves by distillation with rum and with water. They yield an essential oil, which is used to make the rum or to perfume soap, etc.

Bergamot. Citrus bergomia.—Growing in the south of France, Calabria, and Sicily, where the essential oil is expressed from the rind of the fruit, and has a well-known pleasant odor. When fresh it has a green color; air and light soon deteriorate its quality. It should be kept in well-stoppered bottles in a cool dark place. This advice may apply to nearly all perfumes and essential oils except rose, which does not spoil. Bergamot is seldom used alone, but, combined with other essences, adds to their richness, especially to all spice oils.

Bigarrade. Citrus bigarradia.—The Seville orange is cultivated for its oil, which is distilled from the flowers. This neroli is much known and used as a prominent ingredient in eau de Cologne, indeed an indispensable one. It can also be used in bouquets.

Benzoin. Styrax benzoin.—Gum benzoin is a native of Siam and Singapore. It exudes from wounds made in the tree, and soon hardens into a compact mass, has a perfume resembling vanilla, which is usefully and largely employed for tinctures, essences, bouquets, pomades, and toilet powders.

Caraway. Carum carui.—Caraway seed grows in all parts of Northern Europe, and yields a very useful essential oil, which is much used for perfuming soap, in combination with lavender, cloves, or bergamot. The ground seed are valuable for sachet powders.

Cardamom. Aplinia cardamomum.—Is a native of the East Indies, growing wild in hilly countries. The seeds have a very pleasant aromatic flavor which can be utilized for various purposes where a spicy flavor is desired.

Cascarilla. Croton cascarilla.—This shrub grows wild in various parts of the West Indies and Mexico, and the bark yields a pleasant musky odor, especially when burned. Hence it is a useful ingredient in making fumigating pastils or for perfuming tobacco.

Cassia. Lauras cassia.—From China and the East Indies we receive this valuable spice, from the bark of which is distilled a very strong essential oil resembling cinnamon, but is not so pleasant. It is used chiefly in toilet soaps, and in small quantities is blended with other perfumes, is useful in some essences, and is also used to flavor liquors and cordials.

Cassie. Acacia Farnesiana.—Is grown in France and Italy for the odor of its flowers, which have a very valuable perfume, resembling violets but stronger, which is imparted to pomades or oils by the process of maceration described in our last chapter. The fragrance is used in combination with others in numerous essences or extracts for the handkerchief.

Cedar. Juniperus Virginiana.—An evergreen tree found in Syria and the United States, yields an essential oil which is quite pleasant, but not much used. The ground wood is used for sachet powders, and the tincture in some dentifrices.

Cedrat. Citras cedrata.—This plant is cultivated in the south of France and in Italy for its fruit, whose rind yields, by expression, a very fine oil, used extensively in eau de Cologne. Its odor resembles a mixture of lemon and bergamot.

Citronella. Andropogon citratum.—A native grass found in Ceylon, yielding a very strong essential oil, which is procured by distillation, and is consumed in quantities for perfuming common toilet soaps, but is not much liked for anything else.

Civet. Secretion of the vivera civetta.—The civet cat is found in India and Africa, and yields this well-known odor in a glandular secretion. It is very repulsive in appearance and smell when used alone, but when combined with other scents gives them a more flowery fragrance than any other substance known; it resembles musk, but in some bouquets is more useful.

Cloves. Caryophillus aromaticus.—Zanzibar furnishes to commerce the larger portion of this useful spice. The essential oil abounds in the whole plant, but the unexpanded flower bud is the clove of commerce. The oil is distilled in different countries, and is a very useful ingredient in a number of soaps, essences, pomades, and as a flavoring for cordials, etc.

Coriander. Coriandrum sativum.—Is a native of Italy, and yields an essential oil in small quantities, very useful for many purposes, particularly to mouth pastils and tooth elixirs.

Dill. Anethum graveolens.—Is grown in England, and is there distilled as much for medicine as for its perfume, which is little known here. Dill-water is used by some as a cosmetic. The oil can be usefully combined with other odors to make a variety.

Eglantine or *Sweetbrier.*—This well-known plant grows a very fragrant leaf, but does not yield its odor readily by the usual processes, and it is consequently imitated by the perfumer.

Elder. Sambucus nigra.—Grows in Europe and the United States. The odor of the flowers, which is fragrant but rather heavy, can be extracted by distillation. Elder-flower water is thought by many to be a great cure-all, but as a perfume it is seldom used.

Fennel. Anethum fœniculum.—Cultivated in southern Europe for medicinal purposes and for its oil, which is procured from the seeds, and used in toilet soaps, but seldom enters into anything else.

Flag. Acorus calamus.—The sweet flag yields a pleasant-smelling oil from its rizome. Used as a flavoring for some kinds of liquors and tobacco, but not often in perfumery.

Geranium. Pelargonium odoratissamum.—The rose-leaf geranium, whose oil is procured by distillation, has a favorite rosy smell, and is largely cultivated in France. It is used to adulterate otto of rose, and also for many different forms of perfumery, and is generally much admired.

Ginger Grass. Andropogon nardus.—Cultivated in the Moluccas, and often called geranium, but though similar in odor is not so pleasant. It enters into the same substances as the rose-leaf geranium, but in cheaper articles.

Heliotrope. Heliotrope grandiflorum.—Is a native of Peru, though not cultivated for its perfume, which is very exquisite, and which the perfumer has to imitate with other essences, but which is not very difficult to do, as the odor resembles a blending of rose and vanilla.

Honeysuckle or *Woodbine.*—The flowers of this well-known vine have a very strong and pleasant jasmine-like odor, that might be extracted by enfleurage; but it is not, and therefore the perfumer makes an imitation, the formula of which is given under the proper heading.

Hovenia. Hovenia unequalis.—Is a beautiful flowery shrub, a native of Japan, but the odor is not remarkably pleasant, and the perfumer has recourse to his art in its imitation. The odor resembles a mixture of rose, lemon, neroli, and cloves in due proportion.

Iris. *See* Orris.

Jasmine. Jasminum odoratissimum.—Largely cultivated in the south of France, in Italy, Algeria, and Tunis, and is one of the most useful of plants for the perfumer. The odor of the flower is extracted by absorption with oil or pomade, from which the fragrance is procured by infusion with alcohol as before described, and enters into various bouquets.

Jonquil. Narcissus jonquila.—Is also cultivated in France for its flowers, from which the odor is obtained by enfleurage, but, not being abundant, it is generally imitated, and quite successfully. (*See* Formulas.)

Laurel. Laurus cerasus.—Grows in France, Italy, and the United States, and its fragrance is extracted from the leaves by distillation to procure laurel water.

It is but seldom used, as its fragrance resembles bitter almonds, but is not so pleasant.

Lavender. Lavandula vera.—Extensively grown in France and England for its oil, which is distilled from the plant when in bloom. The English oil is very much more pleasant than the French, and of many times its value. At Mitcham, Surrey, England, where it is cultivated on an extensive scale, the best oil is obtained. There is a still greater quantity made in France and Italy, but not so good or so valuable. Lavender water, or essence, has had a great reputation, and deservedly so, as its odor is very refreshing. The oil enters into many formulas, and is particularly well adapted for soaps.

The French also distil an oil from the lavandula spica, spike lavender, or oil of spike. Its odor is not so fine, and it is used for soaps only.

Lemon. Citrus medica.—Calabria, Genoa, Spain, and Sicily all cultivate this useful fruit for commerce. The rind contains the essence, which is procured by expression, and forms a very important article of commerce, as it is used for so many purposes, as a flavoring as well as a perfume. Owing to its rapid absorption of oxygen it should be kept in strong well stoppered bottles and in a dark place. It is an important ingredient in eau de Cologne and some other preparations.

Lemon Grass. Andropogon schœnanthus.—To Ceylon, where the grass is distilled for its oil, we are indebted for this product. It grows, also, in many parts of India. The oil has a very strong odor resembling verbena, for which it is generally substituted, and it is also used for perfuming soaps and pomades.

Lilac. Syringa vulgaris.—Grows abundantly in the United States, England, and elsewhere. Its flowers have a very pleasant odor, which could be extracted by maceration but is seldom done, and is universally imitated. (*See* Formulas.)

Lily. Convallaria majalis.—The lily of the valley is a native of Europe, but grows in all temperate climates. Its odor could be extracted by maceration but is not, so the perfumer has to resort to an imitation. (*See* Formulas.)

Limette. Citrus limetta.—Grown principally in Sicily and the south of France for its fruit, whose rind yields a very fine oil similar to the lemon, though pleasanter. It is an ingredient in good Cologne water and some essences, and its odor is particularly refreshing.

Mace. Myristica moschata.—Is the enveloping rind of the nutmeg, which grows in Java and Penang. The concrete oil is extracted by expression from the refuse nutmegs and mace, and is used in pomade and soaps. There is also a limpid oil procured by distillation, and used in combination to make variety by its spicy odor. The ground mace is also used in sachet powders.

Magnolia. Magnolia glauca.—Is a native of our own country. Its flowers are exceedingly fragrant, but as it cannot be procured, a very good imitation is made with the materials we have. (*See* Formulas.)

Marjoram. Origanum majorana.—Sweet marjoram is found in the United States, England, and France; which latter country cultivates it for its oil, which is distilled from the herb and used only for toilet soaps.

Meadow Sweet. Spireæ ulmaria.—This very sweet smelling herb is found in England and elsewhere, but is not cultivated in sufficient quantities for the perfumer's use, and he therefore makes an imitation.

Melissa. *See* Balm.

Mignonette. Reseda luteola.—The flowers of this favorite plant are cultivated in France, and submitted to the process of absorption with grease or oil, from which the odor is extracted by means of alcohol.

Mirbane. Nitro-benzole.—An artificial oil of bitter almonds is made chemically with rectified benzole and nitric acid in an apparatus consisting of a large glass tube in the form of a coil, divided in the upper end into two tubes terminating in small funnels. The acid flows slowly in one funnel, while the benzole flows in the other. The two substances meeting at the point of union combine with the evolution of heat, and the product being cooled as it flows down the worm is collected at the lower end and washed in a dilute solution of carbonate of soda. When properly made it has a strong odor like bitter almonds, but is principally used in soaps.

Mint. Mentha piperita; Mentha viridis.—These well-known essences are made in Europe and the United States, the former being much used as a flavoring for candies and cord als, while the latter is merely used in soaps in combination with other oils. It also enters into one or two tooth washes. Both peppermint and spearmint may be added to many compounds.

Myrtle. Myrtus communis.—The south of France is the only place where the plant is grown for its perfume, which is procured by distillation to make myrtle water, which enters into a popular perfume on the continent known as eau d'Ange.

Myrrh. Balsamodendron myrrha.—This gum resin, grown in Arabia and India, from ancient times to the present day, is now used by the perfumers only in tooth washes and dentifrices, where it is very useful.

Musk. Moschus moschata.—This very useful and indispensable secretion of the musk deer comes to us from Thibet and China, and is found in a small pod attached to the belly of the male deer. The best quality is received from Tonquin. Musk is an unctuous substance, of reddish-brown color which soon turns black by exposure, of a very powerful odor, and although generally disliked in its pure state, mixed with other odors it is very much admired by most people, and often by those who declare that they do not like musk. To the perfumer musk is invaluable, and enters into a great many preparations, as essences, powders, pastils, soaps, etc. etc.

Musk Seed. Hibiscus abelmoschus.—Ambrette, as it is generally called, comes to us from the West Indies, and is in small kidney-shaped seeds of a grayish-brown color, with an odor similar to musk and ambergris. In the form of a tincture it combines usefully in making low-priced essences.

Narcissus. Narcissus odorata.—This favorite flower, found in nearly all climates, is for its fragrance cultivated to some extent in Algeria. Its delicate lily-like odor is extracted by absorption with pomade, but, as it is rare and expensive, the perfumer makes an imitation.

Neroli, Bigarade; Citrus bigaradia. *Neroli*, Portugal; Citrus aurantium.—Orange-flowers are grown in the south of France, in Italy, Sicily, and Calabria, on an extensive scale, and the oil extracted by distillation is sent to all countries. The citrus bigaradia or bitter orange is the most prized, the essential oil of its flowers having the finest odor. The citrus aurantium or edible orange yields a good odor, but it is not so delicate. These odors are generally much admired, and are necessary in the manufacture of good eau de Cologne. There are also made from the same trees two other oils, one from the leaves called petit-grain, and one from the rind of the fruit called Portugal or orange. The orange-flowers when treated by maceration with oil or pomade yield with alcohol a finer flavored perfume, and quite distinct from the nerolis.

Nutmeg. Nux moschata.—The Indian Archipelago furnishes most of the nutmegs of commerce, which are used throughout the world as a flavoring or as a condiment. The essential oil by distillation is used in combination in many articles when a spicy odor or flavor is desired. The nuts ground into coarse powder can also be used in sachet powders.

Orange. Citrus aurentium.—From Calabria and Sicily we receive most of the oil of orange, which is expressed from the rind of the fruit, and is employed for many perfumes. Like all of the oils from the citrus family, it absorbs oxygen very rapidly when exposed, and should be kept well stopped and in the dark. In pomade it has the same tendency, and does not suit so well as some other perfumes.

Olibanum. Boswellia serrata.—A gum resin found in Arabia and India, and used from the earliest times as incense, and called frankincense. The Catholic and Greek churches still burn it as incense, while the perfumer uses it in fumigating pastils and sometimes in the form of tincture.

Orris or Iris. Iris Florentina.—This rhizoma is a native of Italy and grows in other countries. The odor of the root is used in the form of a tincture in many essences and bouquets, and powdered it is very useful in sachet-powders and dentifrices.

Palm Oil. Elais Guiniensis.—The palm that yields this useful oil grows principally in Africa, whence it is received. It is a fatty oil obtained by expression, and when fresh has a pleasant violet-like odor, but is not available for perfume. It is added to pomades to give a yellow color; but its principal use is to make palm soap, which is justly popular, and which retains the odor of the oil.

Patchouly. Plectranthus crassifolius.—A sage-like plant growing in China and India having a peculiar strong odor much admired by many. The essential oil is distilled from the plant, and is much used by perfumers in making an extract for the handkerchief with the addition of a little rose to soften it. It also enters into some other bouquets and essences.

Petit-grain. Bigarade; *Petit-grain.* Portugal.—This perfume has been partially described under the head of neroli, and is obtained from the leaves of the same plants, and is employed in various ways, but principally in making eau de Cologne and bouquets, soaps, pomades, etc.

Pea, Sweet. Pois du senteur.—The flowers of this well-known garden annual have a pleasant perfumé, but as it is not cultivated for its odor the perfumer makes a compound which he calls by that name.

Pink. Dianthus caryophillus.—Clove pink has a very popular odor, though its cultivation is so limited that the perfumer could not get together enough of them to make a pint of essence, so from his numerous ingredients he makes a delightful imitation. To detect the innocent fraud would puzzle the oldest connoisseur.

Rhodium. Convolvulus scoparius.—Called rose wood because it yields an oil somewhat resembling otto of rose, and which was formerly used to adulterate that valuable article. The wood is imported from South America, and is used principally in sachet powders.

Rose. Rosa centifolia.—This may truly be called the queen of flowers, as it is universally admired for its beauty as well as its fragrance, and, though growing nearly all over the world, is chiefly cultivated for commercial uses in Turkey, India, and France. In France pomades and oils are scented with it for the perfumer's use, and in India and Turkey it is grown for the manufacture of the otto of rose, which is obtained by distilling the leaves with water, and requires about 600 pounds to make a single ounce of the oil. When pure it is exceeding pleasant, and is also invaluable to the perfumer for a great many purposes, for there are few odors with which it will not harmoniously combine. Yet for the finer extracts for the handkerchief the alcoholate from the pomade gives a finer odor, and one that it is impossible to dispense with, for more than half his numerous extracts and bouquets. The dried leaves also enter into powders, pastils, and sachets.

Rosmary. Rosmarinus officinalis.—This useful plant is cultivated in the south of Europe for its oil, which is distilled from the flowers and leaves, and comes to us of several qualities, the best being from the flowers alone. In eau de Cologne it is almost indispensable, for it blends so well with the odors of the citrus species, and it is equally useful in toilet soaps.

Sage. Salvia officinalis.—This plant was formerly much employed in perfumery, but at the present time its oil is sometimes used in soaps, and the dried leaves enter into some sachet powders, but being used as a condiment it is considered common.

Santal. Santalum citrinum.—A tree well known in China, India, and Australia. Its wood is burned in incense in the former countries, and its consumption for that purpose is very great. The oil distilled from the wood is valuable in perfumery in many compounds, and has a lasting property available to the perfumer in many ways.

Serpolet. Thymus serphilium.—Wild thyme, whose odor is quite as pleasant as the cultivated herb, is distilled in the south of France, and enters with advantage into perfumes for soaps.

Sassafras. Laurus sassafras.—A native of North America, having a very pleasant essential oil obtained from the bark of the root; it is exported largely to Europe, and is used extensively to perfume cheap soaps and to flavor various medicinal preparations.

Storax. Styrax officinalis.—This balsam is obtained in Asiatic Turkey, by incisions in the trunk of the tree; it is of several kinds and qualities, the best being in yellowish-white tears mixed with a reddish-brown substance. This is scarce, and can be but seldom obtained. The most common form of storax is a semi-fluid black-and-gray substance, having an odor somewhat like vanilla. Soluble in alcohol, in which form it is sometimes employed in bouquets.

Thyme. Thymus vulgaris.—This herb belongs to a large family, all having a more or less fragrant odor. This species is cultivated in France and Germany for its oil, which is used combined with other perfumes to scent soaps, etc. The herb can also be usefully employed in sachet powders.

Tonquin. Dipterix odorata.—From Para and Angustura, in South America, we receive this valuable bean, which contains a volatile oil, a fatty oil, and benzoic acid. In the form of tincture with alcohol they can be used in boùquets and essences; in powder they are useful in sachets, giving somewhat the odor of new-mown hay. They are largely used to perfume segars and tobacco.

Tolu. *See* Balsam of Tolu.

Tuberose. Polianthus tuberosa.—This exquisite flower is extensively cultivated in the south of France and Italy for the use of perfumers all over the world. Its odor is obtained by enfleurage with grease and oils, and its alcoholate is in constant use in numerous bouquets, and always gives satisfaction when judiciously used.

Vanilla. Vanilla planifolia.—To Mexico we are indebted for this very valuable drug, which has a not less favorable fragrance in perfumery than valuable flavor in confectionery, and for both purposes it is largely consumed. The true vanilla is the bean of a handsome vine, and, made into a tincture, it enters into a great number of fine extracts and bouquets, and also in powder into sachets.

Verbena. Aloysia citriodora.—The lemon verbena is a native of Spain, where alone it is cultivated for commerce. The volatile oil is distilled from the leaves, and is generally admired. Perfumers often use the lemon-grass oil for verbena extract, but it has to be modified with other odors to make the imitation equally delicate. It is principally used in handkerchief bouquets.

Violet. Viola odorata.—There are violet farms near Nice and Florence, where this delicate flower is submitted to the process of enfleurage with pomade or oil, from which the perfumer extracts the odor with fine alcohol; and, when carefully made, it is of exquisite and delicate fragrance. This is the most costly of all flower perfumes, for the plant is small and the flowers few, and it requires a great deal of space and labor in its cultivation, and also because it is but a short time in bloom. The extract is frequently imitated with cassie, orris, etc. etc.

Vitivert. Anatherum muricatum.—Vitivert or kuskus is the rhizoma of an Indian grass, which is made into mats and blinds, called tatty, and when sprinkled with water in that hot climate emits a fragrance which is very agreeable. Its essential oil can be obtained by distillation, but it yields but a small quantity. In the form of tincture, it enters into some essences; in powder, into sachet powders.

Wintergreen. Gaultheria procumbens.—The partridge berry, a small evergreen plant, native to the United States and Canada, yields a pleasant and powerful volatile oil by distillation; but more used to flavor medicines than as a perfume, though in combination it may be used in soap.

Ylang Ylang. Unona odoratissima.—Called the flower of flowers, the blossoms of a very handsome tree growing in India and China, and but lately brought to public notice; but it has proved a great favorite. The oil from the flower is obtained by distillation, and has an odor somewhat resembling the jasmine. Thus far it has been quite costly, but as the demand increases so will its production, which will, no doubt, lead to a reduction in its price.

I have here given the perfumer a sketch of the principal ingredients for perfumery, used in his art; but there are very many more, generally, however, such substances as are of secondary importance, or such as are in common use or can be found at any drug store, and to describe which would be unnecessary. What I have described are generally used and easily procured, and are, as I believe, sufficient for his purposes; but if, in my formulas, I should speak of anything not here described, and with which he is not familiar, he can, by writing to any large wholesale druggist in Philadelphia or New York, easily obtain it or information regarding it.

CHAPTER V.

THE LABORATORY AND ITS REQUIREMENTS.

ALTHOUGH there are many preparations of a chemical nature which require some degree of knowledge of that science, I shall endeavor to avoid the technical terms used by chemists, so that it may be possible for my recipes to be prepared by others as well as by those familiar with chemistry. When treating of a chemical combination it may be necessary to use the chemical term, but if possible I shall give the common name.

The books on perfumery, with which I have met, generally adhere to many old and obsolete forms, and load their recipes with substances at once difficult to procure and unnecessary. I shall try to give such recipes only that there shall be no such difficulty, and shall as much as possible simplify all the formulas and endeavor to give such articles only as are obtainable, and are either the best or the most simple and economical.

In preparing a laboratory for his use the perfumer should have several rooms, as it is essential that some branches should be separate from others. One is required for the manufacture and keeping of various tinctures, essences, spirits, waters, etc., in their various bottles and in systematic order; one or two for stills, water-baths, displacers, receivers, macerators, filters, etc., in fact for all the necessary paraphernalia of his art; as well as a room or a closet, cool and dark, as a store-room for essential oils and other substances which are injured by too warm a temperature, such as his finer pomades, etc. etc.

If he makes toilet soaps he needs the aid of steam, which, in the present state of the art, is almost indispensable, as without it he can seldom properly make many articles which he will need. Soaps should have appropriated to them one or more rooms, light, airy, and free from dampness. Face, sachet, and rouge powders also require a room in which they can be prepared separately, for their own sakes as well as on account of the dust they convey to other goods, and if there is a store it should be neat and cleanly, so that the goods may be stored, and the nicer work of finishing completed by the more delicate hands of females.

It may be thought quite unnecessary to give advice as to a proper system in the arrangement of the laboratory—a certain place for his tinctures, infusions, extracts, essential oils, etc., those most handy that are the oftenest needed; in fact a place for everything and everything in its place. This advice may seem superfluous, yet a perfect system of the kind facilitates all operations of this nature; for this is not a trade in which the necessary tools are found ready to his hand, but an art where care and cleanliness are indispensable.

While giving advice to the perfumer, and particularly to the novice, I must not conclude without a caution to him to avoid all materials that are improper or dangerous to use; to guard all his goods against any ingredients that will injure in any manner the person who uses them. The old books of recipes are filled with formulas that if not silly are pernicious and do much more harm than good. If I give the usual form of preparations for an article of which I do not approve, I shall give my opinion of its merits or demerits with the proper caution in making and using it. In order properly to classify the different articles the perfumer makes, I shall adopt a system and give the recipes for tinctures, then for extracts or alcoholates, waters, oils, vinegars, pomades, powders, rouges, pastes, emulsions, hair dyes, etc.

INSTRUMENTS FOR DISTILLATION. — Distillation is the most important and interesting branch of the perfumer's art, as, by its assistance, the different essences, spirituous scents, essential oils, fragrant waters, eau de Cologne, and the vinegars are made.

The chief utensil is the alembic or still, a vessel of tin or tinned copper, and sometimes of glass. Among the many arts in which alembics are used, no one more frequently requires those of glass than that of the perfumer. This is owing to the volatility of much of the material to be distilled, and the consequent care and nicety requisite in the operation.

The alembic (Fig. 1) consists of three distinct and separate parts—the *body*, the *head*, and the *cooler*.

Fig. 1.

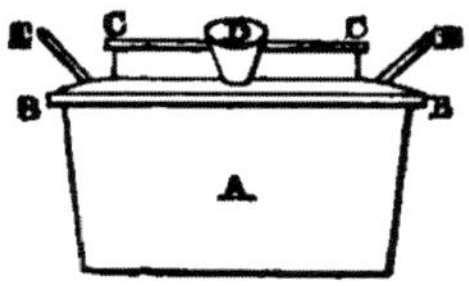

A exhibits the first, which is nothing more than a kettle in the shape of an inverted truncated cone. It is walled up in brick and mortar, the flange *B B* resting on the furnace, and serving to hold the body firmly in its bed. It is generally of equal breadth and depth, with a bottom inwardly convex, so as to give greater heating surface, and a neck *C C* converging towards its opening. On this neck are placed a socket *D*, and the two handles *E E*.

The capital or head (Fig. 2) of the still is made of tinned copper for larger vessels, and of tin or pewter for smaller apparatus. It is cylindrical, terminating in a spherical hood or cup.

Fig. 2.

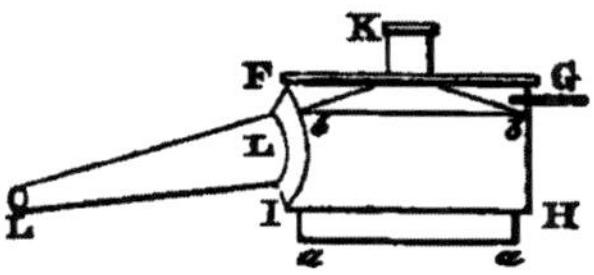

F G H I is the cylindrical part, with a neck *a a* affixed beneath, and so made as to fit nicely into the opening *C C* of the still (Fig. 1). The extreme top is soldered at *b b*, a little below the superior edge of the cylinder. In the centre of this head is a socket

K, and in the side is soldered a slightly conical pipe *L L*, called the *beak* of the alembic.

The materials for distillation are put into the body, the head placed on, nicely adjusted and well luted, and the fire kindled in the furnace. By the action of the heat, the volatile parts are disengaged in vapor, and collect in the capital, from whence they pass through the beak into the cooler or third piece, where they are refrigerated and condensed—hence its name. This refrigerator is of various forms—sometimes a tube extended to some length; then, again, it is spiral, and takes the title of *worm;* but this shape renders its cleansing difficult. Here, below, is a condensing apparatus, economical, convenient, and simple.

Fig. 3.

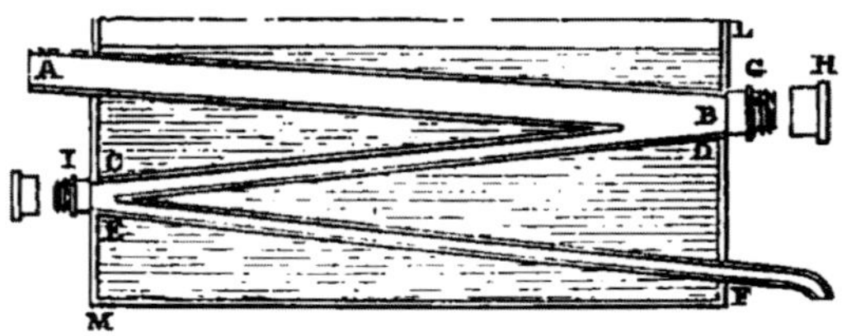

It consists of three cylindrical tubes, *A B C D E F*, each three feet long, and soldered one to the other, so as to form a continued connection. The first is conical at *A*, for the reception of the beak of the still, together with which it is luted: at *B* it is soldered to the end of the second tube *D*, forming a nozzle. These two joined together are soldered to a cylindrical copper ferule *G*, having a screw at its extremity, and covered with a stopper *H*, cut with a corresponding screw, and fixed together with intervening leather washers, so as to insure a hermetical jointure of the two tubes simultaneously. The tubes *C D* and *E F* are similarly adjusted. The whole apparatus is fixed, at the points *A G I F*, in a bath *L M*, which is filled with cold water constantly renewed, during distillation, by the entrance of fresh water at the bottom, which drives off, through a tube, the water which becomes heated, and then always occupying the uppermost part of the bath. The *modus operandi* of this apparatus is easily explained. The vapors enter into the large tube *A B*, and are there condensed and run off slowly in liquid form, into the slightly-inclined tube *D C*, and from that again into *E F*, and, as they are continually in contact with cold water, the liquid soon cools to the temperature of the atmosphere, and falls into the receiver through the tube *F*. If six feet of passage-pipe should be insufficient to cool the liquor, the apparatus can be enlarged by merely increasing the number of tubes. It is not requisite that the breadth of the bath *L M* should be great; for instance, supposing the diameter of the tube *A B* at three inches, then seven or eight inches width are sufficient for the continuous renewal of the water. This bath is of wood, lined with zinc or copper. The connections of the tubes are such as to allow their cleansing at pleasure, by rubbing the interior with hair brushes and water until all smell is removed. At the bottom of the bath is conveniently placed a stopcock, through which to let off the water, after the completion of the distillation.

THE WATER-BATH.—This most useful fixture for distilling very volatile substances enables the perfumer to regulate his temperature so as not to exceed 212° F.

It is a movable cylindrical vessel of tin, or tinned

copper, fitting and sitting in the aperture *C C* of the still *A* (Fig. 1), and resting therein by its collar or flange *N N*, so that its bottom does not reach that of the cucurbit. It is placed in and taken out by the

Fig. 4.

handles *O O*. The neck *a a* of the capital is made so as to be used to the still, either with or without the bath.

Fig. 5 exhibits a water-bath complete, the inner vessel represented by dotted lines being the recipient for the materials, and the outer jacket, the water-holder or heating medium.

The mode of operating by this latter plan is to place the selected materials in the kettle, lute on its head,

Fig. 5.

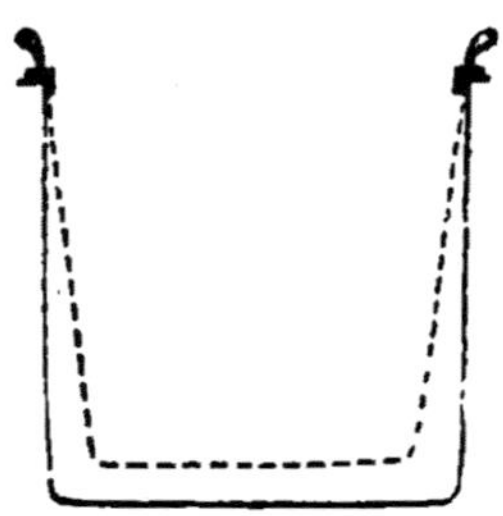

and through the socket *D* (Fig. 1) pour in the water. The top of the capital, being externally concave, is filled with a layer of powdered charcoal, which, as a bad conductor of heat, prevents the condensation of the vapors in that part of the head, and their consequent falling back into the still.

DISTILLATION BY STEAM.—This mode of distillation is particularly applicable for making distilled water from leaves, flowers, roots, and similar substances, and the form of apparatus most convenient for it is shown by Fig. 6. It consists of a tinned

Fig. 6.

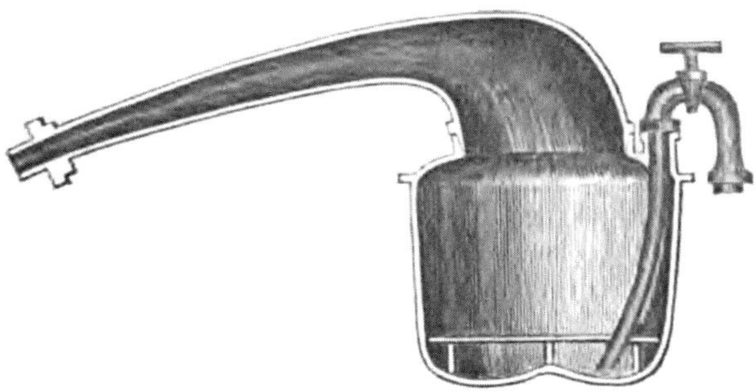

copper body and head, of the form represented by the drawing, with a perforated false bottom Fig. 7,

Fig. 7.

which serves as a platform for the support of the charge of leaves or material. The steam is introduced through the pipe leading beneath the platform, and, passing over through the beaker into the condenser, carries along the oil which is taken up during its transit through the still, and deposits it in the Florentine glass receiver, Fig. 8. The beak is adjusted and luted to the condenser, Fig. 3.

Fig. 8.

Glass Alembics and Retorts.—To procure liquors of a very delicate perfume, recourse is had to rectification, that is, redistillation of the liquid already distilled, and for this purpose the water- or sand-bath is necessary. For the preparation of the vinegars, the acid properties of which are so corrosive of copper, it is always better to use glass or stoneware vessels.

Glass retorts, as shown by Figs. 9 and 10, when of large size, are generally tubulated, that is, provided

Fig. 9.

Fig. 10.

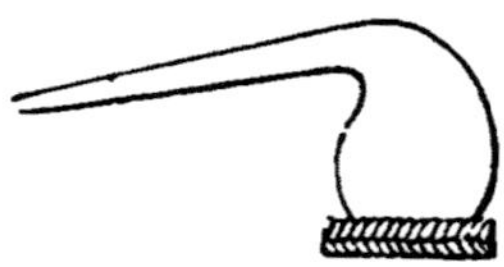

with a stoppered tube at the top of the arch or bend, so as to render their refilling practicable and easy, without moving them from their beds.

The liquid may either be put in all at once through a funnel, or in detached proportions, and gradually, by means of a tube at *S* (Fig. 11) adapted to the opening, and, at the same time, serving as a safety-tube. To give more length to the beak of the retort, there is sometimes added and affixed thereto a glass tube, open at both ends, and bulging in the centre, as shown at Fig. 11.

Fig. 11.

We give the description of a furnace which we can recommend to the perfumer.

Furnace with Hot Water to melt Pomades and Philocomes.

Fig. 12.

A A A A. Masonry work.
B. Hearth, with grate.
C. Ash-pan.
D. Chimney.
E E. Box of sheet-iron, containing water, having at the top three cylindrical apertures, in each of which is placed a pan containing the pomade or

philocome that is to be melted. The diameter of these pans is a little less than that of the apertures, so that they can be easily introduced in the box, and can be taken out after each operation. At two-thirds of their height they have a strong edge which prevents their going to the bottom of the box.

To put this furnace in operation, light the fire on the hearth B. The flame circulates around the bottom and edges of the box, and rapidly heats the water it contains. Then introduce the pans F G H into the aperture.

When the substances they contain are melted, mould in the ordinary way.

This plan enables the perfumer to manufacture different kinds of pomades at the same time, without the inconveniences that attend heating by a direct fire.

CHAPTER VI.

TINCTURES.

Tincture of Ambergris.

Ambergris (gray) . . .	2 ounces.
Loaf sugar	4 "
Rect. alcohol . . .	8 pints.

Rub up the ambergris in an iron mortar with the sugar, adding a small portion of the alcohol at a time, pouring the mixture into the bottle, continuing to add the spirit by degrees until all the ambergris is taken up. Keep the tincture in a moderately warm place for a month in order to facilitate solution.

Tincture of Ambrette. (Musk seed.)

Ambrette, bruised or ground	2 pounds.
Rectified alcohol . . .	1 gallon.

Put together and macerate for two or three weeks, when filter.

Tincture of Archil.

Archil	2 ounces.
Alcohol	1 pint.

This tincture is of a rich, red color, and is used to color hair- and tooth-washes.

Tincture of Alkanet.

Alkanet root	1 ounce.
Alcohol	1 pint.

Alkanet is a fine red color when fresh, but being fugitive will soon fade.

Tincture of Benzoin.

Gum benzoin in coarse powder	1 pound.
Rectified alcohol . . .	4 pints.

Mix the ingredients; keep in a warm place for a fortnight with frequent agitation, when filter.

Tincture of Cinnamon.

Take of cinnamon in powder .	1 pound.
Alcohol	4 pints.

This is useful in mouth-washes and dentifrices.

Tincture of Cedar.

Take of Spanish cedar . .	1 pound.
Alcohol	4 pints.

A useful tincture in dentifrices, and sometimes to color essences.

Tincture of Civet.

Civet (good)	2 ounces.
Orris root, ground . . .	4 "
Rectified alcohol . . .	8 pints.

Rub the civet with the orris in an iron mortar, adding the spirit by degrees, and macerate for a month before using.

Tincture of Cantharides.

Spanish flies, in powder . .	4 ounces.
Alcohol	4 pints.

Used in hair tonics and washes.

Tincture of Cochineal.

Cochineal (ground) . .	2 ounces.
Alcohol	1 pint.

Useful as a coloring tincture in some essences.

Tincture of Gamboge.

Gamboge, in powder . .	2 ounces.
Alcohol	1 pint.

Used to color yellow.

Tincture of Myrrh.

Gum myrrh, in powder . .	2 ounces.
Alcohol, 80°	1 pint.

Useful in tooth washes.

Tincture of Musk.

Tonquin musk . . .	4 ounces.
Loaf sugar	6 "
Rectified alcohol . . .	8 pints.

Bruise the cut-up musk with the sugar in an iron mortar, adding small portions of the spirit at a time until all is taken up; macerate for a month before filtering and using.

Tincture of Santal.

Santal wood, ground . . .	8 ounces.
Alcohol	4 pints.

I have often found this tincture useful in some essences and in tooth elixirs.

Tincture of Patchouly.

Patchouly leaves . . .	8 ounces.
Alcohol	4 pints.

When the leaves are good, this tincture serves to color essences a greenish tint.

Tincture of Styrax.

Styrax	1 pound.
Alcohol	8 pints.

This tincture can be frequently used to advantage in many kinds of bouquets, etc., but being very strong it requires judgment in order to avoid excess.

Tincture of Tonquin.

Tonka bean, ground . . .	2 pounds.
Rectified alcohol . . .	8 pints.

Is a very useful tincture in frequent demand to add to essences, bouquets, etc., which besides the odor tends to give them permanency.

Tincture of Turmeric.

Turmeric, ground . . .	2 ounces.
Alcohol	1 pint.

Tincture of curcuma gives a lemon-yellow color to essences.

Tincture of Tolu Balsam.

Balsam of Tolu . . .	1 pound.
Rectified alcohol . . .	8 pints.

Tincture of Tolu is often a valuable addition to various essences.

Tincture of Peru Balsam.

Balsam of Peru . . .	1 pound.
Rectified alcohol . . .	8 pints.

This tincture is used for the same purposes as the Tolu tincture.

Tincture of Saffron.

Saffron (Sativum) . . .	2 ounces.
Alcohol	2 pints.

A fine yellow tincture, which has a pleasant odor, and is often in request for coloring many preparations.

Tincture of Vanilla.

Vanilla, chipped . . .	1 pound.
Sugar-candy	¼ "
Rectified alcohol . . .	7 pints.
Water	1 "

Beat up the chipped pods with the sugar, adding the water gradually, then the alcohol; macerate the whole together for a fortnight before using. Vanilla is one of the most useful of perfumes, and improves nearly every bouquet it enters into and makes it lasting.

Tincture of Vitivert.

Vitivert root, ground . . .	8 ounces.
Alcohol	4 pints.

Vitivert can be used in this form in several essences and bouquets, and has the property of adding to the perfume and permanency of bouquets.

There are a number of aniline colors that can be usefully employed in coloring many preparations, and of which it may be well to have a supply on hand, for many goods are required to please the eye as well as the nose; but as far as the extracts and bouquets for the handkerchief are concerned, all color as a rule should be avoided.

CHAPTER VII.

EXTRACTS AND BOUQUETS.

I HAVE in the third chapter explained the mode of extracting the odor of flowers by maceration and absorption in the south of France and Italy, and have remarked that the number of flowers cultivated for the purposes of the perfumer is somewhat limited, but that number judiciously used is sufficient, in conjunction with the numerous tinctures and essential oils, to compound almost all extracts and bouquets at present in demand.

There is quite a difference in the names given by different writers to the materials and liquids used, and some works call essential oils essences or ottos. I prefer giving those that are the most common and well known, the term oils; not because it is strictly correct, but because it is the best understood, and usage gives authority to it. And so with the word extracts, — they are called huilles, oils, essences, esprits, and waters. I shall call extracts all the alcoholates from the flower pomades and oils, and all having a simple composition; and bouquets, all that are of a compound nature, and intended to perfume the handkerchief; and waters, all those intended for the toilet as well as the handkerchief, or for general perfuming, such as eau de Cologne, lavender water, etc. When I have occasion to use waters in a formula I shall so call them, as rose-water, etc. So when I speak of extract of rose, for instance, in the formulas, I shall so call it, and allude to the alcoholates by numbers 1 and 2, being the first and second washing of the pomades.

Of these alcoholates, it is always necessary to have a supply ready for compounding the different odors and bouquets, and my system is to wash the pomades or oils with the alcohol twice; hence the numbers one and two, first and second qualities or strengths. Some of the French writers recommend a third washing, but I have never found it necessary, as two operations take out nearly all the odor, and what is left is not sufficient to perfume the pomade when bottled, to which use I always apply it.

Extract of Cassie, No. 1.

Pomade, or oil of cassie .	6 pounds.
Deodorized alcohol . .	8 pints.

Put the pomade, or oil, into a wide-mouthed bottle, or stone jar (or into a tinned-copper churn made for the purpose), and add the alcohol; keep in a warm place, frequently stirring, for a month, when decant off the extract and again subject the pomade to another eight pints of alcohol, and proceed as before to make extract No. 2.

Extract of Jasmine, No. 1.

Jasmine pomade, or oil . .	6 pounds.
Deodorized alcohol . .	8 pints.

Proceed as with the extract of cassie.

Extract of Orange Flower, No. 1.

Pomade, or oil of orange flower	6 pounds.
Deodorized alcohol . . .	8 pints.

Proceed as with the extract of cassie.

Extract of Rose, No. 1.

Pomade, or oil of rose . .	6 pounds.
Deodorized alcohol . .	8 pints.

Operate as for the extract of cassie.

Extract of Tuberose, No. 1.

Pomade, or oil of tuberose .	6 pounds.
Deodorized alcohol . .	8 pints.

Treat the same as extract of cassie.

Extract of Violet.

Violet pomade, or oil . .	4 pounds.
Deodorized alcohol . .	8 pints.

Proceed as for extract of cassie.

There are also pomades and oils of réséda, syringa, hyacinth, and jonquil, but they are seldom imported into the United States for the perfumer. When ordered direct from the seat of manufacture, he may often get the article that is genuine in name only, and which he could as easily have made from the materials already on hand, the formulas for which I give in the chapter on pomades.

The perfumer having followed my system thus far, and having his tinctures prepared and his simple extracts ready, should now supply himself with an assortment of essential oils.

Oil of almonds (bitter).	Oil of lemon.
" aniseed.	" limette.
" bay.	" lemon grass.
" bergamot.	" marjoram.
" caraway.	" mirbane.
" cassia.	" nutmeg.
" cinnamon.	" neroli.
" coriander.	" orange.
" citronella.	" petit-grain.
" cardamom.	" peppermint.
" cedrat.	" pimento.
" fennel.	" palma-rosa.
" gaultheria.	" rose.
" geranium.	" rosemary.
" ginger grass.	" santal.
" lavender.	" sage.

Oil of sassafras.	Oil of thyme, red.
" serpolet.	" thyme, white.
" spike-lavender.	" verbena.
" spearmint.	" ylang ylang.

As nearly all, if not all of these oils are articles of commerce, there is not much difficulty in obtaining them in such quantities as may be required, and those who deal in and import the essential oils have also the distilled waters of rose and orange flowers, with which the perfumer should supply himself.

When he has supplied himself with all these requisite materials, and has them made into the proper form, and arranged with proper regard to convenience and to system, he is prepared to compound his extracts, bouquets, and toilet waters.

It may be necessary here to call the attention of the novice to the importance of studying the nature of his many ingredients, particularly the different odors, with regard to the compatibility of their perfumes. For the making of perfumery is not only a trade, but may justly be called an art, for as the artist blends and contrasts his colors on the canvas, the perfumer can mix and combine his odors so nicely that he can simulate every known fragrance. Moreover he must study the character of his odors. Some are delicate and evanescent, to them he must add some of the many substances he has to give them permanency; others are strong and require modifying with a more delicate or different odor; good judgment and good taste are very essential to success in this art, as they are in all others. Any one may fill a bottle and cork it, but how many will be able to tell the quality of its contents?

While giving the formulas for the extracts, and bouquets for the handkerchief, I shall accompany each odor with suitable remarks, founded on the long experience I have had in their composition, as to their qualities and desirability; as these perfumes are perhaps the most important in the business, and most in request at the present time.

Again, the new beginner may suppose, by a casual glance at the recipes, that there is great sameness; but that would be an error, as a smaller or a larger quantity of one or more ingredients may make a great difference in the result.

Extrait d'Acacia. (Cassie.)

Extract of cassie, No. 1	2 pints.
" jasmine, No. 1	¾ "
" tuberose, No. 1	½ "
Tincture of ambergris	2 ounces.
Orange-flower water (double)	8 "

Cassie is not a favorite perfume by itself, but combined as above is much liked.

Extrait d'Amande Amar. (Bitter almond flowers.)

Extract of cassie, No. 1	½ pint.
Tincture of civet	4 ounces.
Deodorized alcohol	2 pints.
Oil of bitter almonds	3 fluidrachms.
" bergamot	2 "
" cinnamon	½ "
Rose-water (double)	1 pint.

This odor to some is very agreeable, particularly when the other ingredients give it a soft, flowery odor.

Bouquet d'Alhambra.

Extract of tuberose, No. 1 .	2 pints.
" cassie, No. 1 . .	½ "
" orange flower, No. 1	½ "
Tincture of civet . . .	½ "
Oil of rose geranium . .	1 drachm.
Rose-water, triple . . .	½ pint.

A very pleasant perfume.

Bouquet d'Aspasia.

Extract of violet, No. 1 . .	1 pint.
" rose, No. 2 . .	1 "
" jasmin, No. 2 . .	½ "
Tincture of vanilla . . .	½ "
" musk . . .	¼ "
Oil of bergamot	3 drachms.
" cloves	1 "
Orange-flower water, triple .	¾ pint.

Extract d'Ambrette. (Purple sweet sultan.)

Extract of rose, No. 2 . .	1 pint.
Tincture of ambrette . . .	1½ "
" ambergris . .	¼ "
Rose-water, triple . . .	1 "

This formula gives a pleasant variety.

Extract of Auberpine.

Extract of cassie, No. 1 . .	1¼ pint.
" rose, No. 2 . .	1 "
" tuberose, No. 2 .	½ "
Tincture of storax . . .	¼ "
" orris . . .	½ "

Oil of cedar	½	ounce.
" fennel	¼	"
Rose-water, double . . .	½	pint.

This, of course, is a fancy odor, and quite pleasant.

Extrait d'Ambre.

Extract of rose, No. 2 . .	1½	pint.
Tincture of ambergris . .	1¼	"
" vanilla . . .	½	"
" musk . . .	¼	"
Rose-water, double . . .	½	"

Ambergris not having in itself the most agreeable odor, the above combination is very fine, and will last a long while.

Bouquet d'Amour. (Perfect love.)

Extract of rose, No. 1 . .	1½	pint.
" jasmin, No. 1 . .	1	"
" violet, No. 2 . .	½	"
Tincture of musk . . .	¼	"
" ambergris . .	2	ounces.
Rose-water, triple . . .	2	"

This has always been a very popular essence, and one that is always safe to recommend; containing ingredients generally admired.

Brazilian Bouquet.

Extract of rose, No. 1 . .	1	pint.
" tuberose, No. 2 .	1	"
" orange flower, No. 2.	½	"
Tincture of Tolu . . .	½	"
" vanilla . . .	¼	"
" civet . . .	¼	"
Rose-water, double . . .	½	"

Extract of Bergamot.

Oil of bergamot	6 ounces.
" rose geranium . .	½ "
Tincture of musk . . .	2 "
" orris . . .	4 "
Deodorized alcohol . .	3 pints.
Rose-water, double . .	½ "

This compound improves the bergamot, rendering it softer.

Essence Bouquet. (Or nosegay.)

Extract of rose, No. 1 . .	2 pints.
Tincture of orris . . .	1 "
" musk . . .	¼ "
Oil of rose	1 drachm.
" neroli bigarade . .	1 "
" bergamot . . .	2 ounces.
" lemon	1 "
Rose-water, double . . .	8 "

There is no perfume more popular than this, and I consider it an improvement on the English, which contains too much bergamot.

Bosphorus Bouquet.

Extract of cassie, No. 1 .	2 pints.
" jasmin, No. 2 . .	½ "
" orange flower, No. 2	½ "
" tuberose, No. 2 .	¼ "
Tincture of civet . . .	¼ "
Oil of almonds (bitter) . .	½ drachm.
Orange-flower water . .	½ pint.

Centennial Bouquet.

Extract of rose, No. 1 . .	1 pint.
" jasmin, No. 2 . .	¾ "
" tuberose, No. 2 .	¾ "
Tincture of ambrette . . .	½ "
" vanilla . . .	¼ "
" musk . . .	¼ "
Oil of lemon	1 ounce.
" verbena	½ "
" santal	¼ "
Orange-flower water . . .	8 "

A compound odor of my own, which has proved popular.

Bouquet de Caroline.

Extract of rose, No. 1 . .	1 pint.
" violet, No. 2 . .	1 "
" tuberose, No. 2 . .	½ "
Tincture of orris . . .	½ "
" ambergris . .	¼ "
Oil of bergamot	½ ounce.
" cedrat	¼ "
Rose-water, double . . .	8 "

This handkerchief extract has always been a favorite, and there is no reason why it should not continue to be so.

Extract of the Cedar of Lebanon.

Extract of rose, No. 1 . .	1 pint.
Tincture of ambrette . .	1 "
" orris	½ "

Oil of cedar	1 ounce.
" petit-grain	¼ "
Rose-water	8 "
Deodorized alcohol	1 pint.

Extrait de Chypré. (Cypress bouquet.)

Extract of rose, No. 1	1 pint.
Tincture of orris	1 "
" Tonquin	½ "
" vanilla	½ "
" musk	¼ "
" ambergris	¼ "
Rose-water, double	½ "

Caprice de la Mode. (Fashion bouquet.)

Extract of jasmin, No. 1	1 pint.
" tuberose, No. 2	1 "
" cassie, No. 2	½ "
Tincture of benzoin	½ "
" civet	¼ "
Oil of almonds	½ drachm.
" nutmegs	½ "
Orange-flower water, double	12 ounces.

Cashmere Nosegay.

Extract of violet, No. 1	1 pint.
" rose, No. 2	1½ "
Tincture of benzoin	½ "
" civet	¼ "
" Tonquin	¼ "
Flowers of benzoin	½ ounce.
Oil of patchouly	¼ "
" santal	½ "
Rose-water, triple	8 "

Bouquet de Cytheria.

Extract of cassie, No. 1	1	pint.
" jasmine, No. 2	½	"
" tuberose, No. 2	½	"
" rose, No. 2	½	"
Tincture of ambrette	½	"
" musk	¼	"
Oil of orange	1	ounce.
" cloves	¼	"
Rose-water, double	10	"

Cosmopolitan Bouquet.

Extract of tuberose, No. 1	1	pint.
" jasmin, No. 2	1	"
Tincture of orris	1	"
" civet	½	"
Oil of bergamot	1	ounce.
" neroli	¼	"
Rose-water, triple	8	"

Extract of Damask Rose.

Extract of rose, No. 1	1	pint.
" " No. 2	1	"
" tuberose, No. 2	½	"
Tincture of orris	½	"
" civet	¼	"
Oil of rhodium	¼	ounce.
Orange-flower water, triple	12	"

Bouquet des Dames. (Ladies' bouquet.)

Extract of jasmin, No. 1	1	pint.
" cassie, No. 2	½	"
" tuberose, No. 2	½	"

Tincture of ambergris	¼ pint.
" musk	¼ "
Oil of bergamot	1 ounce.
" verbena	¼ "
" cloves	1 drachm.
Deodorized alcohol	1 pint.
Rose-water, triple	½ "

Extract of Eglantine. (Sweetbrier.)

Extract of rose, No. 1	1 pint.
" cassie, No. 2	½ "
" orange flower, No. 2	½ "
Tincture of oris	½ "
" Tonquin	¼ "
Oil of verbena	½ drachm.
" neroli	½ "
Deodorized alcohol	1 pint.
Rose-water, double	½ "

The sweetbrier is a general favorite, and of course all perfumers try to imitate it. This is my idea of the perfume.

Euosmia. (Greek incense.)

Extract of rose, No. 1	1 pint.
" jasmin, No. 1	1 "
" cassie, No. 2	¾ "
Tincture of ambergris	¼ "
" musk	¼ "
" olibanum	¼ "
Oil of cedrat	1 ounce.
" rose	½ drachm.
" santal	½ ounce.
Orange-flower water, triple	8 "

This is an original essence, and deserves the popularity which it has obtained, as its fragrance is soft and lasting.

Flowers of Erin.

Extract of rose, No. 1 . .	1½ pint.
" jasmin, No. 2 . .	½ "
Tincture of orris . . .	1 "
" vanilla . . .	½ "
Rose-water	½ "

Bouquet d'Imperatrice.

Extract of rose, No. 1 . .	1 pint.
" tuberose, No. 1 . .	1 "
" violet, No. 2 . .	1 "
Tincture of vanilla . . .	¼ "
" Tonquin . . .	¼ "
Oil of santal	2 drachms.
" geranium	1 "
Rose-water, triple . . .	8 ounces.

This is a very pleasant odor, that will always please.

Extrait de Frangipani.

Extract of orange flower, No. 1	2 pints.
" rose, No. 2 . .	1 "
Tincture of musk . . .	¼ "
" vitivert . . .	¼ "
" orris . . .	½ "
Oil of santal	1 drachm.
" neroli	1 "
" rose	½ "
Rose-water, triple . . .	4 ounces.

This always popular extract is named after a

Roman family, by whom it was invented about a thousand years ago.

Florentine Bouquet.

Extract of tuberose, No. 1	1½ pint.
" jasmin, No. 1	½ "
" cassie, No. 2	1 "
Tincture of benzoin	¼ "
" civet	¼ "
Oil of rose	½ drachm.
" bergamot	½ ounce.
Orange-flower water, triple	8 "

Bouquet de Fée. (Fairy bouquet.)

Extract of violet, No. 1	1 pint.
" rose, No. 2	1 "
" jasmin, No. 2	½ "
Tincture of orris	½ "
" ambergris	¼ "
" civet	¼ "
Oil of neroli (bigarade)	½ ounce.
" cloves	¼ "
Rose-water, triple	8 "

An original bouquet of pleasant perfume.

Bouquet de Flora. (Nosegay of flowers.)

Extract of rose, No. 1	1 pint.
" jasmin, No. 2	1 "
" orange flower, No. 2	½ "
Tincture of orris	½ "
" civet	¼ "
" ambrette	¼ "
" musk	2 ounces.

Oil of lavender	1 drachm.
" bergamot	2 "
" cloves	1 "
" neroli	½ "
Orange-flower water . . .	6 ounces.

This is a very fine combination, and should be popular.

Extrait des Fleurs des Champs. (Wild flowers.)

Extract of cassie, No. 1 . .	1 pint.
" rose, No. 2 . .	1 "
" jasmin, No. 2 . .	1 "
Tincture of Tonquin . . .	½ "
" civet . . .	¼ "
Oil of bergamot	2 drachms.
" verbena	1 "
Orange-flower water, triple .	4 ounces.

Extrait des Fleurs d'Italie. (Italian nosegay.)

Extract of rose, No. 1 . . .	1 pint.
" orange flower, No. 2 .	½ "
" jasmin, No. 2 . .	½ "
" violet, No. 2 . .	½ "
Tincture of orris . . .	½ "
" musk . . .	¼ "
" benzoin . . .	¼ "
" ambergris . .	¼ "
Rose-water, double . . .	¼ "

This is one of the oldest and best known of essences.

Bouquet d'Indes. (Indian nosegay.)

Extract of rose, No. 1 . .	1½ pint.
" orange flower, No. 2 .	¾ "
Tincture of musk . . .	¼ "
" Tonquin . . .	½ "
" ambrette . . .	½ "
Oil of santal	1 drachm.
" patchouly . . .	1 "
Rose-water, triple . . .	8 ounces.

Extract de Fleur d'Orange. (Orange blossom.)

Extract of orange flower, No. 1	1 pint.
" " " No. 2	1 "
" cassie, No. 2 . .	½ "
Tincture of civet . . .	¼ "
" orris . . .	½ "
Oil of neroli (bigarade) . .	2 drachms.
Orange-flower water, triple .	4 ounces.

Extract of Geranium. (Rose geranium.)

Extract of cassie, No. 2 . .	2 pints.
" rose, No. 2 . . .	½ "
Tincture of benzoin . . .	½ "
" orris	¼ "
" ambrette . . .	¼ "
Oil of rose geranium (true) .	1½ ounce.
Rose-water, triple . . .	8 "

Gypsy Nosegay.

Extract of jasmin, No. 1 . .	1 pint.
" orange flower, No. 2	1 "
" cassie, No. 2 . .	1 "
Tincture of orris	½ "
" musk . . .	¼ "
Oil verbena	½ ounce.
Rose-water, triple . . .	4 "

Hedyosmia.

Extract of rose, No. 1 . .	1 pint.
" orange flower, No. 1 .	1 "
" cassie, No. 2 . .	1 "
Tincture of musk . . .	¼ "
" ambrette . . .	¼ "
Oil of neroli	1 drachm.
" lavender	2 "
" cloves	1 "
" angelica	½ "
Orange flower-water, triple . .	8 ounces.

This is an English odor and has numerous admirers.

Extrait au Heliotrope.

Extract of rose, No. 1 . .	2 pints.
" orange flower, No. 2	1 "
Tincture of vanilla . . .	½ "
" civet . . .	2 ounces.
" ambergris . .	2 "
Oil of almonds	1 drachm.
Rose-water, triple . . .	4 ounces.

Heliotrope is not cultivated for its perfume,

although very fine. This formula is an imitation, and I believe a very good one.

Extract of Honeysuckle. (Woodbine.)

Extract of rose, No. 1	1	pint.
" orange flower, No. 1	1	"
" tuberose, No. 2	½	"
Tincture of Tolu	½	"
" vanilla	¼	"
" musk	¼	"
Oil of neroli, petale	1	drachm.
" almonds	½	"
Rose-water	8	ounces.

Extract of Hovenia.

Extract of cassiè, No. 1	1¼	pint.
" orange flower, No. 2	1	"
Tincture of ambrette	½	"
" orris	½	"
" civet	¼	"
Oil of neroli	½	drachm.
" rose	½	"
" limette	2	"
" cloves	½	"
Orange-flower water, triple	8	ounces.

Hovenia is a native of Japan, but is not a very pleasant odor, but the English perfumers liking the name have compounded an odor which resembles that of the above recipe.

Honeymoon Bouquet.

Like Bouquet d'Amour.

Extrait a la Jacinthe. (Hyacinth.)

Extract of tuberose, No. 1	1 pint.
" rose, No. 2	1 "
" jasmin, No. 2	1 "
Tincture of Tonquin	¼ "
" ambergris	¼ "
Orange-flower water, triple	½ "

Extrait au Jasmin.

Extract of jasmin, No. 1	1½ pint.
" " No. 2	1 "
Tincture of ambrette	½ "
" civet	¼ "
Orange-flower water	¾ "

Jasmin alone is somewhat heavy in odor, but by a slight modification is made pleasant and permanent.

Extrait a la Jonquille.

Extract of tuberose, No. 1	1 pint.
" jasmin, No. 1	1 "
" orange flower, No. 1	1 "
Tincture of orris	½ "
" vanilla	¼ "
" civet	¼ "
Rose-water	¼ "

This, of course, is an imitation, but nevertheless a good one, of pleasant fragrance.

Jockey Club Bouquet.

Extract of rose, No. 1	1 pint.
" cassie, No. 1	1 "
" orange flower, No. 1	½ "

Tincture of orris	½ pint.
" ambergris	¼ "
" musk	¼ "
Oil of bergamot	1 ounce.
" rose	1 drachm.
Orange-flower water	8 ounces.

This is of English origin, and has a great name and a great sale.

Kiss-Me-Quick.

Extract of jasmine, No. 1	1 pint.
" violet, No. 2	½ "
" rose, No. 2	½ "
Tincture of vanilla	¼ "
" vitivert	¼ "
" orris	½ "
" musk	¼ "
Oil of bergamot	1 ounce.
" rose	1 drachm.
" cloves	½ "
Rose-water, double	8 ounces.

A fancy perfume still in vogue.

Extrait de Lilas. (Lilac blossom.)

Extract of tuberose, No. 1	1 pint.
" cassie, No. 2	½ "
" orange flower, No. 2	1 "
Tincture of orris	½ "
" civet	¼ "
Rose-water, triple	¾ "

The perfume of the lilac, like that flower, soon fades; therefore we make an imitation.

Extract of Lily of the Valley.

Extract of tuberose, No. 1 . .	1 pint.
" jasmine, No. 2 . .	1 "
" orange flower, No. 2 .	1 "
Tincture of vanilla . . .	¼ "
" benzoin . . .	¼ "
Oil of almonds	1 drachm.
Rose-water, triple . . .	8 ounces.

This is also an imitation, but, as I think, an improvement on the original.

Extract of Garden Lavender.

Deodorized alcohol . . .	1½ pint.
Extract of cassie, No. 2 . .	1 "
Tincture of ambrette . . .	½ "
" orris . . .	½ "
Oil of Eng. lavender . . .	2 ounces.
Rose-water, triple . . .	8 "

Be careful to use the English oil, as the French lavender is not nearly so sweet.

Extract of Magnolia.

Extract of tuberose, No. 2 . .	1 pint.
" orange flower, No. 1 .	1 "
" violet, No. 2 . .	1 "
" rose, No. 2 . .	½ "
Tincture of musk . . .	¼ "
Oil of cedrat	1 ounce.
" almonds	1 drachm.
Rose-water, triple . . .	4 ounces.

An imitation of a delightful fragrance that will be found excellent.

Extrait des Fleurs de Mai. (May flowers.)

Extract of cassie, No. 1	1 pint.
" tuberose, No. 1	1 "
" jasmine, No. 2	½ "
" orange flower, No. 2	½ "
Tincture of ambrette	¼ "
" vanilla	¼ "
Oil of geranium	2 drachms.
" neroli	1 "
" almonds	½ "
Rose-water, triple	8 ounces.

Bouquet de Mille-fleurs. (A thousand flowers.)

Extract of rose, No. 1	1 pint.
" tuberose, No. 2	½ "
" jasmine, No. 2	½ "
" orange flower, No. 2	½ "
" cassie, No. 2	½ "
Tincture of vanilla	¼ "
" musk	2 ounces.
" ambergris	2 "
Oil of neroli	1 drachm.
" bergamot	2 "
" cloves	½ "
" almonds	½ "
Rose-water, triple	8 ounces.

A perfume that has always been popular and always will be.

Extract of Meadow-sweet.

Extract of cassie, No. 1 . . .	1 pint.
" orange flower, No. 2 .	1 "
" jasmine, No. 2 . .	1 "
Tincture of Tonquin . . .	¼ "
" orris . . .	¼ "
" civet . . .	2 ounces.
Oil of bergamot	1 "
" almonds	1 drachm.
Rose-water, triple . . .	8 ounces.

A pleasant perfume of delicate character.

Extract of Moss Rose.

Extract of rose, No. 1 . .	1 pint.
" " No. 2 . .	1 "
" orange flower, No. 2 .	½ "
Tincture of orris . . .	1 "
" civet . . .	¼ "
Oil of rose	½ drachm.
" rhodium	½ "
Rose-water, triple . . .	4 ounces.

This will be found to be a fine perfume that will improve by age.

Extrait de Musc. (Musk extract.)

Extract of rose, No. 2 . .	2 pints.
Tincture of musk . . .	1 "
" civet . . .	¼ "
" ambergris . .	¼ "
" ambrette . . .	¼ "
" storax . . .	1 ounce.
Rose-water, triple . . .	4 "

This is a general favorite, though many will say that they "cannot bear musk."

Bouquet de Marechale.

Extract of rose, No. 1 . . .	1 pint.
" orange-flower, No. 2 .	1 "
Tincture of vitivert . . .	1 "
" Tonquin . . .	¼ "
" vanilla . . .	¼ "
" orris . . .	¼ "
Oil of neroli	1 drachm.
" vitivert	½ "
Rose-water, triple . . .	4 ounces.

This odor had at one time a great name; its popularity was due to the vitivert. It is still in demand.

Extract of Narcissus.

Extract of jasmine, No. 1 . .	1 pint.
" cassie, No. 2 . .	1 "
" rose, No. 2 . .	½ "
Tincture of vanilla . . .	¼ "
" civet . . .	¼ "
" orris . . .	½ "
Oil of almonds	1 drachm.
Orange-flower water, triple .	8 ounces.

Extract of New-mown Hay.

Extract of rose, No. 1 . .	1 pint.
" cassie, No. 2 . .	1 "
" orange flower, No. 2	½ "
Tincture of Tonquin . . .	½ "
" vanilla . . .	¼ "
" orris . . .	¼ "
Oil of cedrat	1 ounce.
" verbena	½ "
Orange-flower water, triple .	8 "

This is justly a very popular extract, and its odor of the hay will be found very natural.

Extract of Night-blooming Cereus.

Extract of tuberose, No. 1	1 pint.
" rose, No. 2	1 "
" violet, No. 2	½ "
" jasmine, No. 2	½ "
Tincture of vanilla	¼ "
" benzoin	2 ounces.
" musk	2 "
Oil of nutmegs	1 drachm.
" santal	1 "
" neroli	1 "
" almonds	½ "
Orange-flower water, triple	8 ounces.

This imitation has had an extensive sale, and is yet quite popular.

Extrait d'Œillet. (Clove pink.)

Extract of rose, No. 1	1 pint.
" cassie, No. 2	1 "
Tincture of vanilla	¼ "
" ambrette	½ "
" orris	¼ "
Oil of cinnamon (true)	1 drachm.
" cloves	2 "
" petit-grain	1 "
Alcohol	½ pint.
Orange-flower water, triple	½ "

The clove pink has a beautiful odor, which this compound closely imitates.

Bouquet d'Odalisque.

Extract of rose, No. 2	1 pint.
" jasmine, No. 1	1 "
" tuberose, No. 2	½ "
" orange-flower, No. 2	½ "
Tincture of Tonquin	2 ounces.
" musk	2 "
" civet	2 "
" ambergris	1 "
Oil of santal	1 drachm.
" patchouly	½ "
Rose-water, triple	8 ounces.

Extract of Opoponax.

Extract of cassie, No. 1	1 pint.
" tuberose, No. 2	1 "
" jasmine, No. 2	½ "
Tincture of orris	½ "
" benzoin	¼ "
" Tolu	¼ "
" ambrette	¼ "
" musk	2 ounces.
Rose-water	4 "

Under this name there has been a perfume in vogue, though the name applies to a gum.

Oriental Drops.

Extract of rose, No. 1	1 pint.
" tuberose, No. 2	½ "
" jasmine, No. 2	½ "
Tincture of orris	½ "
" vanilla	¼ "

Tincture of vitivert . . .	¼ pint.
" santal . . .	¼ "
" musk . . .	¼ "
Oil of neroli	1 drachm.
" santal	2 "
" patchouly . . .	1 "
" rose	½ "
Rose-water, triple . . .	8 ounces.

This is a good extract, exceedingly fragrant and lasting.

Extract de Patchouly.

Extract of rose, No. 2 . .	1 pint.
" orange flower, No. 2 .	1 "
Deodorized alcohol . . .	1½ "
Oil of patchouly . . .	6 drachms.
" rose	1 "
Rose-water, triple . . .	8 ounces.

Patchouly, so long known and fashionable, is not so pleasant in itself, but when modified as above is very pleasant and permanent.

Extrait de la Fleur de Pesche. (Peach blossom.)

Extract of cassie, No. 2 . .	1 pint.
" orange flower, No. 2 .	1 "
Deodorized alcohol . . .	1 "
Oil of almonds	3 dr'ms.
Rose-water, triple . . .	8 ounces.
Liq. carmine (to color) . .	10 drops.
Tincture of orris . . .	8 ounces.

Extract of Primrose.

Extract of Rose, No. 2 . .	1 pint.
" cassie, No. 2 . .	½ "
" jasmine, No. 2 . .	½ "
Tincture of orris . . .	½ "
" Tonquin . . .	¼ "
" ambrette . . .	¼ "
Oil of almonds	1 drachm.
" bergamot	2 "
Rectified spirit	1 pint.

This will be found to have more odor and to be of pleasanter fragrance than the flower, or an "improvement on nature."

Extrait du Pois de Senteur. (Sweat Pea.)

Extract of tuberose, No. 1 .	1½ pint.
" orange flower, No. 2	1 "
" rose, No. 2 . .	½ "
Tincture of vanilla . . .	½ "
Rose-water, triple . . .	½ "

As we have not the flowers in sufficient quantities from which to make the genuine article, we have recourse to this imitation, which is fine.

Extract of Pond Lily.

Extract of orange flower, No. 1 .	1 pint.
" cassie, No. 2 . .	½ "
" rose, No. 2 . .	1 "
Tincture of vanilla . . .	½ "
" civet . . .	¼ "
" orris	¼ "

Oil of cedrat	½ ounce.
" bergamot	1 "
" cloves	¼ "
" almond	1 drachm.
Orange-flower water, triple .	8 ounces.

This has proved a very popular essence, and deservedly so, as the combination is very fine.

Bouquet de la Reine. (Queen's nosegay.)

Extract of rose, No. 1 . .	1 pint.
" violet, No. 1 . .	½ "
" orange flower, No. 2	1 "
" tuberose . . .	½ "
Tincture of orris . . .	¼ "
" civet . . .	¼ "
Oil of bergamot . . .	¼ ounce.
Rose-water, triple . . .	8 ounces.

Bouquet du Roi. (Royal nosegay.)

Extract of jasmine, No. 1 . .	1 pint.
" violet, No. 1 . .	½ "
" rose, No. 2 . .	1 "
Tincture of vanilla . . .	¼ "
" vitivert . . .	¼ "
" musk . . .	2 ounces.
" ambrette . . .	2 "
Oil of bergamot	1 "
" cloves	2 drachms.
Orange-flower water, triple .	12 ounces.

Extrait a la Rose.

Extract of rose, No. 1 . .	2 pints.
" " No. 2 . .	1 "
Tincture of civet . . .	¼ "
" orris	½ "
Oil of rose	1 drachm.
Triple rose-water . . .	4 ounces.

Extract of Rendelatia.

Extract of cassie, No. 2 . .	1 pint.
" rose, No. 2 . .	1 "
Tincture of ambrette . . .	½ "
" vanilla . . .	¼ "
" musk . . .	¼ "
Oil of lavender, English . .	1 ounce.
" cloves	½ "
" bergamot	½ "
" Rose	½ drachm.
Rose-water, double . . .	12 ounces.

This extract owes its great success to the peculiar combination of the two odors of lavender and cloves, which when mixed form a distinct odor that is universally admired.

Extrait de Réséda. (Mignonette.)

Extract of mignonette, No. 1 .	2 pints.
" cassie, No. 2 . .	½ "
Tincture of orris . . .	½ "
" benzoin . . .	¼ "
" Tonquin . . .	4 ounces.
Rose-water, triple . . .	8 "

Extract of Spring Flowers.

Extract of rose, No. 1 . . .	1 pint.
" violet, No. 2 . . .	1 "
" orange flower, No. 2 . .	½ "
Tincture of orris	½ "
" ambrette	¼ "
" Tonquin	¼ "
Oil of bergamot	1 ounce.
" cedrat	½ "
" almonds	1 drachm.
Orange-flower water, triple .	8 ounces.

Extrait du Bois de Santal.

Extract of rose, No. 2 . . .	1 pint.
" cassie, No. 2 . . .	1 "
Deodorized alcohol	1 "
Tincture of orris	¼ "
Oil of santal	1 ounce.
Tincture of santal	¼ pint.
Rose-water, triple	½ "

Santal has a very pleasant odor, though for the handkerchief it is much refined and improved by the above mixture.

Extract of Sweet Brier. (*See* Ex. Eglantine.)

Extract of Syringa.

Like Orange-Flower Extract.

Extrait Suave.

Extract of jasmine, No. 1 . . .	1 pint.
" cassie, No. 2 . . .	1 "
" tuberose, No. 2 . . .	½ "

Tincture of orris	½ pint.
“ musk	¼ “
“ Tonquin	¼ “
Oil of bergamot	1 ounce.
“ cloves	½ “
“ neroli	¼ “
Rose-water, triple	8 “

Extract of Summer Blossoms.

Extract of orange flower, No. 1	1 pint.
“ cassie, No. 2	1 “
Tincture of ambrette	½ “
“ Tonquin	¼ “
“ tolu	¼ “
“ orris	¼ “
“ musk	¼ “
Oil of bergamot	1 ounce.
“ cloves	½ “
“ almonds	1 drachm.
Ross-water, triple	8 ounces.

Extract of Sweet Clover.

Extract of rose, No. 1	1 pint.
“ cassie, No. 2	1 “
Tincture of orris	½ “
“ Tonquin	¼ “
“ ambrette	½ “
“ musk	2 ounces.
Rose-water	10 “
Oil of petit-grain	½ “
“ bergamot	1 “
“ cloves	¼ “

Extract of Sweet Flag.

Extract of rose, No. 2 . .	1 pint.
" cassie, No. 2 . .	1 "
Tincture of orris . . .	1 "
" Tonquin . . .	¼ "
" civet . . .	¼ "
" tolu	¼ "
Orange-flower water, triple .	¼ "

Sweet flag is another name for Florentine iris, and its odor, which resembles violet, is much admired by many. The recipe improves it very much.

Extract of Tea Rose.

Extract of rose, No. 1 . .	3 pints.
Tincture of ambergris . .	¼ "
" musk . . .	¼ "
Oil of neroli petale . . .	1 drachm.
" rhodium	2 "
Rose-water, triple . . .	8 ounces.

This is a very fine form of rose essence, the rhodium giving a pleasant change.

Extract of Tuberose.

Extract of tuberose, No. 1 . .	3 pints.
Tincture of orris . . .	¼ "
" vanilla . . .	¼ "
Rose-water, triple . . .	½ "

These ingredients added to the tuberose give it softness and permanency.

Extract of Tulip.

Extract of tuberose, No. 1 . .	1 pint.
" violet, No. 2 . .	1 "
" rose, No. 2 . .	1 "
Tincture of orris	½ "
" musk . . .	¼ "
Oil of almonds	1 drachm.
Orange-flower water, triple .	4 ounces.

Bouquet du Turquie. (Turkish nosegay.)

Extract of rose, No. 1 . .	1 pint.
" cassie, No. 2 . .	1 "
" orange flower, No. 2 .	1 "
Tincture of musk . . .	¼ "
" benzoin . . .	¼ "
" Tonquin . . .	¼ "
Oil of bergamot	1 ounce.
" cloves	½ "
" lavender (English) . .	½ "
Rose-water, triple . . .	4 "

A good bouquet of strong and lasting odor.

Extract of Vanilla.

Extract of rose, No. 2 . .	1 pint.
" orange flower, No. 2 .	1 "
Tincture of vanilla . . .	1½ "
" Tonquin . . .	¼ "
Rose-water, triple . . .	¼ "

Vanilla, though entering into so many bouquets, is seldom used by itself. When desired, this formula is of fine odor.

Extrait de Verveine.

Extract of orange flower, No. 2	1	pint.
" tuberose, No. 2	1	"
" rose, No. 2	1	"
Tincture of ambrette	½	"
" orris	¼	"
Oil of lemon-grass	1	ounce.
" limette	½	"
Orange-flower water	4	"

This is a very fine recipe for verbena, and is a very refreshing perfume.

Extract of Violet. (Wood violet.)

Extract of violet, No. 1.	1½	pint.
" cassie, No. 2	½	"
" rose, No. 2	½	"
" tuberose, No. 2	⅓	"
Tincture of orris	½	"
" ambergris	¼	"
Oil of almonds	1	drachm.
Rose-water, triple	4	ounces.

An extract of exquisite delicacy.

Bouquet de Venus. (Venus nosegay.)

Extract of rose, No. 1	1	pint.
" jasmine, No. 2	1	"
" violet, No. 2	½	"
" cassie, No. 2	½	"
Tincture of musk	¼	"
" ambrette	¼	"
" benzoin	¼	"
Rose-water, triple	¼	"

Extract of Volkameria.

Extract of violet, No. 1 . .	1 pint.
" tuberose, No. 1 . .	1 "
" jasmine, No. 2 . .	½ "
" rose, No. 2 . .	½ "
Tincture of orris . . .	¼ "
" ambrette . . .	¼ "
" musk . . .	2 ounces.
Rose-water, triple . . .	6 "

This perfume is an imitation of a fine odor, greatly esteemed by the French, the beau-monde being much attracted by its euphonious name. The plant is a native of India, but we have never seen the genuine perfume.

Extract of Wall-flower.

Extract of orange flower, No. 1 .	1 pint.
" rose, No. 2 . .	1 "
" cassie, No. 2 . .	1 "
Tincture of ambergris . .	¼ "
" Tonquin . . .	¼ "
" musk . . .	¼ "
Oil of almonds	1 drachm.
Rose-water, triple . . .	4 ounces.

Extract of Wisteria.

Extract of rose, No. 1 . .	1 pint.
" cassie, No. 2 . .	1 "
" violet, No. 2 . .	1 "
Tincture of ambrette . . .	¼ "
" civet . . .	¼ "
" orris . . .	¼ "

Oil of verbena	1 drachm.
" santal	1 "
Orange-flower water, triple .	4 ounces.

West-end Bouquet.

Extract of tuberose, No. 1 . .	1 pint.
" jasmine, No. 2 . .	1 "
" rose, No. 2 . .	½ "
Tincture of cedar . . .	½ "
" Tonquin . . .	¼ "
" musk . . .	¼ "
Oil of limette	1 ounce.
" verbena	½ "
" neroli	1 drachm.
Orange-flower water, triple .	8 ounces.

Yacht Club Bouquet.

Extract of jasmine, No. 1 . .	1 pint.
" rose, No. 1 . .	1 "
" orange flower, No. 2 .	1 "
Tincture of civet . . .	¼ "
" orris	½ "
Flowers of benzoin . . .	½ ounce.
Oil of neroli (petale) . . .	2 dr'ms.
Rose-water, triple . . .	4 ounces.

This is a very pleasant bouquet, and has had a long-continued popularity.

Extract of Ylang Ylang.

Extract of jasmine, No. 2 . .	1 pint.
" rose, No. 2 . .	1 "
Tincture of orris . . .	½ "

Tincture of civet	. . . ¼	pint.
Oil of ylang ylang	. . . ½	ounce.
Rectified spirit (65°)	. . . 1½	pint.

This is a new and favorite extract of East Indian source, and is a distinctive odor.

The formulas given are those of the proper strength for usual sale; if the perfumer wishes a cheaper article, he can dilute them with rectified spirit of 65° strength, as he may wish, or with rose and orange-flower water, though they would be difficult to make clear, and it would be a loss of perfume to filter very often. The rose and orange-flower waters I use are those imported from France and Italy, and are far superior to any we distil in this country. It is necessary to keep in mind that as these extracts and bouquets are intended for the handkerchief, all coloring matter that would make a stain must be avoided. In giving the formulas I have endeavored to avoid all articles having any decided color, but if by chance the compound should have too much, filtering through coarsely ground animal charcoal will generally remove it.

It will also be seen that I have given the formula for about four pints of extract, as the most convenient, as I thought, for the manipulator or dealer; should he want a smaller quantity he can easily divide it, or if a larger, multiply it *ad infinitum.*

Few perfumes for the handkerchief should be distilled, for the true delicacy of the flower odor is injured or lost, for any excess of heat will alter if not destroy it. I mention this as a precaution, because many books advise distillation for many such preparations.

The perfumer in this country has several disadvantages to contend with. His alcohol is generally made from corn spirit, while the alcohol used by the French is of brandy spirit, the bouquet of which is so different from ours, and which no doubt gives the peculiarity to their perfumes, especially to the eau de Cologne, that we cannot hope to rival until such spirit is attainable; and yet there are some few odors made from our spirit, when properly deodorized, that have as good if not better fragrance than theirs. But for citrous odors and for lavender theirs is superior. I would suggest, that, when the perfumer wishes to simulate the brandy spirit, a half ounce of acetic ether to each gallon of alcohol will have the desired effect.

In the preceding formulas for extracts and bouquets the reader will perceive I use a small portion of the distilled waters of rose and orange flower. This is because our alcohol comes to us at 95° in strength, which is too strong for the extracts, making them too pungent and volatile. The French recipes call for spirit fully 10° less in strength. Hence the reason for my formulas having the waters to bring them to about that strength. If they should not be clear, a few grains of carbonate of magnesia in the filter will make them so. None of these odors should be bottled or sold until they are three or four weeks old, as all perfumes made of spirit seem to require that length of time to get a proper blending of the odors; and if well made they improve with time.

CHAPTER VIII.

AROMATIC AND TOILET WATERS.

WHILE giving so many recipes for making the handkerchief odors, I may apologize for their great number; but they are selected from at least as many more at my command as being the best, simplest, and most in demand. I have also adopted terms in general use by druggists in this country to designate the materials used, as also the apothecary's or troy weight. I designate a tincture, such as has alcohol as the solvent of the drug. Extracts, all the alcoholates of simple odors from the French oils and pomades, and essential oils I call oils, that term being the best known. I repeat this as a reason for giving simple terms as far as practicable, as I essay to write a practical work, and use only such terms that the operator may not be misled.

I shall now proceed to give the formulas I have adopted for making the weak or spirituous perfumes which I call toilet or aromatic waters, such as eau de Cologne, lavender or Hungary water, bay rum, aromatic vinegars, etc. etc. The old books are filled with formulas, the ingredients of which, if not unknown to modern and improved tastes, are useless except as guides to a better selection suited to present uses.

Cologne water or eau de Cologne, so universally known and used wherever civilization exists, was invented early in the eighteenth century, although at first it was called ésprit de vie, or elixir of life; nor has it lost any of its popularity by being classed among perfumes only.

Innumerable formulas for eau de Cologne exist and are extolled to the skies by their authors, yet the proper ingredients are very simple, for it owes its well-deserved standing in the world of perfumes to the fragrance of the citron plant. As bergamot, lemon, orange, cedrat, limette, neroli, with rosemary, are the chief ingredients—these odors, in greater or less variety, modified to the taste, enter into all genuine Cologne waters. Many writers on perfumery would persuade us that it is necessary to take the whole range of aromatic substances and all the herbs in a book on botany to compound a true Cologne, but it were worse than useless to use such ingredients, for they give an odor foreign to the true eau de Cologne, and deprive it of the refreshing property for which it is esteemed.

Owing to the use of alcohol from the grape spirit by the German and French manufacturers of Cologne, we cannot hope to attain the quality of excellence with our alcohol from the corn spirit, for it would seem that the grape spirit is especially adapted to the citron odors to produce the proper aroma for eau de Cologne. Yet with our spirit properly deodorized, a very good product can be obtained, when good judgment is used in selecting pure and fresh materials.

The most noted manufacturers of Cologne distil the citron oils with the spirit and afterward add the neroli and rosemary. Yet a very good eau de Cologne can be made by merely mixing the ingredients as given by my formulas. As a rule, when the odor is delicate, like jasmine, tuberose, etc., distilling is injurious, destroying its ethereal fragrance and producing a different odor.

No. 1. *Eau de Cologne.* (J. M. Farina.)

Oil of bergamot	4	fluidounces.
" lemon	1½	"
" neroli, bigarade	3	"
" rosemary	3	"
" cloves	½	"
" lavender (best)	½	"
Deodorized alcohol	2½	gallons.
Rectified spirit	1½	"

No. 2. *Eau de Cologne.* (French recipe.)

Oil of neroli (petale)	3	ounces.
" bergamot	3	"
" petit-grain	1	"
" cedrat	3	"
" orange (Portugal)	5	"
" rosemary	3	"
Deodorized spirit, 65°	5½	gallons.

Mix well and allow it to rest seven days before filtering.

No. 3. *Eau de Cologne.* (Second quality.)

Oil of bergamot	4	ounces.
" lemon	4	"
" orange	4	"
" rosemary	3	"
" neroli (petale)	1	"
" petit-grain	2	"
Alcohol, 85°	6¾	gallons.

Cologne water is very volatile, and I have found favor for my own recipes because I have made them more lasting by adding some fixing ingredient, which also tends to correct the odor of the fusel oil which remains in the corn spirit, and is unpleasant.

No. 4. *Eau de Cologne.* (Cristiani's.)

Oil of bergamot	8 fl. ounces.
" cedrat	4 "
" rosemary (flowers) . .	4 "
" neroli, bigarade . .	2 "
" petit-grain . . .	2 "
" cloves	1 "
Extract of orange-flower, No. 1 (from pomade) . . .	1 pint.
Tincture of ambrette . . .	¼ "
" orris . . .	¼ "
Deodorized alcohol, 95° . .	6 gallons.
Orange-flower water, triple . .	1 "

This has given general satisfaction, as it approaches in odor many of the most celebrated German colognes.

Cologne Oil. (Cristiani's Cologne Essence.)

Oil of rosemary (flowers) . .	8 ounces.
" bergamot	8 "
" orange (Portugal) . .	6 "
" lemon	4 "
" cedrat	4 "
" neroli (petale) . . .	4 "
" petit-grain . . .	4 "
" lavender (best) . .	2 "
" cloves	2 "
Alcohol, 95°	5½ pints.

Four ounces of this essence in 7 pints of alcohol and 1 pint of orange-flower water, will make a good cologne water suited to the wants of American buyers.

Eau d'Ange. (Angel water.)

Myrtle flowers	2 pounds.
Rose leaves	½ "
Rectified spirit	8 pints.
Water	2½ "
Salt	1 pound.

Digest together for two days, when distil off one gallon; the salt to be added just before distilling.

Eau de Beauté.

Tincture of benzoin . . .	2 ounces.
" ambergris . .	½ "
" musk . . .	¼ "
Rectified spirit, 65° . . .	½ pint.
Orange-flower water . . .	3½ "

A very cooling and refreshing perfume and cosmetic for the skin. Properly made it will retain its milky appearance, and it is much esteemed for the removal of freckles, tan, etc.

Eau de Bouquet de Fleur.

Oil of cedrat	½ fl. ounce.
" rosemary	½ "
Extract of rose	4 "
" violet . . .	2 "
Tincture of ambergris . .	1 "
Alcohol, 95°	2½ pints.
Orange-flower water . . .	1 "

This is a desirable perfume for the handkerchief or lavatory.

Eau de Grand Duchesse.

Oil of Portugal (orange)	1 ounce.
" rosemary	½ "
" cloves	2 drachms.
" neroli	½ "
Tincture of orris	¼ pint.
Alcohol	3 "
Rose-water	¾ "

Florida Water. (Cristiani's.)

Oil of bergamot	8 ounces.
" orange	4 "
" lavender (best)	3 "
" cloves	1½ "
" cinnamon (true)	¼ pint.
Tincture of orris	½ "
" Peru balsam	¼ "
Alcohol, 95°	4 gallons.
Water	6 pints.

Mix, and let it remain quiet for some days before filtering and bottling. Florida water has a great popularity in the West Indies and South America, whence I have made frequent shipments, and this formula has given general satisfaction.

Eau de Fée. (Fairy water.)

Oil of lemon	1 ounce.
" bergamot	½ "
" rosemary	½ "
" lavender	½ "
" cloves	¼ "
Tincture of ambrette	4 "
" civet	2 "
Alcohol, 95°	3 pints.
Orange-flower water	½ "

This will be found to be a pleasant and economical toilet water, and can also be used on the handkerchief.

Geranium Water.

Oil of rose geranium, French .	2 fl. ounces.
Tincture of orris . . .	4 "
" ambrette . . .	4 "
Alcohol, 95°	3 pints.
Rose-water	½ "

Hedyosmia Water.

Oil of neroli, petale . . .	½ ounce.
" lavender (best) . .	½ "
" cloves	¼ "
" rose	1 drachm.
Tincture of orris . . .	½ pint.
" musk . . .	2 ounces.
Alcohol, 95°	3 pints.
Orange-flower water . . .	¼ "

A modification of an English recipe where the directions are to distil. It is only necessary to filter the above and produce a very fine toilet water.

Heliotrope Water.

Oil of rhodium	1 drachm.
" rose	1 "
" almonds	20 drops.
Tincture of orris . . .	½ pint.
" vanilla . . .	¼ "
" musk . . .	1 ounce.
Alcohol, 95°	3 pints.
Rose-water, triple . . .	4 ounces.

This will be found excellent.

Eau de Lavand. (Lavender water.)

Oil of lavender (best) . .	3 ounces.
" rhodium . . .	1 drachm.
Alcohol, 95°	3 pints.
Rose-water	1 "

Lavender water has had and still retains great favor with many people, and when distilled is very fine. The above formula may be distilled, but if filtered only it will prove good.

Eau de Lavand Ambré. (Amber lavender.)

Oil of lavender (Mitcham) . .	2 fl. ounces.
" rose	1 fl. drachm.
" bergamot	1 fl. ounce.
Tincture of musk . . .	1 "
" ambergris . .	1 "
Alcohol, 95°	3 pints.
Rose-water, triple . . .	1 "

Mix, and let it stand a week, filter, and it will be found excellent.

Hungary Water.

Oil of rosemary	1 ounce.
" lavender (best). . .	½ "
" petit-grain . . .	1 drachm.
Tincture of Tolu. . . .	1 ounce.
Alcohol	3 pints.
Orange-flower water . . .	1 "

Hungary water owes its peculiarity to rosemary, and was invented several hundred years since, when it was supposed to have the power of causing those who used it as a cosmetic to remain young forever.

Eau de Miel. (Honey water.)

Oil of lemon	1 ounce.
" cloves	$\frac{1}{4}$ "
" neroli	1 drachm.
Tincture of vanilla	2 ounces.
" ambrette	2 "
" musk	1 "
Alcohol, 95°	3 pints.
Orange-flower water	$\frac{3}{4}$ "

A very fine fragrant water.

Eau de Millefleur.

Oil of bergamot	$\frac{1}{2}$ ounce.
" neroli	$\frac{1}{4}$ "
" cloves	$\frac{1}{4}$ "
" almonds	1 drachm.
Tincture of orris	$\frac{1}{2}$ pint.
" cedar	$\frac{1}{4}$ "
" ambrette	$\frac{1}{4}$ "
" musk	1 ounce.
Extract of rose, No. 2	2 "
" cassie, No. 2	2 "
Alcohol, 95°	2 pints.
Rose-water, triple	$\frac{1}{2}$ "

This will be found a favorite fragrance, and a very permanent one for the bath or the handkerchief.

Eau de Romain. (Italian flowers.)

Oil of orange (Portugal)	1 fl. ounce.
" neroli, petale	$\frac{1}{2}$ "
Tincture of benzoin	2 "
" vanilla	2 "

Tincture of ambergris . . .	1 fl. ounce.
Extract of tuberose, No. 2 . .	2 "
" cassie, No. 2 . .	2 "
Alcohol, 95°	3 pints.
Rose-water, triple . . .	¼ "

This is from an original Italian recipe, and nothing I ever made in this form has had a greater popularity. It is delicate and lasting, and superior to many of the so-called French extracts.

Eau de Sultana.

Oil of orange	1 ounce.
" rose	1 drachm.
Extract of jasmine, No. 1 . .	2 ounces.
Tincture of vanilla . . .	2 "
Tincture of benzoin . . .	1 "
Flowers of benzoin . . .	1 drachm.
Alcohol	3 pints.
Orange-flower water . . .	¾ "

Eau Hygienique.

Eau bouquet de fleur . . .	2 pints.
Gum camphor	1 ounce.
Alcohol	1 pint.

Used as a wash for the skin.

Eau de Mousseline.

Extract of rose, No. 2 . .	2 ounces.
" jasmine, No. 2 . .	2 "
" orange flower, No. 2 .	2 "
Tincture of vanilla . . .	1 "
" musk . . .	1 "

Oil of cloves	1 drachm.
" santal	½ "
Alcohol	3 pints.
Orange-flower water	½ "

Eau de Violette de Parme. (Italian violet.)

Extract of cassie, No. 2	2 ounces.
" violet, No. 2	2 "
Tincture of orris	4 "
" civet	1 "
Oil of almonds	½ drachm.
" rhodium	1 "
Alcohol, 95°	3 pints.
Rose-water, triple	¼ "

Violet water will be found a delicate and pleasant article for the toilet or the handkerchief.

Eau Vulneraire.

Oil of lemon	½ ounce.
" rosemary	½ "
" peppermint	1 drachm.
Tincture of benzoin	4 ounces.
" musk	2 "
Rectified spirit, 65°	3½ pints.

Eau de Vanille.

Tincture of vanilla	1½ pint.
" Tolu	¼ "
" Tonquin	¼ "
" ambrette	½ "
Alcohol	1 "
Rose-water	½ "

Verbena Water.

Oil of lemon grass . . .	1½ ounce.
" lemon	½ "
" neroli (petit-grain) . .	¼ "
Tincture of orris . . .	4 "
" Tonquin . . .	2 "
Alcohol, 95°	3 pints.
Orange-flower water . . .	½ "

An exceedingly refreshing perfume, and made in this manner will be found better than the generality of verbena water in the market.

Bay Rum.

Oil of bay	½ ounce.
Loaf sugar	2 "
Alcohol, 95°	1 pint.
Rectified spirit, 60° . . .	7 "

Beat up the sugar with the oil and add the alcohol; lastly put in the spirit, and filter. Bay rum can be made better by using N. E. rum instead of the spirit.

I might continue the list of aromatic waters without limit, as there are many more; but they are but modifications of those given, and should others be needed the perfumer can get a very correct idea of their ingredients from those already given.

The expert manipulator with the materials at hand can make almost any desired odor, or can invent one himself and give it any euphonious name he may elect. I must proceed to give formulas for ammoniated and acetic waters or vinegars.

The pungency of vinegar used to be thought a hygienic property, and was naturally used as a prophylactic with satisfactory results; indeed, it is a very valuable form of perfume, as its effects are beneficial when a few drops are added to a bath or the lavatory.

Vinaigre Aromatique. (De Bully.)

Oil of lemon	1 ounce.
" lavender (Eng.) . .	½ "
" rosemary flower . .	¼ "
" cloves	¼ "
Gum camphor	1 "
Tincture of benzoin . . .	2 "
" orris . . .	2 "
" storax . . .	1 "
" Tonquin . .	1 "
" musk . . .	1 "
Alcohol, 95°	4½ pints.
Acetic acid	1 "
Rose-water, triple . . .	1½ "

Dissolve the oils and camphor in the alcohol; add the tincture, then the acid, lastly the rose-water; let it stand a fortnight before filtering.

Cologne Vinegar.

Cologne essence (Cristiani's) .	2 ounces.
Alcohol	3 pints.
Acetic acid	½ "
Orange-flower water . .	½ "

This can also be made by adding a portion of acetic acid, say one-eighth, to ordinary Cologne, when acetated Cologne is ordered. I prefer operating as above, as it makes a nicer preparation.

9

Henry's Vinegar. (English.)

Dried leaves of rosemary, rue, sage, wormwood, mint, and lavender flowers, of each	½ ounce.
Bruised nutmegs, cloves, angelica, and camphor, of each	¼ "
Alcohol, 95°	4 ounces.
Concentrated acetic acid . .	16 "

The materials are macerated with the alcohol two days, when add the acid and macerate in a warm place for a fortnight, when press out the liquid, being careful that it does not come in contact with any metal, as the acid will corrode it and the fluid be contaminated with it. This vinegar is used in vinaigrettes

Vinaigre des Quartre Voleurs. (Four thieves' vinegar.)

Take the fresh tops of rosemary, sage, wormwood, rue, and mint, of each . . .	¾ ounce.
Lavender flowers . . .	1 "
Calamus, cloves, nutmegs, and cinnamon (bruised), of each .	1 drachm.
Camphor	½ "
Alcohol	2 ounces.
Strong vinegar . . .	1 pint.

The camphor is dissolved in the alcohol, added to the other ingredients, and when they have digested ten days the mixture is strained.

Marseilles vinegar has had a great reputation as a cure-all, and no doubt is a good preventive of contagion. It is said to have been invented by four thieves, who robbed the dead at the time of the plague in Marseilles, and by its use escaped the effects of the pestilence. Any druggist can make as effective a preparation by dissolving the essential oils in alcohol and acetic acid.

Vinaigre a la Rose.

Concentrated acetic acid . .	1 ounce.
Otto of rose	½ drachm.

Used like Henry's Vinegar for perfuming vinaigrettes; and it is customary to have a little asbestos in the vials in order to retain the vinegar, or fill a pungent with the crystals of sulphate of potash, and let the vinegar fill the interstices; hence the name of sel de vinaigre or salt of vinegar.

Vinaigre a la Violette. (Violet vinegar.)

Extract of cassie, No. 2 . .	½ pint.
" violet, No. 2 . .	½ "
" rose, No. 2 . .	½ "
Tincture of orris . . .	½ "
White wine vinegar . .	2 "

Digest for ten days and filter. This is a very pleasant form of aromatic vinegar; and we might give twenty more such recipes, as orange flower, tuberose, etc. etc., but, in view of the instructions already given, it would seem unnecessary, as well as from the fact that we have never found much demand for this class of goods.

Of ammoniated products, the demand is equally limited, and is confined to two or three preparations for lavatory purposes, or stronger combinations for perfuming pungents or smelling salts. The latter is much used in headaches or to gratify the olfactories.

Ammoniated Cologne Water.

Cologne essence (Cristiani's) .	1 ounce.
Alcohol	2 pints.
Aqua ammonia, FFF. . . .	2 ounces.

A substitute for spirits of sal volatile.

Aromatic Spirits of Ammonia. (Spirits of sal volatile.)

Oil of lemon	1/8 fl. ounce.
" rosemary	3/4 "
" nutmegs	1/4 "
Spirits of ammonia . . .	2 pints.

A very grateful stimulant and antacid in sick headache, and much used in medicinal practice to assist the action or cover the nauseous taste of medicine. It can be advantageously used in the bath or lavatory.

Eau de Luce. (Succinated spirits of ammonia.)

Oil of amber, rectified . . .	1/2 drachm.
" lavender	1 "
Tincture of benzoin	2 ounces.
" Peru balsam . . .	2 "
Aqua ammonia, FFF. . . .	6 "

Agitate together in a bottle, but do not filter, as it should retain its milky appearance. This preparation is useful as a stimulant and antispasmodic, and as a lotion for the sting of insects and reptiles.

Volatile Essence. (For perfuming pungents or smelling salts.)

Oil of lavender	. . . .	½ ounce.
" bergamot	. . .	½ "
" cloves	. . . .	¼ "
" rhodium	. . . .	1 drachm.
Aqua ammonia, strong	. .	2¾ ounces.

This I have generally found to give entire satisfaction as a perfume for the carbonate of ammonia, commonly used in pungents.

CHAPTER IX.

SACHET POWDERS, ETC.

PERFUMES in the form of powders have been traced to the most ancient times, and they were, no doubt, among the earliest forms of perfume; for among the curiosities of the ancient Egyptians in the British Museum is a vase taken from the tomb of a mummy, probably four thousand years old, that was nearly full of a powder of resins, etc., which still had a pleasant odor; and seems to be such a vase as is still used in many countries to hold a "pot-pourri," a powder of dried flowers and herbs.

The Bible also speaks in sundry places of perfumes and gums and frankincense, and of the "Wise men" presenting to Christ gold, frankincense, and myrrh.

Sachet powders are generally put into silk or satin bags, or into ornamental paper envelopes, and are useful for perfuming clothes, drawers, trunks, desks, letter paper, etc. etc. Under this head I shall also treat of scent balls and beads, cassolettes, fumigating pastils, purfumed leather, etc. etc.

The variety of these powders is large, with the names of nearly all the extracts or bouquets we have given, and some peculiar to themselves. The ingredients should be good and fresh, and contain such substances as have a permanency of odor; otherwise they will lose their perfume very soon after being exposed to the air.

Bouquet Sachet.

Ground rose leaves	1	pound.
" orange flowers	½	"
" lavender	1	"
" orange peel	½	"
" cedar wood	¼	"
" thyme	¼	"
" orris root	½	"
" gum benzoin	½	"
" vanilla	¼	"
" rhodium wood	¼	"

Let these be ground and sieved, but not too fine, as a coarse powder has the advantage of allowing the air to pass through the mass, and of retaining its odor longer. On finishing the powder a few essential oils dissolved in alcohol can be mixed in.

Sachet au Cypré. (Cypress sachet.)

Ground rhodium wood	1	pound.
" cedar wood	½	"
" santal wood	½	"
" rose leaves	½	"

Ground orris root	1 pound.
" gum benzoin . . .	½ "
Oil of rhodium	½ ounce.

Sachet a la Frangipane.

Ground rose leaves	1 pound.
" santal wood . . .	1 "
" vitivert root . . .	½ "
" orris root . . .	1 "
" musk pods . . .	1 ounce.
Oils of neroli, rose, and santal, each	1 drachm.

This sachet is a general favorite.

Heliotrope Sachet.

Ground rose leaves . . .	1½ pounds.
" orris root . . .	2 "
" Tonquin beans . .	½ "
" vanilla . . .	¼ "
" gum benzoin . .	¼ "
" musk pods . . .	½ ounce.
Oil of rose	½ drachm.
" almonds	½ "

I have been accustomed to have each article ground separately, and then when mixed grinding them again all together, as a better means of blending them thoroughly.

Geranium Sachet.

Ground rose geranium leaves .	1 pound.
" orris root . . .	2 "
" rhodium wood . .	½ "
" gum benzoin . . .	¼ "
Oil of rose geranium . . .	¼ ounce.

Magnolia Sachet.

Ground rose leaves . . .	1 pound.
" orange flowers . .	½ "
" orris root . . .	2 "
" benzoin	¼ "
" orange peel . . .	¼ "
Oil of almonds	1 drachm.
" cedrat	2 "

Musk Sachet.

Ground rhodium wood . .	1 pound.
" orris root . . .	2 "
" vanilla	¼ "
" musk pods . . .	2 ounces.
" benzoin	2 "

Millefleur Sachet.

Ground orris root . . .	1½ pound.
" lavender flowers . .	1 "
" orange flowers . .	½ "
" rose leaves . . .	1 "
" benzoin	¼ "
" Tonquin . . .	¼ "
" cloves	¼ "
" vanilla	¼ "
" santal	¼ "
" cinnamon . . .	2 ounces.
Extract of millefleur . . .	2 "

New-mown Hay Sachet.

Ground rose leaves . . .	1 pound.
" orange flowers . .	½ "
" orris root . . .	1 "
" benzoin	¼ "

Ground Tonquin bean	½ pound.
" ambrette	½ "
Oil of almonds	1 drachm.
" verbena	2 "

Patchouly Sachet.

Ground patchouly herb	2 pounds.
" rhodium	¼ "
" orris root	1 "
" benzoin	¼ "
Oil of patchouly	1 drachm.
" rose	20 drops.

Rose Sachet.

Ground rose leaves	1½ pounds.
" orris root	1 "
" rhodium wood	1 "
" santal	½ "
" benzoin	¼ "
Otto of rose	2 drachms.
Brazil wood	1 ounce.

Verbena Sachet.

Ground lemon thyme	1 pound.
" lemon peel	2 "
" orris root	1 "
Oil of lemon grass	½ ounce.
" bergamot	1 "

Violet Sachet.

Ground orris root	2 pounds.
" rhodium wood	½ "
" rose leaves	½ "

Ground black currant leaves	.	½ pound.
" benzoin	. . .	¼ "
" musk pods	. . .	½ ounce.
Oil of almonds	. . . .	½ drachm.

West-end Sachet.

Ground rose leaves	. . .	1 pound.
" orange flowers	. .	½ "
" rhodium wood	. .	½ "
" orris root	. . .	1 "
" benzoin	. . .	¼ "
Oil of neroli	. . . .	1 drachm.
" cedrat	. . . .	2 "

Pot-Pourri.

Bruised lavender flowers	. .	1 pound.
" lemon thyme	. .	½ "
" sage	. . . .	½ "
" rose leaves	. . .	½ "
" orris root	. . .	1 "
" cloves	. . . .	¼ "
" cinnamon	. . .	¼ "
" gum benzoin	. .	¼ "
" marjoram	. . .	¼ "
Salt	. . . . . .	½ "

Pot-pourri is a mixture of flowers, herbs, and spices bruised together, and a little salt added under the supposition that it will keep its odor longer.

Cassolettes, sometimes called printaniers, are little scent balls, inclosed in handsome perforated boxes made of ivory, gold, or silver, and worn about the person or carried in the reticule. Nearly all of the sachet powders can be made into them by mixing with them a mucilage of gum tragacanth, making into balls, and, before they are quite dry, making perforations through them with a large needle.

Perfumed beads are much the same as cassolettes, except that they are colored black with ebony wood or ivory black, and, when dry, polished or carved, and strung and worn round the neck. When well made they are very durable.

Fumigating pastils are a very useful form of perfume, having the property of emitting their fragrance when burned; and they are among the most ancient forms in which perfumes were first used.

Pastilles Fumantes.

Powdered charcoal	2	pounds.
" olibanum	½	"
" Tonquin	¼	"
" benzoin	¼	"
" allspice	¼	"
" cinnamon	¼	"
" cloves	¼	"
" nitrate of potash	¼	"

Mix together and make into a mass with a mucilage of tragacanth, and by means of a mould or with the fingers make them into cones, about an inch long and not quite half an inch at the base. When dry they can be burned on little ornamented bronze stands to perfume the sick-chamber or other apartments.

Santal-wood Pastils.

Ground santal wood	1¼	pounds.
" olibanum	¼	"
" benzoin	1	"
" saltpetre	⅛	"

Ground cassie	¼ pound.
Oil santal	2 drachms.
" cloves	2 "

In most of the burning pastils in which the aromatic roots, woods, and barks are the principal ingredients, the smoke of them is so great as to be objectionable, and, when the aromatic odor has evaporated, leaves an unpleasant burnt odor. To remedy this defect, I will give what I consider a better form for this useful article, in which the volatile substance is evaporated in the air; and there is little smoke, and that a pleasant one.

Fumigating Pastils.

Powdered willow charcoal . .	4 pounds.
Gum olibanum	½ "
" benzoin	½ "
Oils of lavender, caraway, cloves, cinnamon, thyme, geranium, santal, rhodium, of each . .	2 drachms.
Nitrate of potash	2 ounces.

The saltpetre is dissolved in the mucilage of tragacanth, then the whole mixed and beaten into a stiff mass, and moulded into cones or cast into figures with tin cutters.

Cristiani's Pyrosmia (Fumigating Wafers)

Are another form of fumigation that is equally convenient and pleasant, in fact, more handy, being in a more compact form. Take white blotting card unsized, and moderately thick, and saturate it with a solution of two ounces of saltpetre to one pint of rose-water; when dry coat it with the following mixture, applied with a soft, flat brush:—

Tinctures of olibanum, benzoin, Tolu, vanilla, cascarilla, of each	2 ounces.
Oil of rhodium	1 drachm.

After being well dried, the cards are cut into squares of about an inch and packed into small tin-boxes, in the lid of each of which is a small opening to admit the corner of the wafer, which, when lighted, burns away rapidly, leaving a very pleasant odor in the apartment.

Perfumed Leather. (Peau d'Espange.)

Tincture of benzoin . . .	½ pint.
" musk . . .	2 ounces.
" ambergris . .	2 "
" vanilla . . .	4 "
Oil of lavender	2 drachms.
" santal	1 "
" neroli	1 "
" bergamot	4 "

This mixture is spread upon thick buckskin with a soft flat brush, and when dry is cut into equal-sized pieces, and enveloped in silk bags or ornamental paper. This is a very convenient article for scenting letter paper, clothes, chests, etc. etc., and will retain its perfume a great length of time, and will not soil.

There are a great many means resorted to for perfuming apartments. Almost every one is familiar with the odorators made of a rubber bulb with bent tube attached, one end being placed in a bottle of perfume, which latter is ejected in the form of spray on exhausting and expanding the bulb. There is also a lamp that is filled with perfumed alcohol, having in the wick a small coil of platinum wire; this lamp is lighted, and allowed to burn until the wire becomes red hot, when it is blown out, when the platinum remains incandescent while there is any alcohol left, and emits the perfume in a slightly altered condition.

There is also a device of a lamp generating steam that passes through tubes properly bent, and carries with it the contents of a bottle of essence, and so adding moisture with the perfumes. This is applicable to large audiences at concerts, theatres, etc.

CHAPTER X.

PREPARATIONS FOR THE SKIN.

COSMETICS for the skin are a very important branch of the perfumer's art, and in the recipes given I shall try and give such ingredients as are harmless, and, at the same time, efficacious. This class of perfumes is very large, and there are so many nostrums advertised guaranteed to effect the most marvellous results, that a word of caution should be given to careless people not to use any such preparations, unless they know the ingredients, or have perfect confidence in the persons who prepare them. Unprincipled quacks advertise nostrums that, through ignorance or worse, do much more injury than benefit to that delicate organ, the skin.

To prepare cold cream and the emulsions a considerable degree of skill is requisite, as without some practice the novice will find it difficult to get the desired quantity of oil and water to combine with the other ingredients. A little experience and care in the temperature will soon produce success.

Arsenical and mercurial preparations I will omit, as they should not be used except by the advice of a medical practitioner.

Almond Lotion.

Bitter almonds, blanched . .	4 ounces.
Orange-flower water . . .	12 "
Curd soap	½ "
Alcohol, 65°	4 "
Oil of almonds	20 drops.
" bergamot	1 drachm.

Dissolve the soap in a water-bath with the orange-flower water, beat up the almonds in a clean marble mortar, gradually adding the soap and water, strain through a clean washed muslin strainer and return to the mortar, and while stirring gradually add the alcohol in which the oils have been dissolved.

Amandine.

Oil of almonds, sweet . .	2 pounds.
Clarified honey . . .	3 ounces.
White shaving cream . .	1 "
Liquor of potassa, U. S. P. .	½ "
Oil of almond (essential) . .	1 drachm.
" cloves	1 "
" bergamot . . .	2 "
Balsam of Peru . . .	1 "

Scent the oil of almonds with the essential oils and balsam, mix the honey with the soap and liquor potassa in a marble mortar, and while stirring add the oil until it assumes a transparent appearance when put up in China-paste boxes.

Cucumber Lotion.

Blanched almonds . . .	4 ounces.
Shaving cream	½ "
Oil of benne	½ pound.
Expressed juice of cucumbers .	1¼ pints.
Alcohol, 65°	4 ounces.

Manipulate as for almond lotion.

Camphor Lotion.

Spermaceti, white wax, oil of almonds (sweet), of each .	2 ounces.
Shaving cream	1 "
Liquor potassa, U. S. P. . . .	1 "
Gum camphor	1 "
Blanched almonds . . .	4 "
Rose-water	1¼ pints.
Alcohol	4 ounces.
Oil of pimento	½ drachm.
" bergamot . . .	½ "

Make like almond lotion.

Elder Flower Emulsion.

Blanched almonds . . .	4 ounces.
Distilled elder-flower water .	1¼ pints.
Alcohol, 65°	¼ "
Shaving cream, white . .	½ ounce.
Oil of sweet almonds . .	½ "

White wax	½ ounce.
Spermaceti.	1 "
Liquor potassa	2 drachms.

Melt the wax and spermaceti with the oil, soap, and potassa, make the milk as you make that in almond lotion, pouring it into the warm wax, etc., very gradually; lastly add the alcohol, in which are dissolved the camphor and essential oils. If carefully made it will have a uniform milky appearance.

Cosmetic Cream of Lilies. (Cristiani's.)

Bitter almonds, blanched . .	5 ounces.
Orange-flower water, triple .	1½ pint.
Alcohol	½ "
White wax, spermaceti, oil of benne, shaving cream, of each	½ ounce.
Oil of neroli	½ drachm.
" bergamot	1 "
" cloves	½ "
Borax.	½ ounce.

This beautiful preparation I consider an improvement; for when properly prepared and bottled it will keep sweet for years, and its property of improving the complexion is unsurpassed. Prepare it as directed in camphor lotion, dissolving the borax in the orange-flower water slightly warmed.

Balsam of Honey. (Baume de Miel.)

Spermaceti	3 ounces.
White wax.	1 "
Oil of benne	6 "
Shaving cream	2 "
Honey	4 "

Tincture of ambergris . . .	½ ounce.
Oil of pimento	1 drachm.
" bergamot	2 "

Melt the sperm, wax, oil, and shaving cream together in a glazed vessel, and add the honey, stirring until nearly cold, when drop in the essential oil, and put in china pots.

Glycerine Balm.

Glycerine, best	4 ounces.
Rose-water, triple . . .	12 "
Citric acid	½ "
Oil of almonds	½ drachm.
" lemon	1 "

Rub up the essential oils and acid, and while stirring gradually add the glycerine and rose-water. It should be a clear solution, and is an invaluable preparation for whitening and softening the skin, removing freckles and discolorations.

Lait Virginal.

Tincture of benzoin . . .	½ ounce.
" vanilla . . .	2 drachms.
Rose-water	1½ pint.

Add the water to the tincture very slowly, to insure a perfect milky emulsion that will not precipitate. A very fine preparation for whitening and cooling the skin.

Cold Cream. (Cristiani's.)

Benne oil	12 ounces.
Rose-water, triple	8 "
Spermaceti	4 "
White wax	2 "
Otto of rose	20 drops.

Melt the wax and sperm with the oil in a porcelain vessel, which should not be too shallow. When melted, place the rose-water where it can run very slowly into the paste; keep stirring until it is thoroughly mixed, when add the otto of rose; then put it into porcelain jars for sale. When well made it will keep good for a long time.

Cold Cream of Violets.

Substitute oil of violets perfumed by enfleurage for the benne oil. Thus you can make the cold cream of orange flowers, jasmine, tuberose, etc. etc., simply by the difference in perfume.

Cucumber Cream.

Oil of benne	½ pound.
White wax	1 ounce.
Spermaceti	2 "
Green oil	1 "
Cucumber juice	6 "
Oil of neroli	30 drops.

The juice of cucumbers can be obtained from the fruit by expression. When collected it should be heated slightly to coagulate the albumen it contains, and strained. Green oil is olive oil impregnated with the flavor of the fruit by several contacts with it.

Prepare in the same manner as cold cream.

Glycerine Cream.

Mutton suet (clarified) . .	8 ounces.
Spermaceti	2 "
Benne oil	4 "
Glycerine	2 "
Oil of almonds, essential . .	1 drachm.
" cedrat	2 "
" cloves	½ "

Melt the sperm and suet with the oil, and add the glycerine while cooling, then the perfumes, and put into the jars intended for sale.

Camphor Ice, with Glycerine. (Cristiani's.)

Paraffine wax	8 ounces.
Sparmaceti	4 "
Cacao butter	2 "
Castor oil	2 "
Benne oil	8 "
Camphor	2 "
Glycerine	2 "
Oil of neroli	1 drachm.
" bergamot	1 "
" pimento	½ "
" almonds (essential) . .	½ "

Put the camphor with the benne and castor oils, melt with gentle heat, add the wax, butter, and sperm, and when cooling stir in the glycerine, and lastly the perfumes. This is generally moulded into forms with a suitable tin mould, and is a very popular article.

Pistuchio Nut Cream or Lotion.

Can be made in the same manner as almond lotion, substituting the pistuchio nuts.

Aqua Ornatus. (Ornamental water.)

Gum benzoin	½ ounce.
Vanilla	¼ "
Rhatany root	¼ "
Rectified spirits, 60° . . .	1 pint.

Bruise the ingredients and put in the spirit; macerate for a fortnight, when filter. This is a compact form of lait virginal. A few drops are poured upon a wetted cloth, and the face bathed with it. It is a beautiful and harmless remedy for tan, freckles, pimples, etc.

Sulphur Lotion.

Sulphuret of potash (new) . .	2 drachms.
Tincture of benzoin . . .	½ ounce.
Glycerine	1 "
Rose-water, triple . . .	1¼ pint.

Dissolve the sulphate of potash with a portion of the rose-water, add the glycerine and gradually the rest of the water. For pimples, freckles, discoloration, itch, black heads, etc. Though not a pleasant smelling preparation, it is yet quite efficacious.

Eukesis, or Essence of Soap.

Shaving cream	6 ounces.
Liquor potassa (U.S.P.) . .	2 drachms.
Oil of almond (sweet) . .	½ ounce.
Alcohol, 60°	1 pint.
Oil of almond (essential) . .	1 drachm.
" bergamot	2 "
" pimento	½ "

This is a very pleasant and convenient preparation for shaving, and is usually put in tubes of tinfoil, and when wanted a portion is squeezed out on the face, and a lather is easily made with the brush.

Emil Blanc. (White enamel.)

Lavigated talc	3 ounces.
Glycerine	2 "
Rose-water, triple . . .	1¼ pint.

The talc should be exceedingly fine, and be triturated with the glycerine in a wedgewood mortar, and the rose-water gradually added. This is a pleasant and harmless article. Similar preparations are made with the oxide of bismuth, zinc, or lead, that are not so innocent, and as it is the object of this work not to give pernicious recipes, all formulas given can be employed with confidence.

Pomade Divine.

Lard	½ pound.
Almond oil	½ "
Spermaceti	¼ "
Gum benzoin, powdered . .	¼ "
Oil of bergamot	1 drachm.
" cloves	½ "

Melt in a water-bath and add the benzoin in fine powder and the perfume before it stiffens. This preparation has had a great name, and is pleasant, safe, and healing.

Camphor Balls.

Mutton suet	12 ounces.
White wax	4 "
Camphor	2 "
Oil of lavender	2 drachms.

Melt the camphor in a small portion of the suet; add the wax and balance of suet. It is moulded into cakes, and used for softening the skin, chafes, chapped hands, etc. etc.

Rose Lip Salve.

Spermaceti	4 ounces.
White wax.	2 "
Oil of benne	6 "
Castor oil	2 "
Otto of rose	½ drachm.
Vermilion	1 "
Rouge vegetal	2 "

Melt carefully, and when creamy put into small metal, porcelain, or rose-wood boxes.

Blanc de Perle (Pearl white)

Is levigated talc mixed with a little almond oil and mucilage of gum tragacanth, and spread upon porcelain disks for convenient use.

ROUGES AND PAINTS FOR THE FACE.

Rouges and paints for the face and eyebrows, etc., come under the head of cosmetics, and are usually harmless when made of carmine or safflowers, but not so when the aniline colors are used, as they are apt to contain mineral poisons.

Bloom of Roses. (Liquid Rouge.)

Carmine, No. 40 . . .	2 drachms.
Aqua ammonia, FFF. . .	½ ounce.
Alcohol, 60°	2 "
Gum Arabic	½ "
Rose-water, triple . . .	1 pint.
Otto of roses	10 drops.

Rub the carmine and gum with the aqua ammonia in a porcelain mortar, and a portion of the rose-water, when dissolved add the alcohol slowly and the balance of the rose-water. The perfume to be dissolved in the alcohol. Lastly strain.

Vinaigre de Rouge.

Carmine, No. 40	½ ounce.
Aqua ammonia	1 "
Extract of rose, No. 2 . .	2 "
Acetic acid	1 "
Rose-water	4 pints.

Mix the carmine with the ammonia in a mortar; add the extract, then the acid; lastly, and by degrees, the rose-water.

Rouge de Theatre

Is the carthamus rouge (rouge vegetal) mixed with a few drops of almond oil, and with mucilage of gum tragacanth, and spread upon porcelain disks, convenient for use.

Crepon Rouge

Is cotton saturated with solution of carmine or carthamus and dried.

Chinese Card Rouge

Is an unsized paper saturated with carthamus, which when dried assumes a bronze hue.

Pink Saucers,

So long used, consist of the same solution of carthamus or carmine evaporated to a creamy consistence and spread upon saucers.

Lily White or Pearl Powder,

So much used in this country, is generally a mixture of Paris white and kaolin, and formed into cakes and put in fancy boxes. A finer article is made with a mixture of powdered talc and corn starch held together with mucilage. The name of pearl powder has heretofore been applied to the oxide of bismuth, but it is not much used at the present time.

Violet Toilet Powder.

Corn starch	10 pounds.
Ambrette seed	1 "
Orris root in powder . . .	1 "
Tincture of musk . . .	2 drachms.

This is a favorite and perfectly harmless powder, much used for the chafing of infants; it is prepared by keeping the starch in contact with the ambrette seed for about a month, sieving the latter out and adding the orris and tincture.

Rose Toilet Powder.

Corn or potato starch . . .	12 pounds.
Powdered orris root . . .	½ "
Oil of santal	1 drachm.
" rose	½ "
Tincture of civet . . .	1 "

This is simply mixed and sieved and put into boxes or wrappers. Starch powders are the safest and most useful of all toilet powders, as they absorb all excess of moisture, and remedy redness and gloss on the face, besides being indispensable for chafes in infants.

Poudre de Riz.

Rice powder is now much used and is perfumed in the same manner as the starch powders.

Lycopodium Powder. (Club-moss powder.)

Lycopodium	1 pound.
Rose or violet toilet powder .	2 "

Club-moss powder is invaluable as an absorbent, and for excoriated surfaces in infants, etc.

Cosmetic Almond Powder.

Sweet almonds, blanched . .	1 pound.
Potato starch	3 "
Powdered orris root . . .	½ "
White curd soap . . .	¼ "
Carbonate of soda . . .	1 ounce.
Oil of bergamot . . .	2 drachms.
" almonds, essential . .	1 "
" cloves	1 "

First grind the almonds; add the starch, then the soap (previously dried and powdered), and the soda; re-sieve to blend the whole together; lastly, add the perfume. Used as a soap powder, and has a fine effect in whitening and softening the skin.

Sulphuretted Toilet Powder.

Lac sulphur	4 ounces.
Powdered talc	3 "
Corn starch	3 "
Paris white	4 "
Benne oil	2 ounces.
Tincture of orris . . .	1 "
" ambrette . . .	½ "

Mix thoroughly by sieving all together; make into a mass with pure water, and mould into a tablet suited to the box it is intended for. Sulphur is the safest of all mineral substances intended for the skin. Be careful not to use the ordinary flower of sulphur, as it is apt to have some free sulphuric acid in it, and will injure and irritate the skin. This powder will be found useful in almost all cutaneous eruptions.

Meen Fun (Chinese skin powder)

Is a sort of magnesian earth in impalpable powder, very absorbent to all the secretions of the skin.

Cosmetic Gloves.

Cosmetic gloves are sometimes wanted as a remedy for rough and chapped hands; gloves of cheap leather are coated with some such cosmetic creams as we have given the recipes for, but I will add a French formula for chaps and chilblains, etc., as follows:—

Glove Cosmetic.

Mutton suet	2 ounces.
Spermaceti	1 "
Powdered benzoin . . .	½ "
Yolk of two eggs.	
Peru balsam	1 drachm.
White curd soap . . .	½ ounce.
Olive oil	2½ "
Otto of roses	20 drops.

If this mixture is spread upon the inside of the glove, and worn several nights, the hands will be found to be soft and white.

Glycerine Jelly for the Skin.

Almond oil	8 ounces.
White curd soap . . .	1 "
Pure glycerine	2 "
Oil of bergamot. . . .	1 drachm.
" cloves	½ "
" thyme	½ "

Dissolve the soap in the oil in a water-bath, and add the glycerine and perfumes. Used as a cosmetic for softening the hands, and is applied in small quantities after washing the hands, and while they are still moist.

Lip Balm.

Mutton suet	2 ounces.
Cacoa butter	1 "
Almond oil	2 "
Glycerine	1 "
Powdered borax	2 drachms.
Oil of pimento	20 drops.
" neroli	20 "
Powdered benzoin . . .	1 drachm.

Color the oil with a little alkanet-root, and mix by melting all together, adding the perfume before quite cold.

Fard Bleu.

Starch	2 ounces.
Talc	1 "
Oil	2 drachms.
Mucilage	q. s.
Ultramarine blue . . .	3 drachms.

Make into small tablets, for marking the blue veins on the temples or elsewhere.

Fard Noir.

Make as above, using a little soap and ivory black, and rolling into spills or pencils. Used to darken the eyebrows.

CHAPTER XI.

POMADES AND COSMETICS.

In the preparation of pomades and cosmetics great care must be exercised in selecting and compounding the ingredients, which should be fresh and deprived of all impurities or disagreeable smells, or they will be unfit for the purpose. The perfumer uses for pomades tallow, suet, veal fat, lard, and wax. All of these greases contain albumen and membrane, which should be removed before using, as they tend to make them turn rancid in a very short time. The process of washing greases in a small way is performed in this manner. About fifty pounds of lard or suet are put into a clean vessel, which is put inside a larger vessel of water, in which a pound or two of salt is dissolved (a marine bath), or a steam jacket if at hand. The grease is melted with two ounces of powdered alum, and then three ounces of table salt, and the heat is continued until all scum has risen, and is skimmed off, when it is allowed to cool.

The grease has then to be washed with water to remove all alum and salt. This is done in two ways: first, the grease is again melted, and two quarts of pure water are added, and allowed to boil slowly, when the steam carries off all the smell; the alum and salt being deposited at the bottom with the water. In the second process the grease is put in portions on a slab of slate a little inclined, and rubbed with a stone muller, while a stream of clean water pours gently over the grease while being rubbed, just as a painter grinds his colors. When finished it is re-melted to deposit all remaining water.

This is rather a tedious process, and, when the material is wanted in quantity, the perfumer can avail himself of machinery invented for the purpose.

For the purpose of having system, perfumers divide their grease into hard and soft body. The first is generally two parts of lard and one of suet or tallow, the latter is five parts of lard and one of tallow, and may be improved by the addition to each five pounds of an ounce of powdered gum benzoin. In the flower-growing countries of France and Italy, whence we procure the fine pomades of flowers, the purification of grease bodies is of sufficient importance to be made a separate trade, and if the perfumer here has a large demand for pomades, a stock of those prepared greases should be kept on hand, as they enter in different proportions into all of them.

The stock of pomades is not complete without an assortment of the prepared greases or bodies of benzoin, vanilla, balsams of Tolu and Peru, etc. etc.; ready for mixing with the different pomades for the hair.

Benzoin Pomade (or body).

Hard body	10 pounds.
Powdered gum benzoin . .	1 "

Melt in a water-bath for twelve hours and strain.

Tonquin Pomade.

Hard body	10 pounds.
Tonquin beans in coarse powder	1 "

Let them macerate some days, melting occasionally, and then strain.

Vanilla Pomade.

Vanilla beans, cut very fine .	½ pound.
Hard body	10 "

Melt and stir once a day for ten days, when strain. And thus you can make ambrette pomade, using 2 pounds of musk-seed to 10 pounds of body; or musk pomade, using 2 ounces to the 10 pounds; and orris pomade, taking 2 pounds to the 10 of grease; ambergris pomade, 2 ounces to the 10 pounds; etc. etc. They must all be melted several times before all the perfume will be extracted from the substance.

It is also necessary to have on hand coloring body for the different pomades, as red, yellow, green, etc.

Yellow Body.

Roco or anatto-seed . . .	1 pound.
Hard body	6 "

Although the coloring matter is on the surface of the seed, it penetrates somewhat below, and therefore it is best to have the seed coarsely ground; keep it melted several hours in a water-bath, when strain and keep in a cool place for use.

Red Body.

Carmine	2 ounces.
Vermilion	4 "
Hard body	4 pounds.

Green Body.

Spinach leaves	2 pounds.
Hard body	4 "

Put in a water-bath and macerate until the leaves have lost their color. After straining again melt and set aside quietly, that the water of the leaves may go to the bottom. Green of an inferior color can be made with powdered gum guaiacum melted with the grease.

I have made frequent mention of the flower pomades which we have to procure from the south of France and other neighboring places, and also the manner of their preparation. They are, of course, indispensable for making the finest goods. Although all the pomades from which most of the odors have been extracted by means of alcohol can be used, the alcohol, however, tends to hasten rancidity, but can be extracted by pressing through leather, or by melting with a small portion of water; the alcohol, having a greater affinity for the water, will join it and fall to the bottom when the melted pomade is set quietly by.

Pomade d'Acacia. (Cassie pomade.)

Cassie pomade	1 pound.
Hard body	$\frac{3}{4}$ "
Green "	$\frac{1}{4}$ "
Oil of cedrat	$\frac{1}{4}$ ounce.
" almonds (essential) . .	1 drachm.
" cloves	1 "

This is a pleasant pomade of greenish-yellow hue. It may be necessary to mention that the perfumes are not added until the pomade is nearly cold, and also that it should not be filled into bottles until it is chilled into a thick creamy consistence; and again, that the bottles be not too cold, as they cool the pomade too suddenly, and cause it to shrink from the glass and have an uneven appearance.

Pomade Balsamique.

Benzoin pomade or body	1 pound.
Vanilla " "	¼ "
Tuberose "	½ "
Hard body	1¼ "

This pomade can be colored a light-brown with a few drops of caramel.

Bear's Grease Pomade.

Soft body	1½ pound.
Jasmine pomade	½ "
Oil of bergamot	½ "
" cloves	1 drachm..

The genuine bear's grease that has had so great a reputation for promoting the growth of the hair, and is still much favored, is difficult to procure in quantities, and if gotten would soon get rancid and unfit for use, and we, therefore, prepare a substitute which is rather an improvement on the genuine article.

Benzoin Pomade.

Benzoin body	2 pounds.
Oil of pimento	½ drachm.
" orange	2 "
" neroli	½ "

Pomade au Beurre de Cacao.

Soft body	1½ pounds.
Cocoa-butter	½ "
Oil of bergamot	½ ounce.
" thyme	1 drachm.
" cassia	½ "

Color with gamboge.

Castor-oil and Glycerine Pomade.

Hard body	1½ pounds.
Castor oil	¼ "
Vanilla oil	¼ "
Oil of bergamot	½ ounce.
" cloves	¼ "
" neroli	1 drachm.

Gum gamboge to color.

Cowslip Pomade.

Hard body	1½ pound.
Jasmine pomade	½ "
Oil of bergamot	2 drachms.
" cloves	1 drachm.
" petit-grain . . .	½ "
Tincture of ambergris . .	1 "

Crystalline Pomade.

Benne oil	1¼ pound.
Castor oil	¼ "
Paraffine wax	½ "
Oil of bergamot	½ ounce.
" thyme	1 drachm.
" cloves	1 "

Color with gamboge.

I will here take occasion to say that the hard refined paraffine wax is for the uses of the perfumer superior to all other waxes, especially when a semi-transparent appearance is wanted. This pomade is of a very pleasing transparent appearance, and a good hair dressing.

Crystal Pomade.

Castor oil	2 pounds.
Alcohol, 95°	1 "
Curd soap	½ "

Dry the soap, first reducing it to shavings, when put into a clean tin vessel with the alcohol, and dissolve by the heat of a water-bath; warm the oil to about the same heat, and add to the soap and alcohol, and it is finished. Perfume with oil bergamot, lemon-grass, and cloves; see also that the bottles it is put into are warm. The result is a perfectly transparent pomade.

Geranium Pomade.

Soft body	1½ pounds.
Tolu body or pomade . .	½ "
Oil of rose geranium . . .	½ ounce.

Color with yellow body.

Heliotrope Pomade.

Hard body	½ pound.
Rose pomade	½ "
Orris pomade	¼ "
Vanilla pomade	½ "
Tuberose pomade . . .	¼ "
Oil neroli	1 drachm.
" almonds	½ "

Color light brown, if it is not of the proper shade. This is, of course, an imitation, but quite as delicate and pleasant as if it were made from the genuine flowers.

Pomade a la Jacinth. (Hyacinth pomade.)

Hard body	1 pound.
Tuberose pomade	½ "
Jasmine "	½ "
Oil of cedrat	2 drachms.
" cloves	1 "
" almonds	1 "

Color with tincture of archil a light purple.

Pomade au Jasmin.

Jasmine pomade	1 pound.
Hard body	¾ "
Vanilla body	¼ "
Oil of rhodium	1 drachm.

Color light yellow.

Jonquille Pomade.

Jonquille pomade	½ pound.
Jasmine "	¼ "
Hard body	1 "
Tolu "	¼ "
Oil bergamot	2 drachms.

Color yellow with yellow body.

Lavender Pomade.

Hard body	1½ pound.
Cassie pomade	½ "
Oil of lavender (best)	1 ounce.
" rosemary	½ "
" cloves	1 drachm.

Color light green.

As a matter of course it would not be necessary to make an imitation of a flower pomade if the fresh flowers could readily be procured, and we had all the apparatus to conduct the enfleurage, but not having such means, we have to use the best we have, and to exercise our skill in an imitation.

Limette Pomade.

Hard body	1½ pound.
Tuberose pomade	½ "
Oil of limette	½ ounce.
" lemon-grass	¼ "
" cloves	1 drachm.

Color green.

Mayflower Pomade.

Hard body	1 pound.
Tuberose pomade	¼ "
Rose "	¼ "
Cassie "	¼ "
Tonquin "	¼ "

Color yellow.

Macassar Pomade.

Hard body	1½ pound.
Castor oil	¼ "
Ambergris pomade	¼ "
Oil of nutmegs	½ drachm.
" cinnamon	¼ "
" rosemary	½ "
" thyme	¼ "
" rose	30 drops.

Color light red with red body.

Marrow Pomade.

Soft body	1½ pound.
Mace body or pomade	¼ "
Benzoin body	¼ "
Oil bergamot	½ "
" lemon	¼ "
" cloves	¼ "

Color deep yellow.

This pomade is generally stirred very briskly while cooling with a stirrer like an egg-beater to fill it with particles of air, making it light and spongy. This operation gives a peculiar appearance to pomades, and can be done to all such as may be thought proper.

Mille-fleur Pomade.

Rose pomade	½ pound.
Violet "	¼ "
Orange-flower pomade	½ "
Benzoin "	½ "
Musk "	¼ "

Color brown with caramel.

Musk Pomade.

Rose pomade	½ pound.
Hard body	¾ "
Ambergris pomade	¼ "
Musk "	½ "

Color brown with caramel.

Myrtle Blossom Pomade.

Hard body	1 pound.
Jasmine pomade	½ "
Orange-flower pomade	¼ "
Vanilla	¼ "

Color light yellow.

Narcissus Pomade.

Hard body	¾ pound.
Jasmine pomade	½ "
Cassie "	¼ "
Rose "	¼ "
Vanilla "	¼ "
Oil of almonds (essential)	1 drachm.

Color light yellow.

Neroli Pomade.

Hard body	1¼ pound.
Orange-flower pomade	½ "
Ambrette "	¼ "
Oil of neroli (bigarade)	2 drachms.
" petit-grain	1 "

Color light yellow.

Orange-flower Pomade.

Hard body	1¼ pound.
Orange-flower pomade	½ "
Tolu "	¼ "
Oil of Portugal	1 ounce.
" cloves	¼ "

Color yellow.

Oriental Cream.

Soft body	1 pound.
Rose pomade	¼ "
Benzoin "	¼ "
Tonquin "	¼ "
Musk "	¼ "
Oil of santal	1 drachm.
" rose	½ "

Palma-Rosa Pomade.

Soft body	1 pound.
Rose pomade	$\frac{1}{4}$ "
Cassie "	$\frac{1}{4}$ "
Benzoin "	$\frac{1}{4}$ "
Mace "	$\frac{1}{4}$ "
Oil of ginger-grass . . .	2 drachms.
" cloves	1 "

Color yellowish-green.

Philocome Pomade.

Purified lard	1 pound.
Beeswax	$\frac{1}{4}$ "
Cassie oil (from flowers) . .	2 ounces.
Rose oil " " . .	4 "
Tuberose oil " " . .	2 "
Mace pomade	4 "

Color pink or yellow.

Primrose Pomade.

Soft body	1 pound.
Cassie pomade	$\frac{1}{4}$ "
Rose "	$\frac{1}{4}$ "
Vanilla "	$\frac{1}{4}$ "
Benzoin "	$\frac{1}{4}$ "
Oil of petit-grain . . .	1 drachm.
" lemon	2 "
" almonds, (essential) .	1 "

Color bright yellow.

Quinine Pomade. (Tonic pomade.)

Soft body	1⅓	pound.
Rose pomade	¼	"
Vanilla oil	¼	"
Sulphate of quinine	½	ounce.
Oil of bergamot	½	"
" cloves	¼	"

Color light yellow.

Rub up the quinine in a wedgewood mortar with a few drops of aromatic sulphuric acid; add the vanilla oil, and put into the pomade melted by means of water-bath, and stir till cold.

Pomade Romaine.

Roman pomades are of softer bodies than pomades in general, or between pomades and oils; are much liked by many people, and are easily made by a judicious mixture of the pomades and antique oils, and can be made of any odor of the preceding kinds. I will give an example.

Pomade Romaine a la Ambrosie.

Soft body	1	pound.
Vanilla oil	½	"
Musk oil	¼	"
Cassie oil (from flowers)	¼	"
Oil of bergamot	1	ounce.
" cloves	¼	"
" roses	½	drachm.

Mix with the least possible heat, color light brown, and you have a very pleasant hair-dressing of delicate fragrance.

Rondelatia Pomade.

Hard body	1¼ pound.
Cassie pomade	¼ "
Rose "	¼ "
Tonquin "	¼ "
Oil of lavender (best)	½ ounce.
" bergamot	¼ "
" cloves	¼ "

Color pale yellow.

Pomade à la Rose.

Soft body	1 pound.
Vanilla body	¼ "
Rose pomade	½ "
Tuberose pomade	¼ "
Oil of santal	1 drachm.
" rhodium	1 "

Color deep red.

Pomade à la Sultane.

Soft body	1 pound
Heliotrope pomade	¼ "
Tuberose "	¼ "
Jasmine "	¼ "
Tonquin "	¼ "
Tincture of musk	1 drachm.
Oil of pimento	1 "
" cedrat	½ ounce.

Color light brown.

Tuberose Pomade.

Soft body	1 pound.
Tuberose pomade . . .	½ "
Rose "	¼ "
Benzoin "	¼ "
Oil of cedrat	2 drachms.
" almonds (essential) . .	1 "

Color bright yellow.

Vanilla Pomade.

Soft body	1 pound.
Vanilla body	½ "
Rose pomade	¼ "
Ambergris body . . .	¼ "
Oil of rhodium	2 drachms.

Color deep yellow.

Verbena Pomade.

Hard body	1¼ pound.
Cassie pomade	½ "
Benzoin "	¼ "
Oil of lemon-grass . . .	½ ounce.
" lemon	¼ "
" cloves	1 drachm.

Color light green.

Violet Pomade. No. 1.

Soft body	¾ pound.
Violet pomade	¾ "
Cassie "	¼ "
Civet "	¼ "
Oil of rose	½ drachm.
" almonds	1 "

Color light green.

Violet Pomade. No. 2.

Soft body	1 pound.
Cassie pomade	¼ "
Orris "	½ "
Peru balsam pomade . . .	¼ "
Oil of almonds	1 drachm.

Color green.

White Pond Lily Pomade.

Soft body	1¼ pound.
Jasmine pomade	¼ "
Orange-flower pomade . .	¼ "
Vanilla pomade	¼ "
Oil of almonds, essential . .	1 drachm.

No color.

White Rose Pomade.

Soft body	¾ pound.
Rose pomade	¾ "
Jasmine "	¼ "
Vanilla "	¼ "
Oil of rhodium	1 drachm.
" rose	½ "

No color.

Ursalina. (Crystalline bear's grease.)

Oil of benne	1¼ pound.
Castor oil	¼ "
Paraffine wax	½ "
Oil of bergamot	2 drachms.
" pimento	1 "
" santal	1 "
" cloves	1 "

Color with a little gamboge rubbed with a portion of the oil. This is a very pretty looking pomade, and is a good hair dressing.

Phenolin Pomade.

Benne oil	$1\frac{1}{2}$ pound.
Paraffine wax	$\frac{1}{2}$ "
Oil of bergamot	$\frac{1}{2}$ ounce.
" lemon	$\frac{1}{4}$ "
" cloves	1 drachm.

Color with a little carmine, rubbed up with a portion of the oil. A pleasant semi-transparent pink pomade. The paraffin wax, as I have observed, makes a handsome pomade, and is made use of in various new pomades with fancy names, such as vasaline, cosmoline, etc. etc., and is often made with impure paraffine containing some of the benzole, which causes an unpleasant smell that a great amount of perfume will not cover.

Pomade Hongroise. (For the Moustache.)

Diachylon plaster . . .	1 pound.
Rose pomatum	2 ounces.
Oil of bergamot	2 drachms.
" cinnamon . . .	$\frac{1}{2}$ "
" rhodium	$\frac{1}{2}$ "

Put into small bottles or metal boxes.

Pomade Hongroise. (White.)

White wax	$\frac{1}{2}$ pound.
Jasmine pomade . . .	$\frac{1}{4}$ "
Canada balsam	2 ounces.
Oil of cloves	1 drachm.
" bergamot	2 "

Cire a Moustache. (Moustache wax.)

White wax	½ pound.
Oil soap	½ "
Rose pomade	2 ounces.
Oil of cloves	1 drachm.
" lemon	2 "

Mould into small sticks, and color black or brown, or let it remain white, and perfume with the different flavored pomades, in order to give a variety of odors.

Philocome Pomades

Are similar to Roman pomades, except that they are made somewhat harder by the use of lard instead of oil, or about the consistence of the soft body (one part suet to five parts lard). In their composition the perfumer can follow any of the formulas given for pomades. Keeping in view that philocomes must be somewhat softer, and for winter use they are more desirable, I have recommended the infused pomades of amber, benzoin, tolu, etc., to be made of hard body, because they keep better, and if wanted for a softer pomade it is very easy to dilute according to the kind needed. I here give a formula or two as an example of philocome pomades.

Philocome a la Mousseline.

Soft body	2 pounds.
Lard	1 "
Rose pomade	¼ "
Orange-flower pomade	½ "
Musk "	¼ "
Benzoin "	¼ "
Vanilla "	¼ "

Color yellow.

Philocome Moëlle de Bœuf.

Soft body	2 pounds.
Washed flower pomade of any odor	2 "
Oil of bergamot	1 ounce.
" lemon	½ "
" cloves	¼ "

Color deep yellow.

Thus the perfumer can make any desired philocome with the materials at hand.

Cosmetics or Stick Pomatums.

Cosmetics are a still harder product than those we have thus far treated of, and should be made of tallow from which the oil has been pressed at about the temperature of 70° Fahr., for otherwise in our warm summers the oil exudes, and soils the label, making it unsalable. This tallow can be procured of steam candle manufacturers, who are obliged to press out the oil as a preparatory process; but if the perfumer is making soap he had better press it himself, as the tallow oil is very useful in soap-making; a softer soap than the tallow having less stearine in it. This pressed tallow or suet is melted in about the proportion of four pounds to one of wax. As these pomatums are intended for the beard, hardness is of value. They are moulded into batons or sticks with tin moulds of oval, round, or square form. They are open at each end, the upper end being attached to a tin pan, and secured below by strips of tin to prevent them moving, and below there is a similar pan in which a layer of grease is first poured, and the lower ends of moulds placed, and when this grease hardens it prevents the melted grease that you now fill in the moulds from passing through. When all becomes solid the lower pan is removed, and the batons are pushed out, when they can easily be cut to the desired uniform length. The paraffine wax I have found a most useful substitute for beeswax, as it is of that peculiar consistence that causes the sticks to be smooth and slide from the mould as well as to have a smoother surface to envelop with foil. I have made in this manner thousands of grosses of lower priced cosmetics perfumed with essential oils, and sent them to the hottest climates, and they have given entire satisfaction.

For the finer cosmetics, perfumed with the flowers, the French flower pomades are used in such proportions as to insure their remaining solid. For example—

Violet Cosmetic.

Violet pomade	1 pound.
White wax.	½ "

It requires this amount of wax to make it sufficiently solid to keep hard during our summer months.

The pomades of flowers, when washed with alcohol for the extracts and bouquets, can be used with advantage in cosmetics by pressing out the alcohol and some of the oil through leather or canvas bags, when they can be hardened with wax and a portion of essential oils added to give more fragrance; and moulded *en baton.*

CHAPTER XII.

HAIR OILS AND HAIR TONICS.

In all ages, in barbarous as well as in civilized countries, the hair has been the subject of great care and attention, and ointments, unguents, and oils, have from time immemorial been in use for anointing and dressing it. In my history of perfumes these unguents have been mentioned as among the most important of perfumes, and in fact were used long ages before spirituous essences and perfumes were known. Having given a detailed account of the pomades, etc., most in vogue, and selected with care from hundreds of recipes at my command, I shall now give instructions for the preparation of oils and tonics for dressing, fixing, and promoting the growth of the hair, such as antique and hygienic oils, tonics, restoratives, washes, fixatures, depilatories, etc.

The French flower oils, as I have frequently mentioned, are made in a similar manner to the pomades by maceration and absorption; have, or should have, the same amount of odor that the pomade contains, and can be treated in precisely the same manner and in the same proportions with alcohol to extract the odors from them. By some operators they are thought best, as they are certainly most convenient to use.

In compounding the antique and hygienic oils, an assortment of the oils of benzoin, ambergris, musk, and orris, Tolu and Peru balsams, called ambrosial oils, can be prepared in about the same proportions as the recipes call for when pomades are used; for example I will give—

Huile à l'Ambre.

Ambergris	½ ounce.
Benne oil	2 pints.

Rub up the ambergris in a mortar with a portion of the oil. If it adhere to the mortar, a little clean sand can be added with advantage to cause a division of the particles. Put in a bottle, and keep in a warm place, frequently agitating, for a fortnight, or even a month, as it takes a long while for the oil to dissolve it; and in this manner you can prepare all the other oils, in proportion suited to the amount of aroma they contain, or with an eye to their cost.

Antique oils are all the oils of flowers or their combinations, and the base is either fine olive or benne oil. The first is well known to every one, and the latter, which is equally good for the purposes, is obtained from the seeds of the sesame plant, Moringa aptera. It is white, free from odor, and has the property of keeping sweet a long time. I will give the compound antique oils most in vogue.

Huile Antique au Bouquet.

Benne oil	¾ pound.
Cassie oil	½ "
Jasmine oil	¼ "
Rose oil	¼ "
Vanilla oil	½ "
Oil of bergamot	1 drachm.
" neroli	½ "

Huile Antique à la Fleur de Oranger.

Benne oil	1 pound.
Orange-flower oil . . .	½ "
Jasmine " . . .	¼ "
Benzoin " . . .	¼ "
Oil of neroli, petale . . .	1 drachm.

Huile Antique à la Heliotrope.

Benne oil	¾ pound.
Rose oil	½ "
Tuberose oil	¼ "
Vanilla oil	½ "
Oil of almonds, essential . .	1 drachm.

Huile Antique au Jasmine.

Benne oil	1 pound.
Jasmine oil	½ "
Cassie oil	¼ "
Civet oil	¼ "

Huile Antique au Millefleur.

Benne oil	¾ pound.
Rose oil	¼ "
Tuberose oil	¼ "
Jasmine oil	¼ "
Or. flower oil	2 ounces.
Cassie oil	2 "
Vanilla oil	2 "
Styrax oil	2 "
Oil of neroli	½ drachm.
" bergamot	1 "
" cloves	½ "

Huile Antique à la Rose.

Benne oil	¾ pound.
Rose oil	¾ "
Or. flower oil	¼ "
Musk oil	¼ "
Otto of roses	½ "

Huile Antique à la Tuberose.

Benne oil	1 pound.
Tuberose oil	½ "
Jasmine oil	¼ "
Orris oil	2 ounces.
Benzoin oil	2 "
Oil of neroli, petale . . .	½ drachm.

Huile Antique à la Vanilla.

Benne oil	1 pound.
Vanilla oil	½ "
Rose oil	¼ "
Ambergris oil	2 ounces.
Tolu oil	2 "

Huile Antique à la Violette.

Benne oil	1 pound.
Violet oil	½ "
Orris oil	¼ "
Cassie oil	2 ounces.
Benzoin oil	2 "
Oil of almonds, essential . .	1 drachm.

These oils are usually colored only by the flowers in the process of enfleurage, and the perfumer is satisfied with the natural yellow, green, or brownish tinge so imparted. If he desires a color for them, it is easy to impregnate the oils with the different colors needed. I have always kept on hand yellow oils colored with gamboge or roco, red oil with alkanet or carmine, green oils with gum guaiacum or with leaves, which were sufficient for all purposes.

Huile Philocome

Is really another name for the antique oils, although the term is sometimes applied to the soft pomades already noticed.

Huile Hygienique

Is yet another name applied to the antique oils I have already given the formulas for, and the perfumer can, if he has the stock of oils I have recommended, compound and invent almost any oils which the market demands.

Bear's Oil.

Bear's oil, so long and favorably known as beneficial in promoting the growth of the hair, and as improving its appearance, is now very seldom genuine, as all kinds of bland oils, vegetable and animal, have been used under that name, and generally with benefit to the user, as the genuine oil is scarce, and soon becomes rancid in spite of all efforts to prevent it, no doubt because of the large amount of albuminous matter it contains. I usually prepared it thus—

Oil of benne	2 pounds.
" bergamot	½ ounce.
" lemon	¼ "
" thyme	1 drachm.
" cloves	1 "

Color a light yellow.

Aromatic Oil of Flowers.

Benne oil, colored red . .	1 pint.
Oil of santal	1 drachm.
" lemon	2 "
" caraway	1 "
" cloves	1 "
" cinnamon . . .	½ "
" almond	½ "
" thyme	1 "
" bergamot . . .	1 "

Coral Hair Oil.

Benne oil, colored red with alkanet oil	4 pints.
Oil of orange	½ ounce.
" lemon	¼ "
" thyme	1 drachm.
" cinnamon . . .	1 "

Brazilian Hair Oil.

Benne oil	3 pints.
Castor oil	1 pint.
Oil of bergamot . . .	¾ ounce.
" cloves	2 drachms.
" neroli	1 "

Color yellow.

Chinese Hair Oil.

Benne oil	3 pints.
Castor oil	1 "
Oil of rhodium	1 drachm.
" patchouly . . .	½ drachm.
" santal	½ "

Color light green.

This oil I also called Huile de Thé (Oil of Tea).

Grecian Golden Oil.

Benne oil	3 pints.
Cassie "	1 "
Oil of bergamot . . .	¾ ounce.
" cloves	¼ "
" cassie	1 drachm.

Color a deep yellow with the roco oil.

Glycerine Hair Oil.

Pure glycerine	1½ pint.
Alcohol	½ "
Oil of lemon	½ ounce.
" neroli	1 drachm.
" almonds	½ "
Tincture of saffron . . .	2 "

Dissolve the oils with the alcohol and tincture, and agitate with the glycerine, which will become clear in the course of a few hours.

Florentine Hair Oil.

Benne oil	2½ pints.
Orris oil	½ "
Cassie oil	½ "
Benzoin oil	½ "
Oil of Portugal (orange) . .	1 ounce.
" cloves	1 drachm.

Color yellow.

Indian Hair Oil.

Benne oil	3 pints.
Styrax oil	½ pint.
Orris oil	½ "

Oil of orange	½ ounce.
" cinnamon	1 drachm.
" sassafras	2 "

Color yellow.

Japanese Hair Oil.

Benne oil	3 pints.
Rose oil	½ "
Tolu oil	¼ "
Musk oil	¼ "
Oil of geranium	½ ounce.
" santal	¼ "
" pimento	1 drachm.

Color yellow.

Macassar Oil.

Benne oil	3 pints.
Castor oil	1 "
Oil of rosemary	1 drachm.
" rhodium	2 "
" nutmegs	1 "
" bergamot	2 "
" thyme	1 "
" cinnamon	1 "

Color deep red with alkanet.

Huile de Noisette. (Hazelnut oil.)

Hazelnut oil	2 pints.
Oil of bergamot	½ ounce.
" lemon	¼ "
" cloves	1 drachm.
" neroli	½ "

Color light yellow.

Hazelnut oil is imported from France, where it is made for the use of the perfumer, and when sweet and pure is very pleasant.

Rose Hair Oil.

Oil of benne	3 pints.
Castor oil	1 "
Oil of bergamot	½ ounce.
" neroli	1 drachm.
" rhodium	2 "
" geranium	2 "

Color red with alkanet oil.

Rose Hair Oil. (Common.)

Cotton-seed oil (refined) . .	4 pints.
Oil of rosemary	½ ounce.
" orange	1 "
" thyme	¼ "

Color red with alkanet.

Cotton-seed oil, when fresh and properly refined (not bleached), is a very sweet, bland oil, and for low priced hair oils is very suitable. There are great quantities of it bottled and sold as olive oil, but while it has none of the flavor of olive oil, it is yet quite harmless. For making cheap hair oils it is only necessary to select the refined oil of a light bright yellow color, taking care to avoid the oil bleached with sulphuric acid, as the acid oxidizes the oil and gives it a rancid smell.

Hair tonics are a useful class of preparations, that if well made, and with some medicinal properties for improving the growth or beautifying the appearance of the hair, command a ready sale. But the perfumer must be careful that nothing injurious is put into them, in fact nothing that he does not know the effect of. It is necessary for me to give frequent cautions to the operator, to make himself acquainted with the properties and effects of the most important chemical substances. I am aware that many books of formulas and recipes contain improper combinations, hence the occasion of frequent warning.

Cristiani's Chemical Cathairon. (Hair restorative.)

Castor oil	1½ pints.
Alcohol, 95°	6 "
Tincture of cantharides	2 ounces.
Borax	1 "
Water	4 "
Oil of lavender	1 "
" bergamot	½ "
" cloves	½ "

The borax is dissolved in the water by heat, and added by slow degrees to the other ingredients already mixed, and if the alcohol is strong it will not be milky. It is colored slightly with a little caramel. This cathairon has been in the market for twenty-five years, and has been very popular, for it is a useful combination, and a very suitable hair dressing for ladies, as it does not grease the dress.

Cristiani's Cococydonia. (Cocoanut oil and quince seed.)

Cocoanut oil	½ pint.
Castor "	½ "
Alcohol	6 "

Slippery elm bark . . .	1 ounce.
Water	4 "
Oil of bergamot	1 "
" lemon	½ "
" pimento	¼ "
" almonds	1 drachm.

The cocoanut oil is mixed with the castor oil, and the alçohol mixed slowly with them at a slight heat. The elm bark in coarse powder is dissolved in the water and strained, and mixed by agitation with the rest. Lastly it is filtered, perfumed, and colored with a little tincture of gamboge. A popular hair dressing.

Eau Lustral. (Hair restorative.)

Castor oil	1 pint.
Linseed oil	2 ounces.
Tincture of cantharides . .	2 "
Alcohol, 95°	6½ pints.
Oil of bergamot . . .	1 ounce.
" lemon	½ "
" cloves	¼ "
" neroli	1 drachm.

The two oils are mixed together, and dissolved in the spirit by agitation. When combined add the tincture of cantharides and perfumes, and color red with tincture of archil. This has been a standard preparation for many years, and I think a valuable one, as it stimulates the scalp, and gives great softness and glossiness to the hair.

Brazilian Amber Gloss.

Castor oil	1 pint.
Alcohol, 80°	7 "
Oil of geranium	½ ounce.
" cloves	¼ "
" thyme	¼ "

Color with caramel and tincture of roco.

Glycerine and Lime-juice. (Hair tonic.)

Glycerine	2 ounces.
The juice of 6 lemons.	
Castor oil	2 ounces.
Alcohol	8 "
Liquor potassa, U. S. P. . .	½ "
Orange-flower water . . .	4 "
Oil of lemon	2 drachms.

Mix the oil and alcohol, then the liquor potassa and oil of lemon, then mix the lemon-juice, orange-flower water and glycerine, and add to the rest by portions at a time, and agitate frequently. There are no means of making it a perfectly homogeneous compound except by agitation, but it is a beautiful article for the hair, keeping the scalp clean and cool.

Ammoniated Hair Tonic.

Alcohol, 95°	4 ounces.
Castor oil	4 "
Aqua ammonia	2 "
Rose-water	6 "
Oil of bergamot	1 "
" cloves	1 drachm.

This is also a good tonic that has been very popular.

Tonique de Thé.

Black tea, strong	1 pint.
Bay rum	¼ "
Spirits of rosemary	½ "
Glycerine	¼ "

Black tea is supposed by some persons to be a promoter of the growth of the hair. However that may be, my formula, if the tea have or have not any effect, will make a good hair wash.

Glycerine Hair Tonic.

Glycerine, pure	1 pint.
Borax	½ ounce.
Rose-water	2 pints.
Alcohol	2 ounces.
Oil of petit-grain	1 drachm.
" rosemary	2 "
" cloves	1 "

This very pleasant hair tonic is prepared by dissolving the borax in the water, the perfume in the alcohol, and mixing all together. It should be clear, and if colored let it be yellow with tincture of saffron.

Eau Athenian.

Sassafras bark	¼ pound.
Water	2 quarts.
Alcohol	4 ounces.
Oil of cloves	1 drachm.
" bergamot	2 "

This hair tonic has a great reputation, and an extensive sale in Continental Europe, where the sassafras is considered a great cure-all.

Quinine Hair Tonic.

Glycerine	½ pint.
Alcohol	¼ "
Orange-flower water . . .	1¼ "
Quinine	1 drachm.
Oil of rhodium	1 "
" geranium	1 "
" cloves	1 "

Color a light red with tincture of archil.

Dissolve the quinine with a few drops of aromatic sulphuric acid, then the orange-flower water, then the glycerine, lastly add the alcohol in which the oils are dissolved.

Camphor Lotion for the Hair.

Spirits of camphor, U.S.P. .	2 ounces.
Oil of rosemary	½ "
" cloves	1 drachm.
Rose-water	2 pints.

Rosemary Hair Wash.

Spirits of rosemary . . .	1 pint.
Rose-water	1 "
Carbonate of potash . . .	2 drachms.

Bay Rum Hair Tonic.

Bay rum	1 pint.
Borax	½ ounce.
Rose-water	1 pint.

Curling Fluid.

Mucilage of gum Arabic . .	2 ounces.
Salts of tartar	1 "
Rose-water	1½ pint.
Orange-flower oil (from flowers)	4 ounces.

Color with liquid carmine.

Cristiani's Shampoo Lotion.

New England rum . . .	1 pint.
Bay " . . .	¾ "
Glycerine	2 ounces.
Carbonate of ammonia . .	1 "
Borax	2 "

Shampoo Liquid.

Salts of tartar	2 ounces.
Bay rum	2 "
Rose-water	1 pint.
Water	1 "

Bandoline. (l'Amande amère.)

Gum tragacanth . . .	2 ounces.
Orange-flower water . . .	1 pint.
Water	7 "
Essential oil of almonds . .	2 drachms.
Alcohol	4 ounces.

Bandoline à la Rose.

The same, but perfumed with rose-water or otto of rose, and colored pink with liquid carmine.

The gum is dissolved for a day or two in the water, stirred well and strained, and the alcohol with the perfume added.

Quince Seed Fixature or Bandoline.

Quince seed	. . . . .	½ ounce.
Glycerine	. . . . .	1 "
Rose-water	. . . . .	1 pint.

Color if desired yellow or red.

It will be seen that I make frequent use of glycerine (the sweet principle of fat), which I consider one of the most useful substances ever discovered for the use of the perfumer. When pure it is perfectly odorless, and has a specific gravity of 1.28, and its properties are remarkable. It mixes in all proportions with alcohol and water; is very emollient, softening to the skin and hair without greasing; undergoes no change in the air, and dissolves some substances not soluble in oil or syrup.

It is used in medicine as a vehicle for many drugs, is added to poultices to prevent their hardening, besides being soothing in its effects. As a cosmetic it is invaluable, either in lotions or in soaps, gives clearness to the skin, is softening, cooling, and refreshing, and is a remedy for all chafing, chapping, ringworms, hardness, and excoriations of the skin.

I have given a variety of formulas for hair restoratives, and such as I know to be harmless from a long experience in the manufacture of all such preparations, and refrain from giving hundreds that I deem worthless, or of such a nature that in careless hands might do much injury; for they call for caustic alkali, corrosive acids, or dangerous poisonous substances, calculated to do more harm than good, and to bring much dishonor on the perfumer's art.

To judge from the numerous substances that the old and obsolete books recommend as remedies and restoratives for the hair, one would feel that they had gone to both the vegetable and the animal kingdoms, searched heaven and earth, and gone under the earth to find them.

CHAPTER XIII.

HAIR DYES AND DEPILATORIES.

I KNOW full well the difficulties of my position while trying to give formulas that will be effective and at the same time harmless, particularly when it comes to dyeing living hair, for the art of dyeing is a chemical one, and to dye silk and wool there is the experience of hundreds to consult, but the caustic and corrosive substances so used could not be applied to anything attached to the living body without destroying or injuring the skin.

Dyeing the hair has been practised from very early times, as we read of its being universal among the women of Egypt to blacken the eyelids with a black powder called kohl. Indeed they and all eastern nations still use many dyes or stains. Among some it is the custom to ornament the face with blue patches or spots, to blacken the eyelashes, eyebrows, and eyelids; to stain the nails and palms of the hands and soles of the feet an orange-color with the leaves of the henna, and the cheeks they paint red. So in our own time and country the custom of dyeing the hair, mostly by those who hope to conceal the effects of time and age in turning it gray, is very common, and they use great quantities of advertised nostrums that are often deleterious in their effects.

The basis of nearly all hair dye is either lead or silver, and they are susceptible of but few modifications. Bismuth and pyrogallic acid can be used, but their action is not so certain. Copper and iron are used as auxiliaries in some of the formulas.

Lead Dye.

Litharge	2 ounces.
Fresh slaked lime . . .	4 "
Bicarbonate of potash . .	2 "

Mix thoroughly, and keep in well-corked bottles. This powder is mixed with water into a creamy consistence and applied to the hair, with something put over it to keep in the moisture, as it acts only when wet. In about four hours' time it is supposed to dry, and is rubbed out of the hair, when the hair is washed in warm water, oiled, and arranged. Care must be taken to have the hair perfectly clean and free from grease, or it will not dye. I give another, and I think a better preparation.

Indian Hair Dye.

Sugar of lead, powdered . .	2 ounces.
Quicklime " . .	4 "
Starch " . .	2 "

Applied as the last, and will dye in a much shorter time. I submit another in liquid form, and more convenient.

Egyptian Hair Dye.

Litharge	1 ounce.
Carbonate of lead . . .	1 "
Hydrated oxide of bismuth .	½ "
Fresh slaked lime . . .	2 "
Distilled water	1 pint.

This is allowed to stand after being well mixed, and the larger portion of the water poured off; the sediment is the dye, and is very active, dyeing the hair in about half an hour brown or black, according to the length of time it is on it. Another lead dye, very much used at the present time, is made in this manner.

Hair Color Restorer.

Acetate of lead	2 drachms.
Lac sulphur	3 "
Glycerine	4 ounces.
Rose-water	12 "

Perfume to taste.

This is applied daily until the hair changes to the desired shade. This preparation is the usual form of almost all of the advertised nostrums for the purpose, and must be used with care, as its effects on some people are injurious.

Bismuth Lye. (Two preparations.)

No. 1.

Hydrosulphate of ammonia .	2 fl. ounces.
Distilled rose-water . . .	4 "

No. 2.

Nitrate of bismuth . . .	1 ounce.
Aqua ammonia, FFF. . .	q. s.
Distilled rose-water . . .	4 ounces.

For No. 2 the bismuth is put into a glass, and the aqua ammonia added, drop by drop, while rubbing until dissolved, when the balance of the water is added. To use this dye, the hair is thoroughly washed till wet with the first solution, left to dry, and again wetted and dried; when the No. 2 is applied with a soft brush, carefully dividing the hair that all parts may receive it. This is a much safer dye than lead, and with care and skill the hair can be made to look more natural, as it gives a brownish hue.

Colornerus. (Silver dye.)

Nitrate of silver . . .	1 ounce.
Nitrate of copper . . .	1 drachm.
Distilled rose-water . . .	8 ounces.
Aqua ammonia	q. s.

The silver and copper are triturated in a glass mortar, and aqua ammonia added until the liquid becomes of a clear blue color. This dye is applied to the clean hair, and exposed to the light some time, when a black or brown color comes according to the strength; for brown it is usual to dilute it.

Another Silver Dye.

Oxide of silver	1 ounce.
Aqua ammonia	q. s.
Distilled rose-water . . .	6 ounces.
Sap green	10 grains.

Triturate the oxide of silver with the sap green, dropping in the aqua ammonia till dissolved, when add the last of the water. This is similar in its effects to the last, and used in the same manner.

Silver Dye. (Two preparations.)

No. 1. Mordant.

Sulphuret of potassium . .	1½ ounces.
Distilled water	8 "
Liquor potassa, U. S. P. . .	½ "

To be kept well stopped, and free from the light.

No. 2.

Nitrate of silver . . .	6 drachms.
Distilled rose-water . . .	8 ounces.

This is the most popular form of dye, and with a little skill is very effective.

I give another form of silver dye that is called instantaneous, as it dyes at once.

Another Silver Dye. (Two preparations.)

No. 1. Mordant.

Pyrogallic acid	1 ounce.
Distilled water	6 "
Rectified spirit	2 "

Mix and filter.

No. 2.

Nitrate of silver . . .	1 ounce.
Distilled rose-water . . .	1 "
Indigo	10 grains.

If not clear let it stand a day or two.

This is an instantaneous dye, and makes a very black color. If wanted brown, the mordant and the dye should both be diluted with one part of rose-water to two of the mixture.

These dyes, being of lunar caustic, dye the skin as well as the hair, and care should be taken to keep them off the hands, etc. If they should so stain, it can be removed with a strong solution of iodide of potassium in water. Should the finger-nails get stained, it will be necessary to use a sharp penknife to scrape them off.

Italian Hair Dye. (Two preparations.)

No. 1.

Hydrosulphuret of ammonia .	7 drachms.
Liquor potassa	3 "
Distilled water	10 "

No. 2.

Nitrate of silver . . .	1½ drachm.
Nitrate of iron	½ "
Distilled water	2 ounces.

This, when skilfully applied, dies a fine black.

The Turks dye their beards a very fine rich brown or black by means of a metal found in the East, said to be iron pyrites, but that is doubtful. I think it is an alloy of iron and copper in a state of oxide. They use for a mordant roasted Aleppo galls with some henna, and mixed with starch. In dying the beard they first mix up the gall powder into a paste with water, and thoroughly rub it into the beard, letting it dry, and if wanted jet black it is necessary to repeat this application, taking care not to get it on the skin. After the lapse of some hours the metal dye is treated in the same way, and gently rubbed into the beard, when a fine color is produced, according to the quantity used or the length of time used in its application. After this operation henna is sometimes applied to give a richer hue and soften the beard.

Vegetable Hair Dye.

Pyrogallic acid	1 ounce.
Warm water	6 "

This dye is applied daily for about a week, and turns the hair a brownish or reddish hue.

German Vegetable Hair Dye

Is a strong tincture of the green walnut hulls scented, and will stain some hair a rich brown hue.

As the most of these dyes are chemical, it is necessary to give a word of caution to those who prepare and to those who use them. I have given the most harmless, for many formulas contain cyanides, etc.

The frequent use of the litharge dye injures the hair, the lime acts upon the hair bulbs and destroys them. The liquid lead dye, if used a great length of time, will produce the painter's colic or other and worse afflictions. The silver dyes are not so dangerous, though we read of many bad effects produced by their constant use. Yet I have never observed any, if I may except an effect upon the eyesight by a constant dyeing of the beard for a number of years.

The recent rage among fashionable ladies for blonde hair has caused many nostrums to be advertised for changing the hair to that desired shade, but this is a more difficult operation than that of making it black or brown. Caustic alkali has a partial effect in destroying the natural color of the hair, but unfortunately a few applications will take out all the hair. And then again dyeing red and yellow is recommended in the manner of dyeing cloths those colors, but they are, if successful, very unnatural colors. The only harmless method I can recommend, is to use some powder or pomade, holding some blond pigment, but it is a temporary expedient and quite troublesome. I will, however, give some formulas.

Powder Blond. (Yellow powder for the hair.)

Levigated talc	1 pound.
Yellow lake	q. s.

Perfume as required.

Pommade Blonde. (Yellow powder.)

Soft body	1 pound.
Yellow lake	q. s.

Perfume as desired.

In preparing them, it is only necessary to make a thorough combination.

The Circassian beauties of the Sultan's harem are said to dye their hair an orange-red with henna, and from what I know of this plant, it may be possible to do so, but it would be to our eye an unpleasant hue. In early times the ladies of Rome used to repair to their house tops and expose their hair to the influence of the sun's rays after wetting it with an alkali. This would appear to be the most feasible expedient known.

Depilatory powders for removing superfluous hair are in demand by ladies having such disfigurement upon their arms, neck, and lips; these are chemical preparations, and sometimes very poisonous, yet with care and properly used are effective.

Pouder Epilatoire. (Depilatory powder.)

Hydrosulphuret of sodium .	1½ ounce.
Quicklime	5 "
Starch	5 "

Keep in well-stoppered vials.

When used, a small portion and sufficient only for the time, is made into a paste with water, applied and kept on until the smarting is painful, when it is washed off with warm water, and cold cream or glycerine is applied to the part.

Poudre Subtile.

Orpiment	½ ounce.
Quicklime	5 "
Starch	6 "

This is very poisonous, and should be used with care, and on but a small portion of the surface at a time, to avoid absorbing the sulphuret of arsenic. Used as the other, being careful not to blister the skin.

Depilatory Liquid.

Sulphuret of barium . . .	3 ounces.
Water	12 "

A little powdered starch is wetted with this solution, and immediately applied, and when dry it can be removed and takes the hair with it. A safe preparation.

Depilatory Pomade.

Quicklime	2 ounces.
Soda ash	2 "
Soft body	4 "

Rubbed together in a mortar. This is not so rapid in its action, but safer for tender skins. Oriental rasma is a similar preparation in the second recipe given, and much used by the Turkish women, and again I call attention to the danger attending its use.

Eyebrow Pencil.

Suet	1 pound.
Curd soap	½ "
Ivory black	q. s.

This is rolled into spills about the size of a lead pencil, covered with colored foil, or put in a metal case.

Perhaps some of the numerous dyes for yellow might be applied to giving a blonde shade to the hair, as I see a formula for the purpose that first gives the acetate of lead for a mordant, and afterwards a solution of chlorate of potash. This would give a bright yellow that might be toned down with a little Goulard's extract of lead.

And another in which sulphate of iron is used as a mordant, and when dry the hair is washed with lime-water; this gives a more natural hue or a yellowish brown. But as I have remarked, it may be easy to dye wool and hair when off the head, but extremely difficult when on the person.

CHAPTER XIV.

THE TEETH, THE GUMS, AND THE BREATH.

I SHALL now return to a more agreeable class of articles, and in giving my formulas for the numerous powders and washes for the teeth, I cannot forbear some remarks on these most useful preparations, for by a careful and prudent use of them, the many causes of early decay and loss may be prevented. The accumulation of tartar, the softening and swelling of the gums, and the undue acidity of the saliva are the general causes of their injury and destruction. In view, therefore, to overcome these causes, we study to have the proper ingredients. In powder we require something sufficiently insoluble and gritty to remove the tartar; some substance of an astringent nature to harden the gums, and, when there is much acidity of the mouth, an alkaline substance must be used to neutralize it. In the mouth washes we can only, of course, endeavor to overcome the two last causes.

Regarding the choice of the proper kind of tooth-brush to assist the cleansing power of the powder, there is but little to say, as each person should be a judge of the kind which he himself requires. Of the substances used in tooth-powders, charcoal and pumice-stone, bath brick, cuttle-fish bone are, for constant use, almost too resisting and hard, and are apt to injure the enamel. I think prepared or precipitated chalk is the best basis for the powders, unless the teeth have been very much neglected, when some substance of a more gritty nature should be used, for which I recommend powdered cuttle-fish bone.

Rose Tooth Powder. (Cristiani's.)

Precipitated chalk . . .	1½ pound.
Powdered white sugar . .	¼ "
" orris root . . .	¼ "
" cuttle-fish bone . .	2 ounces.
Carmine	½ "
Oil of rose	½ drachm.
" bergamot . . .	½ "
Tincture of musk . . .	¼ "

The chalk, orris, sugar, and cuttle-fish are all mixed together. The carmine is mixed in a mortar with a few drops of aqua ammonia to bring out the color, and the mixed powder is added by degrees. Lastly the perfumes are added, and the whole sieved to effect a thorough combination. This is a very pleasant powder, of handsome appearance, and fine flavor, and is generally liked, though it lacks any astringent property, but is well suited to keep good teeth in good order.

Poudre Dentifrice Allemande.

Sugar of milk	1 pound.
Levigated pumice . . .	2 ounces.
Sulphate of quinia . . .	2 drachms.
Prepared chalk	12 ounces.
Carmine lake	2 drachms.
Oil of lavender	1 drachm.
" lemon	2 "
" cloves	½ "

Mix and sieve.

Poudre Dentifrice de Menthe.

Precipitated chalk	. . .	$1\frac{1}{4}$ pound.
Powdered sugar	. . .	$\frac{1}{4}$ "
" orris root	. . .	$\frac{1}{4}$ "
Oil of rosemary	. . . .	2 drachms.
" peppermint	. . .	3 "

Mix and sieve.

Detergent Tooth Powder.

Precipitated chalk	. . .	$1\frac{1}{4}$ pounds.
Powdered myrrh	. . .	2 ounces.
" borax	. . .	2 "
" sugar of milk	. .	4 "
" orris root	. . .	4 "
Oil of cloves	. . . .	1 drachm.
" cinnamon	. . . .	$\frac{1}{2}$ "
" coriander	. . .	$\frac{1}{2}$ "

Camphorated Dentifrice.

Precipitated chalk	. . .	1 pound.
Powdered orris root	. . .	$\frac{1}{2}$ "
" sugar	. . .	$\frac{1}{4}$ "
" camphor	. . .	$\frac{1}{4}$ "

Rub up the camphor in a mortar with a few drops of alcohol and add the other powders.

Charcoal Tooth Powder.

Powdered charcoal	. . .	$1\frac{1}{4}$ pound.
Prepared chalk	. . . .	$\frac{1}{4}$ "
Powdered catechu	. . .	2 ounces.
" orris root	. . .	4 "
" cassie	. . .	1 "
" cloves	. . .	1 "

Mix and sieve.

Coral Tooth Powder.

Prepared chalk	1¼ pound.
Powdered cuttle-fish	2 ounces.
" red coral	½ pound.
Bole Armenia	2 ounces.
Oil of cloves	1 drachm.
" cassia	½ "
" fennel	½ "
Tincture of vanilla	1 "
" musk	½ "

Mix and sieve.

Aromatic Tooth Powder.

Prepared chalk	1 pound.
Cuttle-fish bone	2 ounces.
Carmine lake	½ "
Powdered sugar	4 "
" calamus	1 "
" cloves	2 "
" cassia	2 "
" ambrette seed	2 "
" cinchona	2 "
" bicarbonate of soda	2 "

Poudre Dentifrice Hygienique. (Cristiani's.)

Precipitated chalk	1 pound.
Powdered sugar of milk	½ "
" cuttle-fish bone	1 ounce.
" orris root	4 "
Carmine lake	1 "
Benzoin acid	1 drachm.
Sulphate of morphia	½ "

Oil of rose	30 drops.
" cloves	10 "
" coriander	20 "
" fennel	10 "
Tincture of vanilla . . .	30 "
" musk . . .	20 "

This powder is deservedly popular, as it contains every requisite of a good tooth powder, and its flavor is very pleasant.

Peruvian Tooth Powder.

Powdered yellow bark . .	½ pound.
" orris root	¼ "
" myrrh . . .	2 ounces.
Precipitated chalk . . .	1 pound.
Bole Armenia	2 ounces.
Oil of cloves	1 drachm.
" caraway	½ "

Soap Dentifrice.

Precipitated chalk . . .	1 pound.
Powdered orris	¼ "
" myrrh . . .	2 ounces.
" white soap . .	3 "
" saffron . . .	1 "
Oil of lavender	2 drachms.

As a matter of course, every druggist thinks he can make the best tooth powder, though he may indiscriminately put into it bath-brick, pumice-stone, and charcoal, which, if the purchaser will use perseveringly, will wear out all the teeth that nature gave him; and so in tooth pastes I will give only such as meet my approval.

Rose Tooth Paste.

Prepared chalk	1¼ pound.
Rose pink	¼ "
Powdered rose leaves . .	¼ "
Honey	q. s.
Otto of rose	½ drachm.
Carmine liquid	½ "
Tincture of musk . . .	20 drops.

The powders are all put together and then made into a soft mass with the honey, and put into China boxes.

Coral Tooth Paste.

Powdered red coral . . .	½ pound.
Cuttle-fish bone . . .	2 ounces.
Prepared chalk	1 pound.
Cochineal	2 ounces.
Cream of tartar	2 "
Honey of roses	q. s.
Oil of cloves	½ drachm.
Alum	2 ounces.

Make into a fine powder, and into a mass with the honey of roses.

Charcoal Tooth Paste.

Powdered willow charcoal .	1 pound.
" orris root . . .	¼ "
" myrrh . . .	2 ounces.
Prepared chalk	½ pound.
Oil of peppermint . . .	½ drachm.
Honey	q. s.

Aromatic Tooth Paste.

Precipitated chalk . . .	1 pound.
Bole Armenia	¼ "
Powdered orris root . . .	¼ "
" cloves . . .	2 ounces.
" cinnamon . . .	2 "
" coriander . . .	2 "
" cuttle-fish bone .	2 "
Honey of roses	q. s.

Peruvian Tooth Paste.

Prepared chalk	1¼ pound.
Powdered orris and myrrh, each	2 ounces.
" yellow bark . .	4 "
" cuttle-fish bone .	2 "
Honey	q. s.

Soap Tooth Paste.

Powdered white castile soap .	½ pound.
Precipitated chalk . . .	1 "
Powdered cuttle-fish . .	2 ounces.
" aquilla bark . .	2 "
Oil of coriander . . .	30 drops.
" pimento	50 "
" lavender	20 "
Honey	q. s.

Violet Tooth Paste.

Prepared chalk	1¼ pound.
Powdered orris	¼ "
" sugar of milk . .	¼ "
" cuttle-fish . .	2 ounces.
Extract of violet . . .	½ "

Oil of almonds, essential	¼ drachm.
Honey	q. s.
Tincture of archil	½ ounce.

Odontine Paste. (Cristiani's.)

Precipitated chalk	1¼ pound.
Powdered orris	¼ "
" cuttle-fish	2 ounces.
" castile soap	2 "
Benzoic acid	1 drachm.
Carmine lake	2 "
Oil of coriander	1 "
" cloves	½ "
" rose	½ "
Clarified honey	q. s.

Opiate Tooth Paste.

Prepared chalk	1¼ pound.
Powdered orris	¼ "
" myrrh	2 ounces.
" rose leaves	2 "
Sulphate of morphia	½ drachm.
Brazil lake	1 ounce.
Oil of cloves	20 drops.
" nutmegs	20 "
" rhodium	30 "
Honey	q. s.

Tooth pastes are a very pleasant mode of cleansing the teeth, and nearly as efficacious as powders. They are always put up in earthen, glass, or porcelain jars or pots, and neatly labelled. They are used by rubbing the moistened tooth-brush over the surface of the paste until sufficient adheres. We will now give some formulas for teeth and mouth washes, a form of dentifrice particularly adapted to strengthening the gums and arresting decay, besides sweetening the breath.

Eau Botot.

Tincture of cedar wood . .	½ pint.
" cinchona . . .	½ "
" myrrh . . .	¼ "
" rhatany . . .	¼ "
Oil of spearmint	20 drops.

These tinctures should be made of rectified spirits of 60°.

Opal Dentiline.

Tincture of myrrh . . .	2 ounces.
" rhatany and Tolu, each . . .	1 ounce.
Orange-flower water . . .	1¾ pint.

Made by gradually adding the water to the tincture, with frequent agitation, so that when made it presents a uniform milky appearance without precipitate.

Camphor Balsam for the Teeth.

Camphor	½ ounce.
Tincture of myrrh . . .	2 "
" Peru balsam . .	2 "
Rectified spirit	1 pint.
Oil of spearmint . . .	10 drops.

This is an excellent and convenient wash for cleansing the teeth and scenting the breath.

Detergent Tooth Wash. (Cristiani's.)

Tincture of pyrethra	4	ounces.
" rhatany	4	"
" myrrh	4	"
" benzoin	4	"
" vanilla	4	"
" aquilla bark	8	"
Extract of millefleur	2	"
Tincture of cochineal	1	"

I have made this dentifrice for the past twenty-five years, and it has met the approval of all who have used it. Like all the rest of these tooth washes, a few drops are sprinkled on the wet tooth-brush and the teeth rubbed briskly, using water to rinse out the mouth. I would advise a metal sprinkler put into the perforated cork for convenience in using the washes, and also one of larger orifice for the tooth powder, as being the latest improvement for this class of goods.

Elixir Odontalgique.

Tincture of rhatany	4	ounces.
" cinchona	1	"
" cedar wood	8	"
" vanilla	2	"
" myrrh	2	"
" cloves	2	"
" cinnamon	2	"
" cochineal	2	"
Extract of rose, No. 2	2	"

Under this name a preparation has had a great sale in England and on the continent. I give this formula as my idea of its component parts.

Oriental Styptic.

Tincture of rhatany, myrrh, pyrethra, cloves, of each	4 ounces.

Particularly recommended for soft or bleeding gums.

Pyrethene Tooth Wash.

Tincture of pyrethra	4 ounces.
" myrrh	4 "
" cinnamon	2 "
" coriander	2 "
" cloves	2 "
" saffron	2 "
" cochineal	2 "
Borax	1 "
Rose-water	4 "
Rectified spirits	8 "

Dissolve the borax in the rose-water and add to the mixture, agitating frequently.

Opiate Tooth Wash.

Tincture of myrrh	4 ounces.
" rhatany	8 "
" opium	2 "
" camphor	1 "
Extract of millefleur	1 "

Very useful for toothache and neuralgia.

Violet Tooth Wash.

Tincture of orris	8 ounces.
" myrrh	4 "
" aquilla bark	8 "

Tincture of archil . . .	1 ounce.
Extract of violet . . .	2 "
" rose	2 "
Oil of almonds	10 drops.

This formula gives a wash leaving a pleasant taste in the mouth, and giving a perfume to the breath.

The formulas given for compounding all these powders and washes are original, and can all be safely recommended for the purposes intended.

Pastilles for cleaning the teeth have been somewhat in vogue, and I think might be still more used, as they possess some advantage over all other forms of dentifrices; not the least one is their cleanliness, as each lozenge is of the size to cleanse the teeth when dissolved in the mouth, and there is no waste or soiling, as there is likely to be with powder or paste unless much care be exercised. I have made several styles, and will give a few forms. Any person may readily modify them.

Dental Pastils. (Cristiani's.)

Precipitated chalk . . .	1¼ pound.
Powdered orris	¼ "
" sugar . . .	½ "
" cuttle-fish bone . .	2 ounces.
Carmine	1 drachm.
Aqua ammonia	q. s.
Mucilage of gum tragacanth .	q. s.
Oil of rose	20 drops.
" cloves	10 "
" coriander . . .	10 "
" nutmegs	10 "

These pastils are made by combining the powders, intimately rubbing the carmine in a large mortar with a few drops of aqua ammonia to bring out the color, and stirring in the mixed powders, and with the mucilage of tragacanth (fresh), making into a stiff mass, rolling out into thin sheets, and cutting out the forms with a tin mould in any device desired. Each lozenge should weigh about half a drachm.

Chlorine Pastils.

Powdered white sugar . .	1 pound.
Chlorate of potassa . . .	3 ounces.
Powdered gum tragacanth .	2 "
Oil of cloves	20 drops.
Rose-water, triple . . .	q. s.

The powders should be thoroughly mixed and sieved, and made into a mass with the rose-water, and into lozenges. Exceedingly useful as an anti-scorbutic, and for sore mouths and foul breath.

Masticatories are those substances taken into the mouth and slowly chewed, such as tobacco, opium, betal-nut, etc. In view of this habit, common to so many people and countries, the perfumer has made use of this means to introduce substances that are efficacious as remedies for bad teeth and breath, sore mouth and throat; and they can be so made as to be a very useful article for a masticatory for sore mouth and soft gums, or bad breath. I make one in this manner:—

Pellitory Masticatory Pastils. (Cristiani's.)

Gum mastic, powdered . .	2 ounces.
Pellitory root, " . .	2 "
Balsam Tolu	1 "
Paraffine wax	11 "

Melt the wax and the balsam together, and, while cooling, stir in the mixed powders, and before it is quite cold cut into dice about ⅓ inch square.

Aromatic Opiate Masticatory Pastils.

Powdered gum mastic	. .	1 ounce.
" orris	. . . .	1 "
" pellitory	. . .	1 "
" opium	. . .	⅓ "
" vanilla	. . .	¼ "
Paraffine wax	. . . .	1 pound.
Tincture of musk	. . .	1 drachm.
" ambergris	. .	1 "
Carmine	. . . . .	1 "

The carmine is blended with the powders and stirred into the melted wax; when perfume, and cut into squares each weighing 10 grains troy.

Aromatic cachous for perfuming the breath are a very useful article, much used, and impart a fragrance to the breath when dissolved in the mouth, and destroy any unpleasant taste from whatever cause.

I have for many years made a specialty of these articles, and can speak knowingly of their great usefulness. They are generally spherical granules of small size, and usually coated with silver-leaf, or colored pink with carmine, made into a small lozenge, colored to suit the ingredient.

Cachou Aromatisé. (Cristiani's.)

Powdered catechu	. . .	1 pound.
" extract of liquorice	.	3 "
" liquorice root	. .	6 "
" gum Arabic	. .	2 "
" white sugar	. .	8 "

These powders being mixed, and with syrup made in a mass and into granules not weighing over half a grain, perfume with the following:—

Oil of cloves	. . . .	1½ ounce.
" coriander	. . .	1 "
" caraway	. . . .	1 "
" peppermint	. . .	1 "
" nutmegs	. . . .	½ "
" lemon	. . . .	1 "
" allspice	. . . .	½ "
" rose	. . . .	½ "
Tincture of musk	. . .	1 "

When made they are coated with pure silver-leaf in this manner: Two wooden globes are provided, screwing together at the centre. In one the pills are coated with some of the cachous, dissolved in rose-water, and highly perfumed, and poured out upon trays to dry. This must be repeated until the surface is smooth. When glazed in this way they are put into the second globe, filling it about one-third full, and shaken with a portion of the glazing to get them slightly wet, when the silver-leaf is put in with layers of cachous and well rolled around. Sufficient silver must be put in until they are thoroughly coated. This process is more difficult to describe than to perform, and it requires some practice to give dexterity in the manipulation.

Arome du Bouche. (Mouth aromatic.)

Powdered white sugar	. .	11 pounds.
" gum tragacanth	.	1 "

Made into a mass with syrup and perfumed with the cachou perfume, and colored with carmine and formed into star-shaped lozenges not over a quarter of an inch in diameter. They are a very nice article for perfuming the breath, and can also be made with the appropriate perfume into

Cachous du musc.
" à la rose.
" à l'amber.
" à l'œillet.
" à la violet, etc.
" à la canella.
" of cardamom.
" de giroffle.
" of rhatany, etc. etc.

Colored to suit the material used.

Cachous des Dames. (Cristiani's ladies' cachous.)

Powdered white sugar . .	8½ pounds.
Chlorate of potash . . .	½ "
Powdered gum Arabic . .	2 "
" tragacanth .	1 "
Carmine	q. s.

Flavored with

Oil of rose	4 drachms.
" coriander . . .	2 "
" cloves	4 "
" nutmegs	2 "
" neroli	1 "
Tincture of musk . . .	2 "
" ambergris . .	1 "

These are made into very small diamond-shaped lozenges, and are exceedingly pleasant and useful—keeping the mouth healthy.

LOZENGES are somewhat out of the line of the perfumer in this country. But in Europe, the better class of druggists and apothecaries have a great many different kinds prepared, for which they find ready sale; and they could be made a feature in all first-class drug stores in this country with but little trouble, for they are exceedingly useful. I will make a few suggestions. The quantity of medicinal substance in each, every druggist should know.

Alum lozenges, astringent.
Bark lozenges, tonic astringent.
Rhatany lozenges, tonic astringent.
Borax lozenges, healing and antacid.
Camphor lozenges, anodyne.
Catechu lozenges, astringent.
Black-currant lozenges, pectoral.
Chalk lozenges, acidity and diarrhœa.
Charcoal lozenges, heartburn, etc.
Chlorate of potash lozenges, antiscorbutic.
Lavender lozenges, stomachic.
Magnesia lozenges, heartburn and dyspepsia.
Myrrh lozenges, astringent and for the gums.
Nitrate of potash lozenges, for scurvy, etc.
Opium lozenges, toothache and anodyne.
Pellitory lozenges, toothache and neuralgia.
Quinia lozenges, tonic and for foul gums.
Soda lozenges, for acidity of mouth and stomach.
Peppermint lozenges, for flatulency and nausea.
Ginger, etc., lozenges, for flatulency and nausea.

Here let me suggest to the enterprising perfumer to give some study and attention to the class of ingredients that enter into all preparations for the mouth and teeth, for, while there are a great many useful substances, there are also a number that should not be used, and require close attention lest he may use something that would cause injury to these delicate organs.

CHAPTER XV

ESSENTIAL OILS AND THEIR TESTS.

As essential oils are perhaps the most important articles used in perfumery, I think it necessary to devote a chapter to them, and endeavor to give the perfumer an insight into their several qualities as well as advice in their selection, and tests for their quality and purity, for without this knowledge he may often be imposed upon when purchasing of some one equally ignorant of their quality or unscrupulous or fraudulent enough to adulterate these valuable substances.

Volatile oil occurs in every part of odorous plants, whose aroma they diffuse by exhalation, but in different parts or organs of different species. In herbaceous plants, such as thyme and lavender, it is distributed throughout all parts of them, but in others it may be only in the blossom, the seeds, the leaves, the tube, or the root; and it sometimes happens that different parts of the same plant produce different oils; the orange, for instance, has three: one in the flowers, one in the leaves, and another in the rind of the fruit.

The quantity of oil varies, not only with the species, but also in the same plant, with the soil, and especially with the climate, as in warm countries it is generally the most profuse.

In several plants the odor is contained in peculiar orders of vessels that contain it so closely that it does not escape in the drying, nor is it lost in keeping the plant for many years; in others, and particularly in flowers, it is formed continuously on the surface, and flies off almost or quite at the moment of its formation.

Volatile oils are usually obtained by distillation. For this purpose the plant is put into a still; water is poured upon it and the heat applied, when the oil is volatilized by the aid of the watery vapor at the temperature of boiling water, and carried over with the steam, which is condensed in the worm, and as it cools the oil separates and rises to the top, or sinks to the bottom, and is received in an appropriate vessel.

Most of the essential oils employed are extracted from the dried plants, but a few, such as the rose and orange-flower, are obtained from the fresh or salted flowers. Some oils of a less volatile nature require a higher heat than 212° Fahr. to raise them in vapor, and it must be developed by adding common salt to the water, thereby raising the heat some 15° more, when they readily come over.

When too much water is used, no oil will be obtained, as it may be partially soluble in water, and thus produce only an aromatic water. If, on the other hand, too little water is used, the plant may adhere to the bottom of the still, get partially charred, and impart a burnt odor to the product. Thus the best mode of conducting these distillations, in my opinion, is to fill a perforated cylinder, and suspend it in the still, and let the steam pass through it. The stills and cylinder should be made of strong tinned copper.

Some plants yield so little oil by the ordinary process that the same water is re-distilled several times with a fresh portion of the plants; repeating until a certain quantity of the oil is obtained, which being taken off, the saturated water is kept for a future like distillation. Some oils, like aniseed and fennel that become concrete at low temperatures, should not have the water of the refrigerator lower than 45° Fahr.

These oils are condensed and received at the end of the worm, and collected in what is called a Florentine receiver (see fig. 8), which is a conical vessel standing on its base, with a bent pipe rising out of the side close to the bottom, and curved a little above the middle like the spout of a teapot. The oil and the water collected in this vessel soon separate according to their specific gravities; if the water be the denser it occupies the bottom, and overflows from the spout, while the lighter oil is left in the receiver. Should the oil be the heavier, the receiver should be a large inverted cone with a stopcock at the apex to run off the heavier oil that has settled by repose. In some cases it is necessary to use ice in the condenser, for the water will thus part with more of the oil with which it is impregnated.

There are some essential oils that are obtained by expression, as the oils of lemon, bergamot, and orange. The pellicle of the ripe fruit is submitted to pressure, and the oil comes out with the water of the peel, and is collected from the surface.

The odors or oils of odoriferous flowers are confined so loosely that they speedily exhale, and, therefore, another process has to be resorted to for their extraction. I speak of such flowers as the jasmine, violet, etc. These flowers are placed in contact with oil or grease, and the operation is repeated with fresh flowers until they are sufficiently perfumed, when by putting strong spirits with the oil or grease we extract its fragrance, the alcohol having a greater solvent power for the odor than the grease. This process of absorption or enfleurage has been more particularly described in another chapter, as also the process of maceration of other flowers as the rose and orange-flower, which is done by thus infusing with oil or grease at a moderate heat.

The physical properties of essential oils differ very much from each other; some are colorless, others yellow, brown, or red, some are green, and a few blue. They have a more or less powerful and agreeable odor, and when quite fresh are sometimes a little rank. Very few are as agreeable as their respective plants. They have a hot acrid taste, but generally agreeable when largely diluted with water or other substances. They have not the unctuous properties of fatty oils, but generally make the skin feel rough. They are nearly all lighter than water, some few having more density, although called volatile oils. The tension of their vapor, as well as its specific heat, is much less than that of water. Their boiling point differs with the different kinds, but is generally about 320° Fahr. When distilled by themselves they are partially decomposed, and the gaseous products decomposed always carry off a little of the oil. They distil readily with water, because the aqueous vapor formed on the surface of the boiling fluid carries along with it the vapor of the oil produced, in virtue of the tension which it possesses at the 212° Fahr.

In the open air volatile oils burn with a shining flame, which deposits a great deal of soot, and their congealing point varies greatly; some do not solidify until cooled to below 32° Fahr., while some are concrete at the ordinary temperature of the atmosphere.

When exposed to the air they absorb oxygen, and become darker in color. This absorption continues until their fragrance also is changed from a pleasant to an offensive one. Light also contributes to this effect; the oil turns gradually thicker, loses its pleasant smell, and is formed into a resin which, by continued exposure, becomes solid. Oil of lavender, recently distilled, has been found to absorb in four winter months, fifty-two times its volume of oxygen, and had disengaged twice its volume of carbonic acid gas; and oil of aniseed in a year had absorbed seventy-eight times its volume of oxygen gas, and exhaled thirteen times its volume of carbonic acid gas. When an oil has begun to experience such an oxidation, a resin is formed, and the oil can be separated by distilling with water. So it is to avoid these changes that it is necessary to fill the bottle full of essential oil, cork and seal or have close fitting glass stoppers, and keep in a cool dark place.

Volatile oils are little soluble in water, yet enough so to impart to it their smell and taste when agitated with it, while the water distilled with it is generally a saturated solution. Such waters are used in medicine and perfumery as distilled water, and are exceedingly useful. They often contain other volatile substances of the plant from which they are distilled, and are apt to putrefy when close stopped in bottles, but if left slightly open to the air these substances exhale, and they will remain sweet. Those waters that are made simply by agitation with the essence will not spoil by being so confined.

Essential oils are soluble in alcohol, and the more so the stronger the spirit is. Some that are devoid of oxygen, as the oils of turpentine and citron, are but sparingly soluble in dilute alcohol, while others, as lavender, etc., are considerably so. Thus we infer that they are more soluble in alcohol the more oxygen they contain. In their combination with alcohol to form the odoriferous spirits, which are incorrectly called waters, as eau de Cologne, etc., when water is added to them they turn milky, as the alcohol has a greater affinity for the water, which combines and liberates the volatile oils.

With the salifiable bases these oils do not combine, except oil of cloves and pimento. Some will partially combine with caustic alkali, for, when oil of turpentine is triturated in a mortar with fused caustic soda, the oil being added slowly to the alkali, it forms a sort of soap. They will generally absorb about six times their bulk of ammoniacal gas; and lavender absorbs 47 times its bulk of it. They will combine in any proportion with all the fatty oils, gums, and resins.

Commercial essential oils are often adulterated, and some knowledge of the tests for ascertaining these adulterations may be useful. When fatty oils, resins, or balsams are present, they may be detected by putting a drop or two of the oil on white paper, and exposing it to heat. If pure, the essential oil will evaporate and leave no stain; but, if any of these substances be present, there will be a transparent stain upon the paper. If fat oil be present it can be detected by mixing with alcohol, say 1 part to 3 of alcohol of specific gravity 0.840, when it will remain undissolved. Resins can be easily detected by distillation, when the resin will be left in the still. Oil adulterated with alcohol will form a milky solution on the addition of water, the alcohol being absorbed by the water, and the oil afterwards forming on the surface; a graduated glass tube will show the quantity of adulteration.

When essential oils are adulterated with cheaper oils, the difficulties of detection are much greater. Then the smell and the taste are our principal guides. We put a few drops of the suspected oil upon a piece of paper or muslin, and smell it from time to time. In this way we may be able to tell the difference of the smell from the beginning from that which exhales at the end—a method that is sure to detect such oils as turpentine or fixed oils; and, again, when the suspected oil is mixed with alcohol of the specific gravity of 0.840, most of the turpentine will remain undissolved. If two oils be mixed, one of which is heavier and the other lighter than water, by adding that fluid and agitating in a vial they will separate when the mixture is allowed to rest.

As it may be necessary for the perfumer to be able to test the different essential oils which he uses, I will give some tests for nearly all such as are likely to be adulterated, or which he has occasion to use.

Oil of almonds has many peculiarities by which its purity may be easily shown. My test is sulphuric acid; a few drops of which on a watch-glass will color it red, but cause but little decomposition, which would ensue if any adulteration were present.

Oil of aniseed, with the same test, congeals into a solid mass with increase of heat; if any other oil be present, this latter oil will separate from the genuine oil.

Oil of cloves, when dissolved in an alcoholic solution of caustic potash, congeals into a crystalline mass, losing its clove odor. If any other oil be present, it will separate.

Oil of cinnamon is not often adulterated, except with the cheaper Chinese oil (oil of cassia). When sulphuric acid is added to the Ceylon oil, it forms a solid mass, changing to a deep black. With the Chinese oil the substance is softer, and of an olive-green color.

Oil of bergamot is generally protected from adulteration by its fine odor, except with the other citron oils whose elements are the same. If alcohol be present, water will absorb and separate it.

Oil of lavender.—Alcohol is the usual article of its adulteration, and can be detected by water and the test-tube. Iodine causes a quick and violent fulmination with the pure oil. The inferior oil will not fulminate.

Oil of roses is principally adulterated with geranium oil or spermaceti. The first can be detected by putting a few drops on a watch-crystal, with as many of sulphuric acid, and stirring with a glass rod. If pure it suffers no change, but, if there is any geranium or other oil in it, the color will become dark and acquire a strong, disagreeable odor. Spermaceti can be detected by alcohol, which will not dissolve it.

Oil of sassafras can be considered pure when it

remains clear with iodine; and sulphuric acid forms with it a green color not produced by any other oil.

Oil of thyme.—Iodine has but a slight reaction upon this oil, but if any other be present it is violent.

These tests may serve a good purpose, and would be necessary when the quantity was great and a strict examination would be justified; but the experienced perfumer, who has handled and used many fine oils, scarcely ever requires any other test than his nose, his eyes, and his tongue.

The quantity of essential oils yielded by the various plants is here given, derived from the best authority.

Cake of bitter almonds,	100	pounds yield	7 ounces.
Aniseed,	100	"	30 "
Bergamot peel,	100	"	12 "
Calamus root,	100	"	10 "
Caraway seed,	100	"	4 pounds.
Cassia bark,	100	"	1 "
Cinnamon,	100	"	12 ounces.
Cloves,	100	"	12 pounds.
Geranium leaves,	100	"	3 ounces.
Orris root,	100	"	14 "
Origanum,	100	"	10 "
Peppermint,	100	"	15 "
Lavender,	100	"	20 "
Nutmegs,	100	"	10 pounds.
Thyme,	100	"	6 ounces.
Orange-peel,	100	"	12 "
Lemon-peel,	100	"	12 "
Cedar wood,	100	"	1 pound.
Melissa bark,	100	"	4 ounces.
Myrtle leaves,	100	"	25 "
Patchouly leaves,	100	"	25 "

Rose leaves,	100 pounds yield	2 drachms.	
Rhodium wood,	100 "	6 ounces.	
Santal wood,	100 "	30	"
Vitivert root,	100 "	10	"
Ylang Ylang flowers,	100 "	4	"
Wintergreen leaves,	100 "	25	"

This table may be useful to get an idea of the value of an oil, or to see what margin of profit would result from distilling it should the opportunity offer. As the manufacture of most of these essential oils is now confined to Europe or other countries of the growth of the plants, it might be well to call the attention of our countrymen to the culture of some of these plants; for with our varied climate and soil it would seem to be quite feasible, and with experience prove profitable. Besides which we have such a variety of indigenous plants, many of which are profuse in flowers and fragrance, that we might with but little trouble be able to obtain some new perfumes that would rank with those so generally esteemed, and which we now have to import from distant countries. In Florida, for instance, we are constantly increasing the culture of the orange and other tropical fruits; would it be more than a short step to cultivate the plants for their flowers, and another to distil their oil, or, by maceration and absorption with grease or oil, give to commerce another source of the supply of these useful articles?

California, whose climate is suited to so many fruits and flowers, has in some districts almost the same climate as Italy. Why cannot we then give attention to the culture of flowering plants that may prove a source of pleasure, health, and wealth to thousands of our people?

I give these hints to a population constantly on the look-out for novelties and ever trying to invent something new, so that, when they have exhausted all other fields without the anticipated success, they may venture into this.

CHAPTER XVI.

DISTILLED WATERS AND ESSENCES.

NEARLY all aromatic plants impart to waters distilled from them their peculiar fragrance, their volatile oil rising with the aqueous vapor, which is condensed with it in the receiver. Many of the plants contain so little of the volatile principle that the first product is very feeble in odor, it is, therefore, necessary to redistil the same water with a fresh portion of the plant a second or a third time.

In the distillation of leaves and flowers it is generally preferred to have them fresh, though rose leaves can be preserved by mixing them with one-third their weight of common salt before they dry, as in drying they lose a great portion of their fragrance. In fact this mode of preservation is preferred by many, as the water distilled from the leaves so preserved is free from a certain rankness, that the product from the recent leaves always retains, but which is in a great measure lost when the water is kept.

Many vegetable substances, on the other hand, yield their fragrance much better when dried, and in some, indeed, it is not developed until they are perfectly dry, and are then only fit for distillation, and if the oil is required, yield much more and of better quality.

The stills or alembics are too well known to need a description here (we have given several cuts of them elsewhere), except to notice that late improvements are made in having a perforated cylinder or wire basket suspended in the still to hold the substance to be distilled in such a manner as to cause the steam to pass through it and carry over with it the aromatic principle, as otherwise, when put immediately into the still, it sinks to the bottom, and adhering becomes charred, and imparts an empyreumatic odor to the product, which it retains a great length of time. A still better mode is to have a steam pipe or coil inserted in the still, and reaching nearly to the bottom, and causing a flow of steam to pass gently through the water and substance, and in that manner avoid all danger of scorching.

It is necessary to observe that the greatest care must be taken to have the still, the head, and the worm or receiver perfectly clean, and free from all foreign odor, to clean it perfectly before and after use, that the article distilled may not be contaminated with any other odor; and to observe not to have too large a quantity of the material for the capacity of the still, as the water may overflow into the receiver. Also if the substance be hard and dry, to have it previously bruised or ground and macerated in the water, some hours previous to the operation. When all is ready, the fire should be brisk, so that the water may quickly be brought to a state of ebullition, and so remain until the end of the process, and to reject the first waters that come over, and to leave sufficient in the still to avoid contaminating the whole with the burnt odor of the last. For if carried too far the product is apt to get slimy or to adhere to the sides of the alembic and be exposed to decomposition. But as careful as you may be, it is difficult to have distillations from plants free from all empyreumatic odor, though by exposing them to the air for a few hours they are generally freed from it.

When these distilled waters are bottled and closely stopped, they are apt to become full of ropy rancid matter, which decomposing produces acidity; there are many remedies proposed to prevent this contamination, such as the addition of spirit before or after distillations, but I have preferred to distil the water a second time to free it from such substances, and have found such waters to keep for years.

Should any volatile oil come over and form on the surface of the water, it can be removed with the pipette. It is also recommended that these waters be filled into bottles or cans completely full and perfectly stopped to exclude the air, and kept in a cool, dark place; and that copper, lead, and zinc should not come in contact with them, as they oxidize those metals and the waters become unfit for use.

The distilled waters of rose and orange-flower imported from France and Italy are very superior to any we can make, as they are made on the spot where the flowers grow, and the last is distilled for the extraction of the essential oil, while the rose is principally for the water alone, for the otto of rose is made almost exclusively in Turkey and India, they having for a long time devoted much space and time to its manufacture. These distilled waters are imported in tinned copper cans, or in bottles inclosed in wicker, and are called double or triple according to the number of times they have been distilled with the flowers, for, as I have remarked, it is necessary to redistil the water with fresh flowers that it may be saturated with the perfume. In distilling for the oil of neroli, the water from which the oil has been taken is called triple, because it usually requires that number of distillations to set the oil free. The flower, though somewhat strong in odor, does not yield it readily, and besides, a large portion of the oil is soluble in the water, so that after these operations the oil begins to separate. The rose-water, though it may receive that number of distillations, seldom has any oil upon it, so much of the aroma does the water absorb. I use these waters extensively in my manufactures, as they contain two of the most important odors used by the perfumer.

Distilled waters for medicinal purposes, that used in former times to be recommended by the different pharmacopœias, are now made by means of the essential oils of the plants needed. In fact the United States Pharmacopœia discards almost altogether the process of distillation, and directs the essential oil to be triturated with carbonate of magnesia and filtered. But the perfumer will find it difficult to obtain a water of sufficient strength for his purpose by this process, and besides in the two most important ones for him, the rose and the orange-flower, the perfume from them is quite different and inferior to the distilled water made as already mentioned.

There are but few distilled waters needed by the perfumer at the present day, though there might be some that he might especially need for some original compound or bouquet of his own invention that might please the fancy of his customers; hence I give these instructions as a guide. If he had the facilities for procuring the flowers of roses or of elder it might be sensible and profitable to distil, for of the former nearly every druggist wants a supply, and if he has any judgment he will not use the water made from the oil if he can get a good distilled one.

The distillations of eau de Cologne and lavender water, and in fact nearly all the aromatic toilet waters and vinegars I have given in my chapter on that subject, would be exceedingly useful, and would produce a better product. Yet there are many odors that distillation does not improve, such as the jasmine, tuberose, violet, etc , and, therefore, for the extracts and bouquets the heat requisite for distillation injures them. I, therefore, use the strongest alcohol as a solvent for the proper material, and when the formula is compounded, I add of the rose or orange-flower water sufficient to bring the extract to a proper strength.

Yet when the toilet water admits of distillation, the process tends to make a better blending of the aroma that is much more pleasant than by other means.

Yet again where the extract may be for flavoring or cooking, the still could be used to great advantage in extracting with spirit the flavor of the plant, in a much more pleasant form than the mere admixture of the oil with the spirit. I shall speak further of this when I come to extracts for flavoring.

The druggist has frequent recourse to the still in many preparations in which alcohol is the solvent, yet has to be used in the form of a weaker spirit, or of a syrup, when he distils it to recover the alcohol, which would otherwise be lost, and which can again be used in manufacturing some other article.

There are some substances rich in oil that the perfumer might distil with profit, such as cloves and other spices, provided he had all the necessary apparatus, but this must be left to his own judgment. I have, when such spices were cheap, distilled them in a steam alembic, driving steam through the spices, and with a large yield of the essential oil; in fact I obtained nearly every atom of the essence by this means.

The reader is referred for illustrations of the different apparatuses for conducting distillation to Figs. 1, 2, 3, 4, 5, 6, 7, 8, 9, 10, and 11.

CHAPTER XVII.

FLAVORING EXTRACTS AND FRUIT FLAVORS.

IT has long been thought that chemistry in its constant researches would finally discover and make artificially all the odors necessary for the perfumer; but thus far few substances have been discovered, with all the experiments of chemists, that can properly bear the name of perfumes. It is true that we can make from oil of amber a substance having somewhat the odor of musk, and from the oil of gaultheria an oil somewhat like the rose in smell, yet none of these organic chemical substances come near to the original article for practical purposes, if we may except the artificial oil of bitter almonds, the oil of mirbane or nitro-benzole; but it is so inferior to the genuine oil that it is only used in the cheapest soaps.

Yet from organic substances there have been prepared many ethers that have the smell and the taste of fruits in a remarkable degree, and are used for making nearly all flavors of the fruits; and are in constant use for flavoring candies and syrups, and in such minute quantities as to be harmless.

While as yet there are but few of these substances that can be properly called perfumes, it would be hazardous to declare that such discoveries are impossible and cannot be, as of all sciences chemistry is the most progressive, and hundreds of able minds are constantly discovering new methods and new substances, or, by experiment, some principle in the old not before thought of.

It is well known that fruit essences are ethers from organic substances, as we have the apple oil and several liquor flavors made from the disagreeable oil of grain, fusel oil, the pineapple oil from putrid cheese, the quince essence from the oil of rue; in fact, all these peculiar flavors are the result of chemical experiments on organic matters, to give details of the exact manufacture of which would require too much space, for, unless the reader were a chemist, he could not understand or practise these chemical processes. But if he should wish to investigate the subject fully, I would refer him to some good author on organic chemistry.

Heretofore these fruit essences have been made best in Germany, from whence we still get them, and I have always found them the most reliable, and usually of such uniform strength that the formulas I give will be graded to their employment in preference to those made in this country, many of which I have found carelessly made or else very dilute.

Extract of Almonds.

Purified oil of bitter almonds .	½ ounce.
Alcohol, 80°	1 pint.

Oil of bitter almonds when not redistilled is apt to have a portion of prussic acid in it, and it is necessary to use an oil known to be free from it. The artificial oil known as oil of mirbane is sometimes recommended, but it has not the pleasant flavor of the true oil.

Extract of Apricot. (The same as almonds.)

Extract of Apple.

Apple essence (full strength) .	1 ounce.
Citric acid	½ "
Alcohol, 72°	1 pint.

Extract of Banana.

Banana essence	1 ounce.
Citric acid	½ "
Alcohol, 70°	1 pint.

Extract of Blackberry.

Apple oil	½ ounce.
Quince oil	½ "
Tincture of orris	½ "
Tartaric acid	½ "
Alcohol, 70°	1 pint.

Extract of Celery.

Celery seed	2 ounces.
Acetic acid	½ "
Alcohol, 70°	1 pint.

Extract of Cinnamon.

Oil of Ceylon cinnamon . .	½ ounce.
Alcohol, 75°	1 pint.
Caramel	20 drops.

Extract of Cherry.

Oil of bitter almonds . .	1 drachm.
Apple oil	½ ounce.
Citric acid	½ "
Alcohol, 70°	1 pint.

Extract of Cloves.

Oil of cloves (fresh) . . .	1 ounce.
Alcohol, 80°	1 pint.
Caramel	10 drops.

Extract of Cocoa.

Take half a pound of chocolate, dissolve in a pint of boiling water, set it aside to cool; remove the cocoa butter, add 2 ounces of glycerine, and bottle; to flavor ice-cream, etc.

Extract of Coffee.

Take half a pound of the best fresh-roasted coffee, pour upon it 1 pint of cold water, let it macerate at a gentle heat for ½ hour, bring to a boil, when take from the fire; let it cool gently for two hours, when strain and add 2 ounces of glycerine; to flavor ice-cream, etc.

Extract of Ginger.

Take four ounces of unbleached Jamaica ginger, bruise and add 8 ounces of strong alcohol, put in a displacer, and pour on by degrees 10 ounces of diluted alcohol; properly made, you will have a pint of very strong extract.

Extract of Jargonelle Pear.

Pear essence	1 ounce.
Citric acid	½ "
Alcohol, 80°	1 pint.

Extract of Lemon.

Oil of lemon (new) . . .	1 ounce.
Tincture of lemon-peel . .	1 pint.

Grate the outer rind from a dozen fresh lemons and put with a pint of alcohol, 95°, and you have tincture of lemon-peel.

Extract of Nutmegs.

Oil of nutmegs	½ ounce.
" mace concrete . . .	1 "
Alcohol, 95°	1 pint.

Triturate the concrete oil in a marble mortar with the alcohol, and add the oil of nutmegs and filter.

Extract of Orange.

Take a dozen fresh Valentia oranges and grate the outer rind from them, and put into 18 ounces of alcohol, 95°, and filter after macerating for 10 days. The orange oil is so seldom new and good that it is not reliable for flavoring.

Extract of Orange Flowers.

Oil of neroli petale . . .	2 drachms.
Acetic ether	½ "
Alcohol, 85°	1 pint.

This will not be good unless the oil is very fresh; if so, it is a delightful flavor; a tablespoonful will flavor two quarts of pudding.

Extract of Peach.

Oil of almonds	2 drachms.
Pineapple oil	2 "
Tartaric acid	2 "
Alcohol, 80°	1 pint.

Extract of Pineapple.

Pineapple essence . . .	1 ounce.
Citric acid	½ "
Alcohol, 80°	1 pint.

Extract of Plums.

Oil of bitter almonds . .	1 drachm.
Apple oil	2 "
Tartaric acid	2 "
Alcohol, 80°	1 pint.

Extract of Rose.

Otto of roses	1 drachm.
Alcohol, 95°	14 ounces.
French rose-water, triple . .	2 "
Liq. carmine	10 drops.

Extract of Raspberry.

Raspberry essence . . .	6 drachms.
Tincture of orris . . .	½ ounce.
Extract of rose, No. 1 (from pomade)	½ "
Citric acid	½ "
Alcohol, 85°	1 pint.
Liq. carmine	30 drops.

Extract of Strawberry.

Pineapple oil	1 ounce.
Tincture of orris . . .	½ "
Tartaric acid	½ "
Alcohol, 80°	1 pint.

Extract of Vanilla.

Take of vanilla bean ½ an ounce and cut it up fine; put in a mortar with an ounce of loaf sugar; take four ounces of rose-water and twelve of alcohol, 95°; mix and add a portion to the vanilla and sugar and put in a displacer, and pour on the balance of the diluted alcohol till all is through; if not dark add a few drops of caramel.

These extracts for flavoring are used for ice-cream, jellies, puddings, cakes, candies, and syrups, and with a few exceptions are as good as the natural fruit; a tablespoonful or half an ounce is sufficient for two quarts of cream or syrup.

As I have previously remarked, distillation might be advantageously employed in making some of these useful extracts, particularly the spice flavors. The product would be stronger and more intimately blended, consequently more pleasant.

16

CHAPTER XVIII.

TOILET SOAPS. IMPLEMENTS AND INGREDIENTS.

TOILET soap is comparatively a modern product, for even in the last century it was little known until the latter half, and then of such a quality and in such quantities that it is scarce worthy of notice, while common soap may be said to have been known from the middle ages, though previous to that time it seems to have been but little known. Yet in the excavations of the ruins of Pompeii a soap boiling factory or room was disclosed with some of the soap still preserved.

The Bible in two instances uses the word soap, but I think it a modern translation for the alkaline earth known to Arabia and Egypt, and which the Egyptians with their usual luxury perfumed for use in their baths.

Marseilles, in France, has been from its first settlement by the Phoceans the great centre of the soap-making art, being naturally so situated as to have the alkali from the barilla and sea-weed, and in close proximity to the home of the olive tree, or at least where it was most cultivated for its oil. It still re-retains the name of making the best soap in the world, as they have always tried to maintain superiority and integrity in its manufacture. Of superior toilet soaps, Paris may be called the centre, and for more than fifty years has excelled in the art, though England now manufactures them upon true scientific principles, yet for the finest quality we still go to Paris. Germany makes a great deal of fancy soap, but by the use of an excess of cocoa-nut oil its quality is inferior.

Toilet soaps form a very important item in the list of articles now made by the perfumer, and being chemical compounds have kept pace, if not excelled all the other branches of his art, for upon no other article can be founded a better reputation then by producing a superior class of this useful and indispensable article of goods, nor can he give it too much care and attention.

Heretofore it has been the custom for the perfumer to purchase soaps made by the large manufacturers, and re-melt and manipulate them to his wants, and under certain circumstances this might be the best plan, but by making his soap by what is called the cold process, he has the advantage of making it in small or large quantities to suit his business. He does not then require the large amount of space, nor the expensive machinery necessary to conduct the business where soap is made in large quantities by boiling, though that process I think the only proper and correct one; and the only one that produces a perfect combination of the materials.

Soap is manufactured on an extensive scale, forming an important article of commerce in all civilized countries, and is a compound resulting from the combination of oils and greases, both vegetable and animal, with the salifiable bases of potassa and soda. Soaps made with soda are hard, those made with potash are soft, the degree of hardness depending upon that of the fats with which they are made; thus the hardest is made of stearine and soda, and the softest with oils and potash; the first is too hard for practical use, while the latter is too soft, and it is this as well as many other things that the maker of toilet soap has to consider.

Oils and fats chiefly consist of oleine and stearine, as in tallow, suet, and several vegetable oils; of margarine, that occurs in many other animal and vegetable greases and oils; of palmitine, found in palm oil and other substances; there are still other principles, according to the nature of the material used by the soap-maker. The fats and oils are seldom composed of any one of those principles, but of several in varying proportions, oleine being constantly found in all of them.

Chemically considered, fats and oils are really salts, and may be called "glyceryles," oleine being the oleate of the oxide of glyceryle, and stearine the stearate of the oxide of glyceryle; that is to say, they are combinations of acids, oleine, stearine, margarine, etc. etc.

Glycerine is a combination of oxide of glyceryle with water, which in that case acts the part of an acid to form a hydrate of oxide of glyceryle. So when neutral fats are mixed with solutions of caustic alkali, their constituents react upon each other, and combine and form a gelatinous mass, which is nothing more nor less than an aqueous solution of soap mixed with glycerine, which is set free by the process.

My space will not permit me to give a thorough chemical description of every article used in making soap, nor of every change that takes place in the process, yet while giving practical instruction in the art it will be almost impossible to do so without using some chemical terms.

The manufacturer of toilet soaps at the present time can have nearly all his material prepared ready for his use; he can buy his lard, tallow, and oils in quantity and quality suited to his needs, and so with his alkalies, they being prepared by the chemist in a caustic and concentrated state, ready for his use. So that unless he wants to manufacture upon a large scale he has little occasion to understand all the processes of the preparation of his material. Yet it is well for him to know how and what methods are used to make them suitable for his use.

The use of steam in the manufacture of toilet soaps is at this time almost indispensable, for without it he has very much more labor, and his product is not so uniform in quality as he should desire, nor can he hope to compete with others who have that advantageous aid. The laboratory for making soaps should be divided into two rooms, one where the soap is made, containing the lye tanks and kettles or steam jacket, engine and boiler, etc.; another where it can be placed on racks to dry, and be milled, plaited, moulded, etc., and where he has room to use all modern appliances, for without them he will find it next to impossible to make toilet soap of good quality that will yield him a good profit for his labor. The cuts at the end of this chapter illustrate most of the implements and machinery needed.

Having his laboratory supplied with all the requisite machinery and in working order, he will proceed to get a supply of the materials, viz., alkalies, tallow, lard, veal fat, olive oil, cocoa-nut oil, palm oil, cotton-seed oil, tallow oil, perfumes, colors, etc. etc.

Should he decide to make his own alkalies (for his facilities may be such that he may economize by it), he will need to have an iron vat, square or cylindrical, of the capacity of about 150 gallons, or sufficient to dissolve a drum of caustic soda of about 500 pounds, which is broken up into as small lumps as possible, and put in the vat with about 75 gallons of water, when steam is let on through a pipe reaching to within a few inches of the bottom, and the contents frequently stirred, and when in the course of a few hours the alkali is melted, put in 50 pounds of fresh-burnt lime in as small pieces as possible, and by degrees. Continue the steam some time longer, while the lime is dissolving and being thoroughly incorporated, when turn off the steam, cover the tank, and allow it to rest a day or more to let the lime precipitate to the bottom.

When the lye has become clear proceed to test the strength of the solution, which is done by a Baumé hydrometer (see Fig. 13). If you want it for cold soap you will have to evaporate it by steam or fire in another vessel, to 36° Baumé; while for boiled soap you require weaker lyes of various strengths. Potash lye is prepared in very much the same manner, but as the manufacturer will not be likely to want it in the same quantities that he does the soda, a small iron pan can be used, say 50 gallons capacity, sufficient for one or two hundred pounds of the alkali, which is treated in the same manner, a little more lime being needed, as commercial potash, or still better, pearl-ash has more carbonic acid. As it is impossible to procure alkalies in a state of purity, it will be necessary to study some of the elements of alkalimetry, and have suitable instruments for testing the amount of caustic lye his salts contain. Though generally if he procures his alkali of a well-known brand or maker, the quality is likely to be uniform, and with the hydrometer and thermometer he can arrive at a sufficient knowledge of its strength and purity by simple tests and calculations.

Having his alkalies provided, and deciding to make his soaps by boiling, it will be necessary to have a large kettle set in masonry, with furnace underneath, or a steam jacket, which is a double kettle with space between for the steam to circulate (see Fig. 17). Frames to put the finished soap into are generally made of wood, in sections placed one upon the other, and fastened with an iron clamp, the whole forming a sort of oblong square well; when the soap sets or becomes hard, a section is lifted off and cut off with fine brass wire, which section is again cut transversely in bars or wedges. (See illustrations of tools for making soap, pp. 253 *et seq.*)

The different oils and greases used seem to require almost as many different modes of working, as tallow will make a certain kind of soap and olive oil another, yet the process may be considered the same slightly modified to suit the several conditions, and in this lies the art of making soaps properly, for, as I have already remarked, soap is a chemical compound, and the more scientifically it is prepared the better should be the product.

The writers on toilet soaps seem to have had more theory than practice in their art, for they tell you to make a soap of tallow and soda, called curd soap, or a soap from lard, etc. etc.; tallow or curd soap is white when new, losing its white color as it acquires age, and becoming so hard as to be almost insoluble in water. Many of you have no doubt found in travelling, a small waxy mass on the washstands of the hotels, that was so hard and stubborn that the utmost coaxing could not raise a lather; and it was no doubt economical, as it lasted a long time, each traveller in turn doing his best to make it of service. This was curd or tallow soap, and a soap made entirely of lard, though not so hard, yet has very little lathering property. It seems singular that there is no one oil or grease used in soap that makes as good a soap as when modified with some other substance having a slightly different property, and is not very much improved thereby.

So with the soaps made of olive oil, the celebrated castile soaps, they are found to acquire great hardness when made of the pure oil, and, therefore, they now have at least ten per cent. of rape-seed oil combined with them to qualify that tendency. The rape-seed oil, being a drying oil, makes a softer soap, like all drying oils, and tends to keep the castile soap of a more plastic consistence. In some districts where barilla is used, the soap is plastic without the addition of rape-seed oil, which is due to having a portion of potash in it, which has the desired property of making a softer and more soluble soap.

Cocoa-nut oil makes a peculiar soap, very much esteemed in Europe, though the effect of saponifying it is to produce a very unpleasant rancid smell, which does not leave it in spite of all perfumes added to cover it. This soap has the property of holding in suspension a large quantity of water, 60 or 70 per cent., and which causes a copious lather; it also has the property of washing with sea-water, which gains it the name of marine soap. This oil enters into all the German recipes for toilet soap, but does not improve their quality, though it gives them a semi-transparent, waxy appearance, very pleasing to the eye. The French also use it, but sparingly, in many of their soaps, but chiefly for its emollient property, which is very advantageous, particularly in shaving soap. Cocoa-nut oil, though perfectly pure and sweet when used, acquires this disagreeable odor upon saponification by the formation of caprylic acid, which when not in great quantity can be partially disguised by strong perfumes.

Resin or rosin, so largely used in soaps, will not by itself form a soap, through its insolubility in alkali, but requires the addition of greases, or rather, as it is the least in quantity, it may be said to be added to the fats, or, correctly speaking, to the soap, for it is generally put in with the last lye, after the soap has been well boiled and nearly complete, and then put in but a small proportion to the amount of fats used—a quarter or at most a third of the amount. Rosin is not much used for soaps for the toilet; in fact, it is difficult to introduce it into soaps made by the cold process, as many of these soaps are made; and when it is required, as it sometimes is, it is combined by means of the mill, by using a part of boiled rosin soap and other soaps made cold.

Palm oil is one of the most useful fats for toilet soap, its constituents being oleine and palmitine; its natural pleasant smell is an advantage, as it resembles the smell of violets; it has a great deal of yellow coloring matter, which is sometimes available, though it has to be in a great measure destroyed before or during saponification. This bleaching is done in several ways, either by exposure to the air or by means of chemicals; in the first method, the melted oil has pipes inserted into it and air blown through it. Whatever unpleasant odors arise are carried into the chimney above the pan by means of a funnel inverted over the pan. Of the chemical processes for bleaching, several methods are employed, though I think that the use of chromate of potash is the simplest. To each 100 pounds of the oil half a pound of chromate of potash, dissolved in a quart of warm water, is stirred into the melted oil for an hour, using a crutch or paddle filled with holes for the better means of rapid mixing, when the oil is allowed to rest; and the coloring matter is deposited, or at least sufficient of it to render the soap made of it a natural fawn color, and avoid the disagreeable yellow color; this when in excess is very objectionable to the soap.

Lard, as I have said, makes a very beautiful soap, similar to olive oil, the constituents being identical, though derived from such different sources. Castor oil also makes a fine soap; as also does benne oil; and ground-nut oil is also a very good soap material, though by itself it is almost too soft for general use. Cotton-seed oil, now used for a great many purposes, has few equals as an article for soap. A great deal of this oil is now made in the Southern and Western States, and, when properly refined, is exceedingly useful. Combined with lard, tallow, palm oil, etc., it forms a fine basis for toilet soaps, and has the great advantage of economy, as the price is usually much lower than any other material. Veal fat is exceedingly useful to the perfumer; the toilet soap made of it has great whiteness and fine emollient properties. Mutton fat, being rich in stearine, is a useful addition to many soaps, supplying a hardness often needed in other materials, though by itself and with soda it becomes too hard, and turns yellow with age.

From my experience, it seems that there are few oils or greases that will by themselves give as good a soap as when other oils or greases are combined with them to alter or improve their qualities. There are other fats and oils that can be used in soap, though often difficult to procure, as hemp-seed oil, poppy oil, mustard oil, sunflower-seed oil, rapeseed oil, butter of cocoa, etc. etc., all of which could be used with advantage, provided they could be purchased at a price that would make an economical soap, or that by experiment would yield a soap of superior quality.

Besides the alkalies and oils and greases the toilet-soap maker requires a number of other chemicals, drugs, etc., such as sulphuric, nitric, and muriatic acids, sulphate of iron, chromate of potash, oxide of manganese, sulphate of soda, chloride of soda or common salt, etc., besides a supply of materials for coloring; for red he requires vermilion, cudbear, and some kinds of aniline red; for yellow, anatto, gamboge, and aniline; for blue, ultramarine and indigo; and for brown, umber, cutch, sienna, caramel, etc. The other shades can all be made by an admixture of these, as green is yellow and blue, purple is red and blue, etc. etc. But generally the least coloring matter in a soap the better your customers will like it, though to please the eye, and to assimilate the soap to its name, a certain portion of color seems necessary, but people of intelligence avoid all soaps known to contain color, for they imagine that color is added to cover some sophistication. Therefore, let the maker of good toilet soaps endeavor to get the purest materials, and observe much neatness and cleanliness in the details, so that his products may be known to be, as they appear, perfectly pure.

Of the perfumes required for scenting soaps, it is needless to speak here, as they have nearly all been described, being the same as are used in the other branches of the perfumery business, though many can be used in soaps that are almost useless for other purposes. This will be seen when I give the different formulas, though I might here remark that nearly all the spice and herb oils can be used as soap perfumes, while the citron oils are not so economical, the alkali somewhat impairing their fragrance. The French manufacturer makes the finest soaps from the flower pomades, that they may have the delicate odor of the flowers, but of course such soaps have to be made by the cold process, as the greater heat of boiling would destroy all their delicate odors; they also resort to the use of the mucilage of gum tragacanth to impart emolliency and solubility to their soap, which addition is a great benefit to fine soaps for toilet purposes. Gum tragacanth is a very useful article in many trades, and is often used by the perfumer in several preparations. For soap, a few ounces are soaked overnight in water or perfumed water, stirred until dissolved, strained and added to the soap before finishing, or combined with the soap and colors in milling.

It is hardly necessary to speak of the many substances that are used and can be used in the adulteration of soap, for it is not well for the toilet soapmaker to employ such sophistication in his soaps, for he must endeavor to make the best article possible, and try to excel all others in quality and style, and avoid all adulterations that would injure his products and his reputation. On the contrary, let him take such pride in his art as to emulate the highest in it, and not by the use of adulterations destroy the character of this product, and bring all perfumed soaps into disrepute, but let him persevere in the good qualities of his manufactures, and he will eventually profit by it.

I will here illustrate the most important implements and machinery needed in the art of making toilet soap.

The siphon should be of half-inch lead pipe, and may be made after Coffee's pattern, for moderate volumes of liquid, as it possesses many advantages over the usual forms in delivering the liquid without any inconvenience to the operator. It is shown by

Fig. 13.

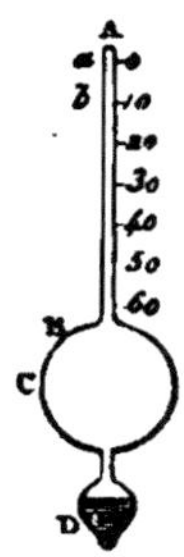

Baumé's hydrometer for alkalies.

Fig. 14.

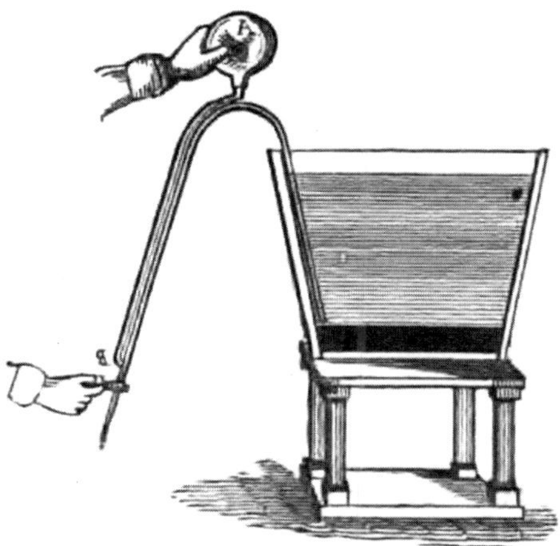

Siphon for lye, etc.

Fig. 14, and consists of a bent tube, one leg of which is longer than the other, and a smaller lateral tube B, capped with a large, hollow India rubber ball A. The long leg has also a stopcock near its lower end. It is put in operation by closing the cock, compressing the bag, and quickly immersing the short leg in the clear lye, to within an inch or less of the subsident carbonate of lime, as represented in the drawing. The act of compressing the ball produces diminution of the elastic force of the internal air by expelling the most of it, so that as soon as the hand is removed from the ball, the outward pressure of the air drives the liquid up to the highest point of the bend, whence it drops, by the force of gravitation, on the opening of the cock, and flows out in a continuous stream, as long as the mouth of the short leg is covered by it.

Large tuns lined with sheet lead, and with cullendered false bottoms, Fig. 15, are perhaps the best

Fig. 15.

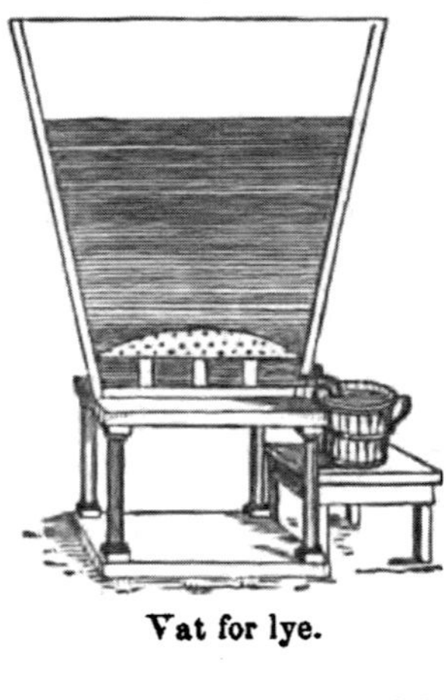

Vat for lye.

and most durable fixture of this kind that could be put up. In this case there is a cock fitted near the bottom of each tun, and through it the clear lye collecting in the lower part of the vat, between the diaphragm and the bottom, can be drawn off into tubs below, for use as may be wanted. Close by these vats there must be a pump or hydrant, with its outlet spout conveniently arranged for a supply of water, in quantity as required.

Fig. 16 shows a kettle. Should there be several, they are placed on a line with each other, and over

Fig. 16.

Soap kettle with fire hole.

a furnace beneath. To the caldron a tube of about two inches diameter is adapted, which serves as an outlet for the waste lye which remains under the boiled paste. At the mouth of the furnace is an arcade; and at the bottom of this vault iron bars are placed as supports for the fuel which is to heat the caldron. The arrangement of the masonry work is generally, however, left to the skill and ingenuity of the bricklayer. These soap pans or caldrons are cast with a flange at their top, so that, when necessary, an adjunct cylinder of wood, in the shape of a cone, may be fastened to them.

A (Fig. 17) is the interior of the cast-iron kettle, surrounded by brickwork. B is the outer cast-iron caldron, which should fit to the inner kettle tightly, so as to prevent any escape of steam. D D is the tube leading from the steam boiler, and conveying the steam to the kettles. It is fitted with a cock, which is opened or shut, according as the steam is to be let

Fig. 17.

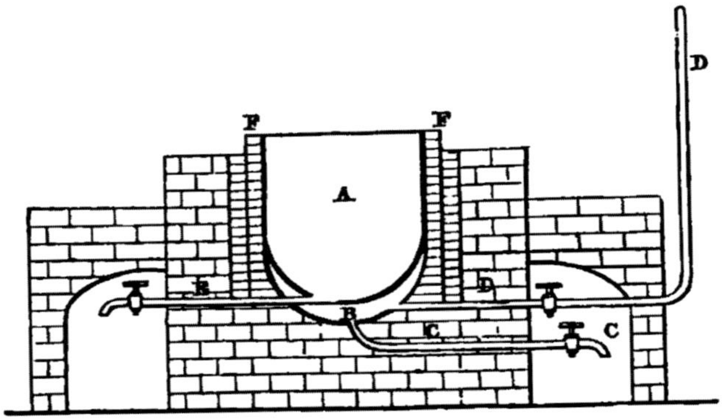

Steam kettle or jacket.

on or off, for accelerating or retarding the boiling of the soap. C C is the tube by which the condensed vapor is discharged. The cock in this tube can be left slightly open so as to operate as a safety-valve, when one of these necessary appendages is not affixed to the apparatus. The tube E is the discharge-pipe of the caldron.

In this country, frames are made of pine wood, for light-colored and fine soaps. The iron frames need not exceed half an inch in thickness; but those of wood should be made of two-inch stuff. The shape is that of a parallelogram, as shown by the drawings; and the dimensions of the opposite sides and ends are respectively 36 and 12 to 15 inches. They should be about 36 inches deep, and smoothly jointed, so that when they are placed on top of each other in piles of three, four, or five (Fig. 18), they may form a water-tight well, which will hold the hot paste without leaking. The iron are of the same

Fig. 18.

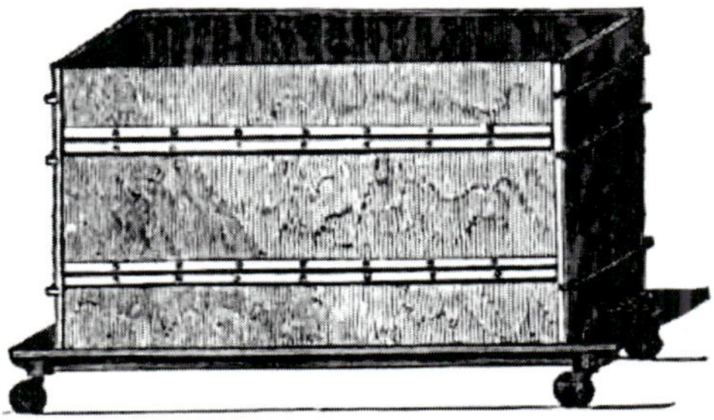

form as the wooden frames; but differ in size. The sides are of wrought-iron plate, and the remaining portions of cast iron. Fig. 18 presents a side view, Fig. 20 the bottom, and Fig. 19 a top view of them;

Fig. 19.

Fig. 20.

a

and the clamp, which fits on the ends, and which holds them together, is shown by *a*. They are drawn to a scale of three-eighths of an inch to a foot. Being mounted on wheels, these frames can readily be moved from place to place. The good conducting power of the metal promotes the cooling and solidifying of the soap paste.

The wooden frames are lifted off, one at a time,

Fig. 21.

and the soap remains upon the movable bottom ready to be divided into bars, as shown by Fig. 21. Fig. 22, 1, shows the well of five frames, ready for receiving the soap paste. The bottom of the well and a single frame are severally presented in Fig. 22, 3 and 2.

Fig. 22.

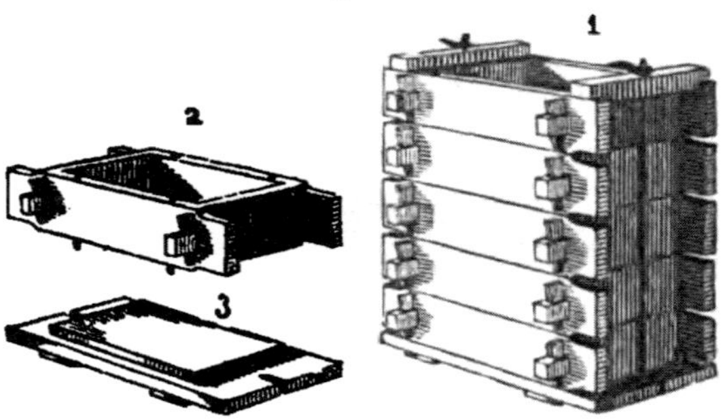

Frames for soap.

The German frames, like those of this country, are also constructed so that they may easily be separated into pieces, being set up by nuts and screws, as shown in Figs. 23 and 24. Their floor is also movable; and

Fig. 23.

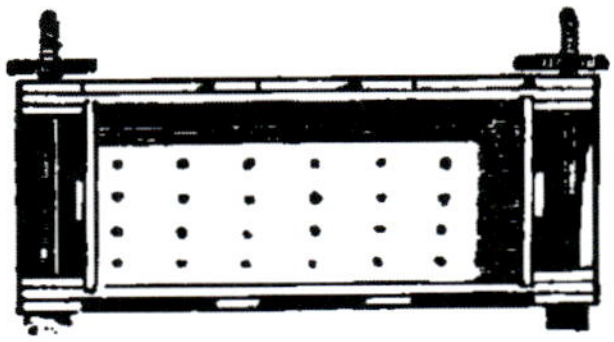

Fig. 24.

is shown in longitudinal section by Fig. 25, and in breadth by Fig. 26. It consists of two layers of deal boards, in the upper of which are four grooves, fitting with the projections in the sides. The two

Fig. 25.

Fig. 26.

narrow sides are also supported on the inside by cross-pieces. All the sides are strengthened by supports. When the several parts are put together, the bolts, screw cut at the other end, have only to be inserted through the projecting parts of the longer sides, and made fast by the nuts at the ends, to form the whole into a solid box. A cloth spread over the bottom prevents any soap from passing the holes,

Fig. 27.

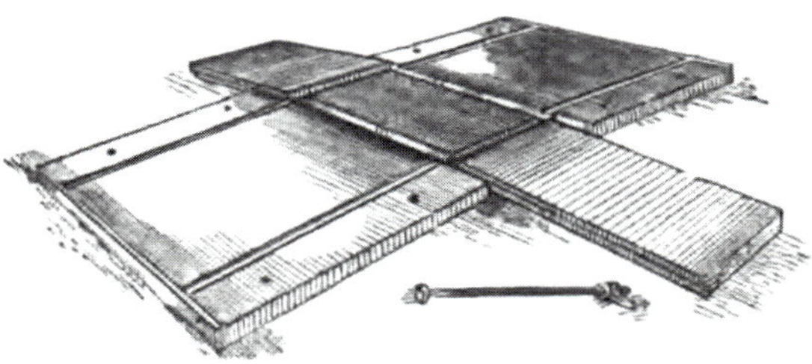

through which the lye drains off. A frame with its sides and ends down is shown by Fig. 27. By the side of it is the clamp used for holding the different parts in position when the frame is set up.

Minor Implements.—The minor implements of the soap laboratory are, a crutch, Fig. 28, composed of a long wooden handle adjusted, at the end, to a board,

Fig. 28.

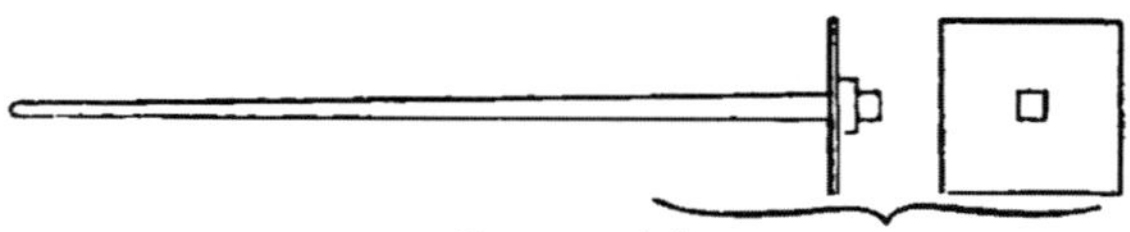

Soap crutch.

and used for stirring the soap paste in the operation of "*mottling;*" large, cullendered, iron ladles, with long, wooden handles (Fig. 29), for dipping out the

Fig. 29.

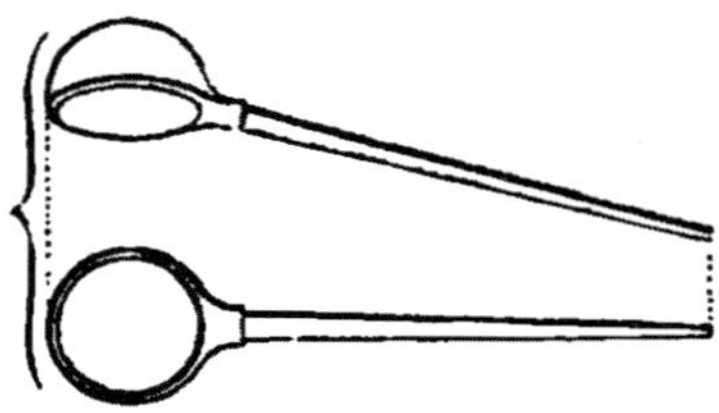

Fig. 30.

Ladles and bucket.

hot paste from the kettles, and copper buckets (Fig. 30) for conveying it to the frames.

Every manufactory of soaps should also be supplied with presses, for compressing the tablets of soap. One suitable for toilet soaps is shown by Fig. 34, which clearly exhibits its construction. It has two spiral springs, A and B, by which the cake of soap is immediately expelled from the box C as soon as it is pressed. The workman knocks it off with the tablet that is to take its place; and so the pressing goes on without any delay in removing the tablets of soap as fast as finished. D is a rope suspending a wooden rod,

Fig. 31.

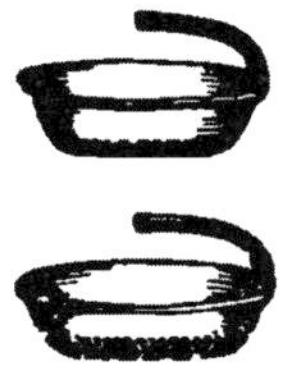

Soap ladles.

Fig. 32.

Gauge.

Fig. 33.

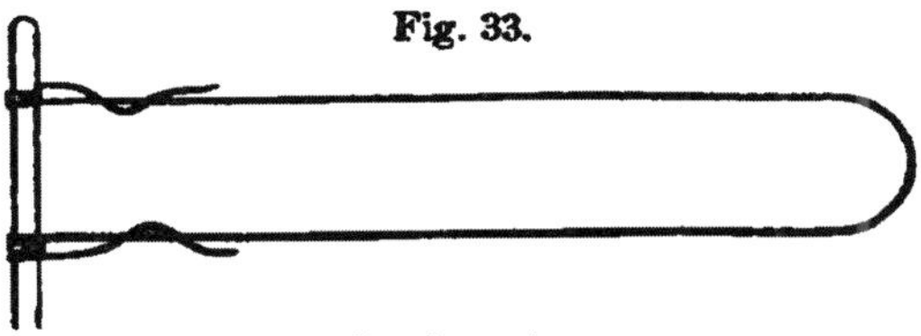

Cutting wire.

Fig. 34.

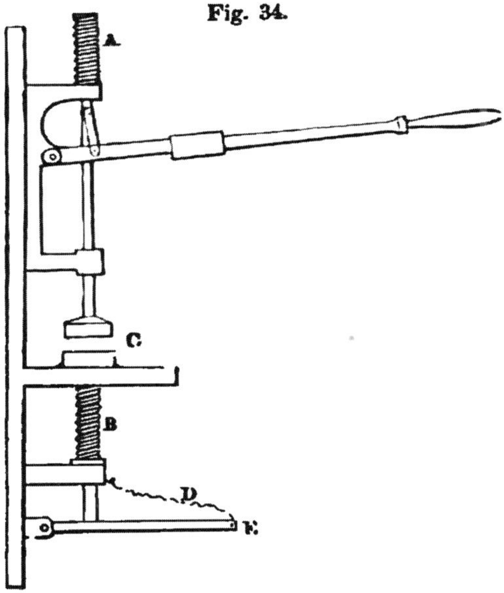

Soap press.

E, which serves as a support to the bottom of the die during the pressure. The box C is movable, being merely fastened by screws; and, when necessary, may be replaced by others of different sizes. This is a great convenience, for the size and form of the tablets may be varied by merely changing the box. The die from which the tablet is to receive a device, or the impress of the manufacturer's name, is screwed to the top of the box C, and may also be changed, as fashion, caprice, or taste shall dictate.

Fig. 35.

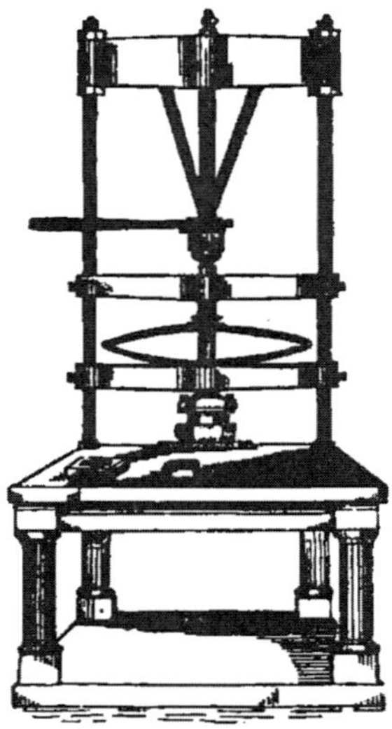

Soap press with spring.

Screw Press.—When the soaps pressed in the first mould are entirely dried, they are slightly scraped at the surface and dipped into alcohol; they receive their definitive shape by means of a second mould which is placed under a screw press.

Figure 36 represents this press.

Fig. 36.

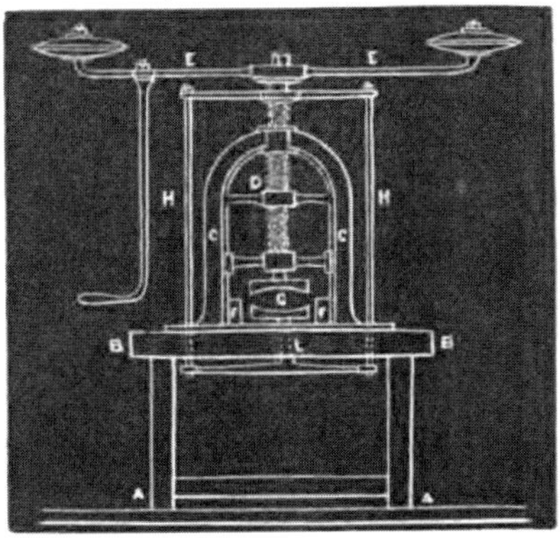

Screw press for toilet soaps.

A A. Oak posts supporting the press.

B B. Strong oak board used to receive the press.

C C. Frame of the press.

D. Iron screw provided at the end with a groove to receive the upper shell of the mould.

E E. Fly. It is surmounted with a ball at each end.

F F. Cast-iron matrix used to receive the copper mould.

G. Copper mould formed of two pieces.

H H. Rods of wrought iron adapted by means of screws to a horizontal bar below E E; these rods pass under the cast-iron matrix F F, and raise the movable rod L, after each pressure; then this raises the mould G, fixed in the cast-iron matrix. In this way, after the pressure has been given by the screw, the soap can be taken from the mould and another substituted.

The other accessories which complete the establishment of a toilet soap factory are the drying-room:

1. A scale to weigh the bars of soap.
2. Another scale to weigh small quantities.
3. Several large wooden boxes lined with lead, to mix the shavings of soap with the colors and the oils.
4. Several tables covered with marble for balling the soap.
5. Several marble mortars to grind and pound the soap.
6. Several fine drum sieves to pass the colors to be incorporated into the soap.
7. Boards for drying the soap.
8. Scrapers and knives: the former for cleansing the surface of the bars of soap, the latter for dividing the soap into small cakes.

Slatwork frames, made of wooden uprights and cross-pieces, as shown by Fig. 37. The openings between the slats permit the free access of the air, and thus promote the drying.

Fig. 37.

Soap rack.

Figure 38 shows a kettle for cold soaps.

Figure 39 represents a kettle or jacket with a double bottom, heated by steam. This kettle is of

Fig 38.

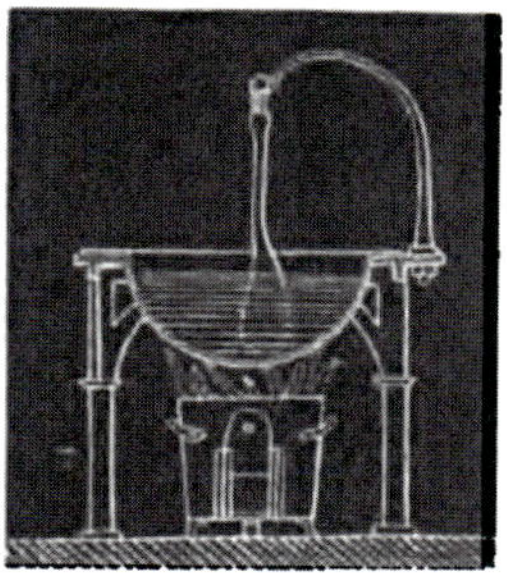

Fig. 39.

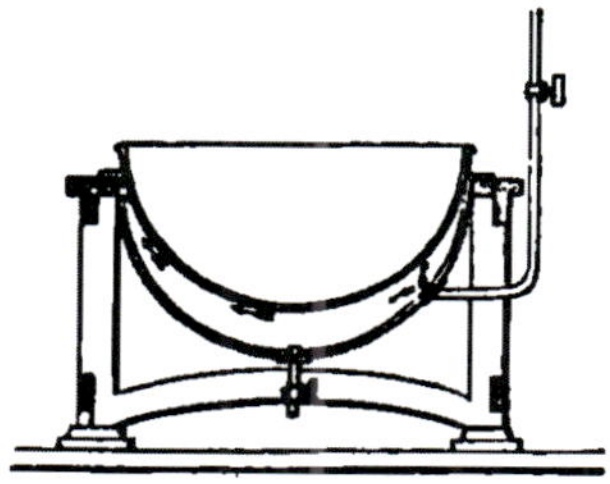

Kettles for soaps by the cold process.

tinned copper, and may be used also to purify tallow and greases.

Fig. 40.

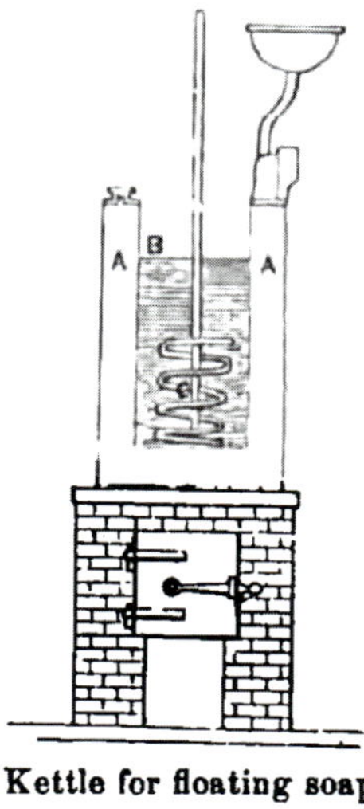

Kettle for floating soaps.

A A (Fig. 40) is a cucurbit.

B is a tinned copper water-bath.

C is a beater or stirrer, to which a movement of rotation is given.

The capacity of the water-bath for twenty pounds of soap must be twenty-five gallons. The soap is put into the water-bath B, with the necessary quantity of water, and when it is melted, the beater C is put in motion. For the operation to succeed well, the temperature of the mixture must be between 158° and 176°.

Fig. 41.

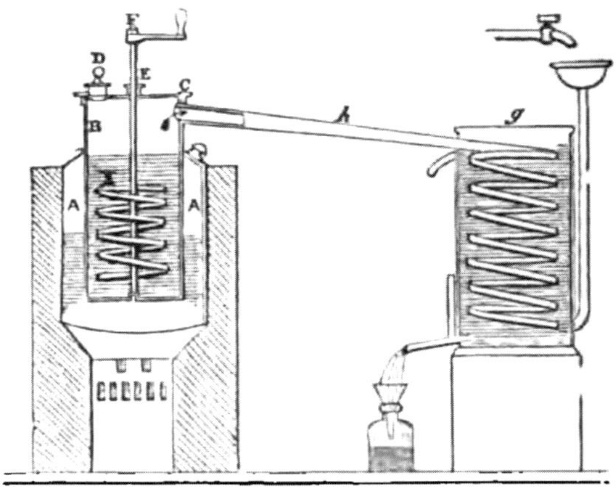

Still and water-bath for transparent soaps.

A A (Fig. 41). Cucurbit of copper fixed on a brick furnace.

B. Water-bath which exactly fits into the cucurbit; the solution of the soap is operated in the vase.

C. Cover of the water-bath. It has two apertures, D, E. The first is closed by a large cock, the other gives passage to the stirrer X, F.

F. Stirrer.

g. Worm of copper or tin, destined to condense the alcoholic vapors.

h. Copper pipe, serving to make the connection between the alembic and the worm.

Fig. 42.

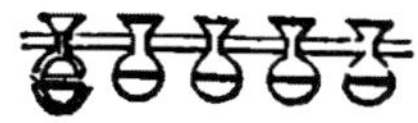

Moulds for transparent soap balls.

Copper dippers, with handles of two feet length, Fig. 43.

Fig. 43.

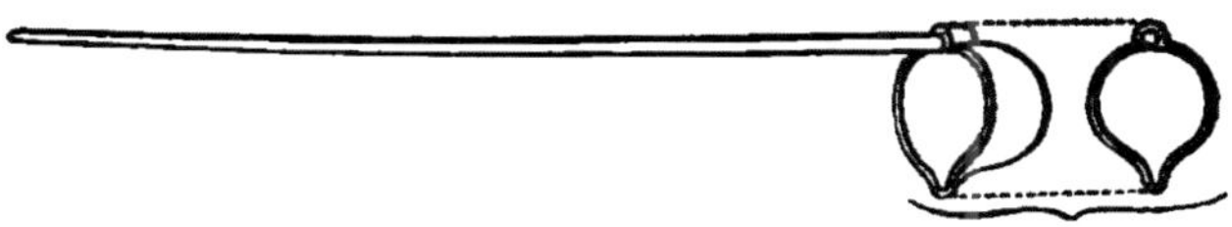

Figure 44 represents the cutting or stripping machine.

Fig. 44.

Soap cutter or stripper.

A (Fig. 44). Cutter.

B. Iron shaft which traverses the centre of the cutter and carries a handle C, at one of its ends; this handle is used to give motion to the machine.

D D. Frame of wood or cast iron, on which the shaft of the cutter rests.

E. Inclined plane of wood, on which the soap is placed to be cut into shavings; F, is the cake of soap.

G. Large wooden box to receive the shavings of soap.

The method of using this machine is very simple. The cake of soap to be cut being laid on the inclined plane E, and touching the cutter at one end, a movement of rotation is given to the machine by the handle C. During the rotation, each time the blades of the cutter touch the cake of soap, they take off a shaving which falls into the box. The first cake being cut, substitute a second, and so on.

This machine renders immense service in the manufacture of toilet soaps. A man with it can reduce 200 pounds of soap to shavings in one hour.

Fig. 45.

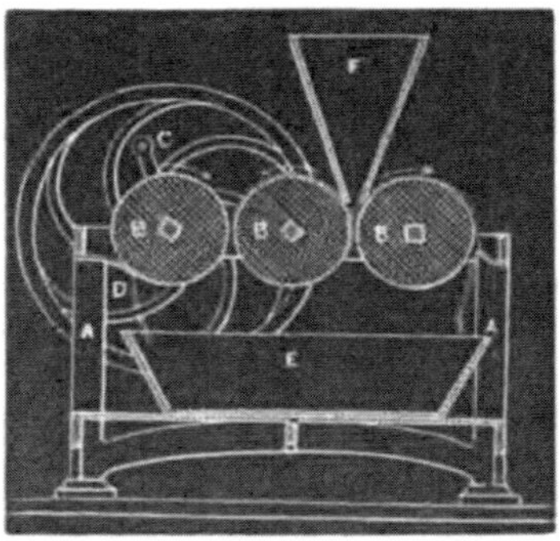

Soap mill.

The soap-mill is represented in Fig. 45. It consists of three cylinders of porphyry, from five to six inches in diameter, by twelve or fourteen inches in length. They are separated from each other; the distance between them is regulated by screws, at will. They are set in motion by a system of gearing, the unequal dimensions of which, produce also an unequal rotation for each cylinder. We give the indication of the principal pieces which compose it.

A A. Frame of cast iron which supports the cylinders.

B B B. Cylinders to grind the shavings.

C. Crank fixed on the axis of the first cylinder; used to put the machine in motion.

D. Scraper. It is formed of a large steel blade, fixed horizontally against the last cylinder, which it traverses in all its length. The use of this blade is to scrape off the soap adhering to the cylinder.

E. Large wooden box lined with lead. This box receives the soap which has been crushed between the cylinders.

F. Movable hopper of wood lined with zinc. Its object is to receive the shavings of soap and transmit them to the cylinders.

CHAPTER XIX.

TOILET SOAPS. MANIPULATION.

THE exact causes of the saponification of oils and greases with alkalies are yet obscure; and, no matter what may be the experience of the operator, he will find at all times something to learn that will either improve his goods or facilitate his methods. Thus we hear people say that no soap can be properly made without boiling. While I admit that boiling is as yet the best known means of making a proper chemical combination of the ingredients, I am not prepared to say there may not be discovered other means to produce a better article, so that, if the maker of toilet soap is progressive and attentive, he may discover such improved process that may benefit himself and those who may follow him.

To know how to make a good soap is very necessary, and, as boiled soap is the best, we must try and give the proper mode of making it. Being assured by proper tests of the purity and causticity of his alkalies, let him have ready lyes of the different strengths required—some to mark 10°, 15°, 21°, and 27° Baumé—or an average of about 21°; and to make a good white soap for stock, take

Tallow or veal fat . . .	30 pounds.
Lard, refined	45 "
Cotton-seed oil	25 "

In all 100 pounds.

Let them be put into a kettle of about 40 gallons' capacity, heated by furnace or by steam. The heat is applied, and, when the fats are melted, about 50 pounds of soda lye at 12° Baumé are poured gently in, with constant stirring and boiling for some hours, when 20 pounds of lye at 18° are added, and, after boiling about an hour, it is allowed to rest, the steam turned off or the fire withdrawn; this is called the parting operation or empatage, and requires constant stirring to form into a perfect homogeneous mass, and forms a perfect mixture having no grease at the top or alkali at the bottom.

After some hours' rest, you proceed to the second operation or separation, which is done by means of alkalies, having pure common salt in solution, and marking 20° to 25° Baumé, and the object is to separate the soap formed from its excess of water—you turn on the heat gently and pour in gradually 25 pounds of the salted lye. Keep stirring until the soap separates in grains or curds, when, after this separation appears complete, turn off the heat and allow it to rest for some 6 hours, when remove the lye from the bottom, which lye may not have much causticity, but may be useful to use again for the same operation by adding a little caustic lye to make it mark the requisite strength.

The third operation or coction is conducted by pouring into the soap about 30 pounds of caustic lye at 25°, and bringing to a boil, constantly stirring to keep down the scum that will form, and will appear less as the soap boils and is near completion. After boiling some three or four hours turn off the heat, and in two or three hours draw off the lye.

The liquidation or cleansing is the fourth operation, and is done by pouring into the melted soap 30 or 40 pounds of lye marking 6°, and boiling gently for a few hours until the soap is dissolved into a paste of a grayish shade and is neutral; when the fire is withdrawn, and the soap stirred briskly for some time and allowed to rest until the next day, when the lye is drawn off and the scum removed, and ladled into the frames, being careful not to stir up the darker soap that forms at the bottom, which with the scum soap can be used for another operation, or for soaps that have color, as the palm, rosin, etc.

When in the frames it can be colored, perfumed, or allowed to cool in its natural white state, and cut up into bars and kept for stock to make various soaps by means of the mill, or by remelting with other kinds of soap to form the different varieties desired.

To make a good palm soap, I take

Palm oil (purified and bleached)	60	pounds.
Tallow oil	20	"
Cocoa-nut oil	20	"

100 pounds in all.

Begin with the first process, called parting, with about 15 gallons of caustic lye at 12° or 15°, keeping it stirred, but not boiled too violently, as it might cause the cocoa-nut oil to separate, which, if it did occur, can be combined again by adding a gallon or two of cold, weak lye. Boil for three or four hours, adding by degrees stronger lyes of about 20°. Keep stirring until towards the end of the boiling, add 2 gallons of lye at 25°, when remove the heat and stir briskly until thoroughly mixed, when let it rest.

After resting some hours, proceed to the second process of separation, which is rendered somewhat more difficult in all soaps containing cocoa-nut oil; we now pour in little by little salted lye of about 25°, and when by boiling we see the soap forming into grains and floating in the lye the heat is turned off and the stirring is stopped, and, after letting it rest to separate, the lye is drawn off.

For the third operation, or coction, add about 8 gallons of lye at 27°, and when it begins to boil a great deal of froth will form, which must be beaten down, and it will disappear as the boiling continues; and when after some hours' boiling the soaps begin to form into a curdled mass, a portion taken out forms, when pressed between the fingers, a hard scale; the heat and stirring are stopped and the soap allowed to rest, when it will form upon the top, and the lye can be withdrawn from the bottom.

In finishing, or what some call fitting, the soap in the kettle is then diluted with about 10 gallons of weak lye at 5°, and boiled and stirred; when, after a thorough mixing, if it should separate, weak lye at 2° is added, and it again becomes pasty, and the darker soap at the bottom begins to rise to the surface, when it may be considered finished. When the heat is removed the pan is covered up and allowed to rest five hours; the scum is then removed and the soap is ladled into frames, taking care not to take the dark soap from the bottom. This operation should yield about 160 pounds of soap of a handsome yellow color, which can be employed as a body for many colored toilet soaps.

Another useful soap as an ingredient or body for cheaper, yet very good, toilet soaps of 2d quality, is

Palm Soap with Rosin.

Palm oil	30	pounds.
Cocoa-nut oil	20	"
Tallow oil	35	"
Rosin	15	"

Melt the oils by gentle heat, pouring slowly in 8 gallons of caustic lye of 12°, stirring and gently boiling for three hours, when add 5 gallons of stronger lye of 17°, and boil three hours longer, or until it become a perfect pasty mass, when put in 3 gallons of lye at 21°, stirring well and removing the heat, when let the paste rest.

To separate with the salted lye at 25°, pour in while stirring another 6 gallons until it forms into grains, and the lye separates, when let it rest five hours and draw off the lye.

In the third operation lye of 25°, amounting to about 6 gallons, and the rosin previously melted and strained, are now poured in, keeping down the froth by occasional beating, stirring when the scum disappears, and after boiling about six hours the grains look hard, and crumble between the fingers; draw the heat and let it rest, and after some time draw off the lye.

This soap will still have to be finished by a fourth operation, which is divided in two: 1st, add 6 or 7 gallons of lye at 7°, stirring and boiling for five or six hours, and if it has any tendency to grain add a gallon or two of cold water to give it consistency. Yet it is necessary that the soap should separate, which can be seen by the lye running off separately on the stirrer, when stop the heat and cover up. 2d, as the soap will still be too caustic, it can be neutralized by adding (after drawing off the lye of the first operation) 3 gallons of solution of sal soda, marking 5°, and boiling and stirring to a smooth, syrupy fluid, until the soap from the bottom appears to rise somewhat discolored, when turn off the heat, having added a portion of water to supply the evaporation. After a day's rest the scum is taken off, and the soap dipped into frames, when the gray soap at the bottom is mixed with the scum, and can be kept for the next operation, or boiled together with weak lyes for an inferior soap.

Cocoa-nut Oil Soap.

I have remarked that this soap has peculiar properties, and that of washing in sea-water is a great advantage, and gives it the name of marine soap.

To prepare this soap a little potash lye added to the soda lye is an advantage, for when about 12 per cent. of the potash lye is mixed with the soda, it not only makes the soap more plastic, but improves its qualities for all purposes. This potash can be added to the soda before it is made caustic, or (which is the better plan) they can be separately prepared and mixed before beginning the operation of saponification. This potash lye is so useful that, even if the toilet soap-maker did not make soft toilet soaps, he would find it essential in imparting an emolliency to his best soaps by their greater solubility.

To saponify 100 pounds of cocoa-nut oil, take 90 pounds of soda lye at 30°, and 10 pounds of potash lye at 30°, and mix, and after the oil has been well purified, let it be melted, raising the heat gradually while adding the alkali, and bringing to a boil. The soap, which at first appears to granulate, gradually becomes syrupy and perfectly united.

If, during the process, the soap separates into grains, a few pints of water added while stirring will generally correct it and supply evaporation; when the paste is perfectly homogeneous and transparent, it may be considered finished, and when the heat has somewhat subsided it can be put into the frames.

This soap, being of a brilliant whiteness, and of a translucent, waxy aspect, takes the colors very nicely. To color red take vermilion or orange mineral in the proportion of a drachm to the pound, mixing in a small mortar with a portion of the soap, and stirring in the frame. It can also be mottled or marbled with the different colors, red, yellow, and blue, and by a little practice very handsome effects are produced.

The aniline colors can be used for this soap to

great advantage, but they are added cold by the milling process, when the perfumes are added, and they make very attractive colors.

This process of milling, which will be more fully described in another chapter, permits of the mixing of the different kinds of soaps, and, as cocoa-nut oil soap is not much favored in our country, and yet has some advantages in combination with the others, they can be combined in all proportions to make an endless variety of kinds and colors, and of various perfumes suitable to their names. This addition of cocoa-nut oil has the advantage of giving great emolliency and a profuse lather to all the other soaps, and should when well perfumed make them acceptable to almost every one.

CHAPTER XX.

TOILET SOAPS BY THE COLD PROCESS.

Soaps of this class, though rarely so perfect in quality as those made by boiling, yet, properly and carefully made, give good satisfaction, and in some respects they have an advantage, especially when soaps are wanted to have the fine fragrance of the flowers, the delicate odors of which would be destroyed by boiling. Though these odors could be added to the boiled soap by milling, it would have to be in the form of extract or alcoholate, which would be in many ways objectionable, causing the cakes to shrink and warp in the process of drying.

Again, a great many objections have been made to these soaps becoming very hard and insoluble, and as soon losing their perfume, and being caustic and irritating to the skin, leaving an unpleasant roughness after using. Nearly all these objections can be overcome, for when they exist it is because of the carelessness or ignorance of the manufacturer; for if he knows his business properly he can by this process make a soap that has none of these faults.

The proper lye for most of these soaps is the caustic soda lye, with about ten per cent. of potash lye of the same strength and causticity. Making soaps by this process would be more economical than boiling, if the lyes did not require as much fuel and trouble to concentrate them as is experienced in the boiling of the soap, yet, as I have said, these lyes can be purchased of the manufacturing chemist already prepared, and of the strength of 36°, the strength usually employed and prepared especially for this purpose. But, if the manufacturer has not the convenience of procuring them, or the cost of transporting is too great, he will have to make them for himself by concentrating the soda lye prepared as directed in my last chapter, and the potash lye in the same manner as heretofore described; and, as he will require to make soft soaps as well as hard, it would be well to prepare stocks of each of these alkalies of the requisite strength, and keep them on hand ready for his use; they must mark 36° Baumé at a temperature of 60° Fahr.

These soaps have borne the name of "little pan" soaps, because they can be manufactured in small pans with as much facility as large ones, or in fact more conveniently, for one person can manage a kettle with from 100 to 300 pounds with ease. Figure 38 represents a portable kettle, the heat for which is communicated by a small charcoal furnace, which can be withdrawn at any moment to regulate the heat. In a kettle of this description, holding about 50 gallons, a person can easily make 200 to 300 pounds of soap in two or three hours, so that if his materials be ready to his hands, he can easily turn out 1000 pounds of soap in a working day.

As said in speaking of boiled soaps, the toilet-soap-maker, who wishes to make soaps in variety and of good quality, will provide himself with a stock of each of the kinds requisite for a good white soap, palm soap, half palm soap, cocoa-nut oil soap, etc.; so that by a judicious combination he can make all the different kinds needed.

To make a fine white soap suitable for most of his colored soaps by the cold process, mix the greases in about the following proportions:—

Lard, purified	30	pounds.
Veal fat, purified . . .	40	"
Cocoa-nut oil	10	"
Cotton-seed oil	20	"

100 pounds in all.

Having seen that all are of good quality and clean, melt them together, and bring them to a heat of about 112° F.; and, if convenient, warm the alkali, consisting of 45 pounds of caustic soda and 5 pounds of caustic potash, both at 36° Baumé, to about 90° F., and place in such a manner as to cause it to run slowly into the melted grease, while a person is constantly stirring, stopping occasionally to see that the heat does not get above the point named or the lye does not run too fast, as either event would cause the contents to separate. Continue the stirring, after all the lye is in, until it is too thick to work, and the two substances are completely united, when turn into a frame, which had better be lined with a soft, clean cotton cloth, large enough to bring over the top of the frame and cover the soap. The perfume can be put in before the soap hardens in the pan; and, for almond soap, should be—

Oil of bitter almonds . .	12 ounces.
Oil of lemon	4 "

In a few hours after the soap is in the frame, a singular spontaneous reaction takes place with these soaps; their particles seem to react and cause the temperature to rise to about 180° F. But this phenomenon does not impair their quality, but, on the contrary, is a means of a more intimate combination of the particles, and the soap is thereby improved.

In a day or two, according to the quantity and size of the frame, the soap can be cut up and *platted* and racked, and in a week it is ready to be pressed.

This soap should be of a beautiful clear white, and but slightly caustic, and give a fine lather. If made into almond soap, each cake should be wrapped in foil. But it would be well to have a stock of this white soap in bars to use for making soaps of other colors and perfumes, such as rose soap, etc.; and also a yellow soap, made as follows:—

Yellow Soap.

Palm oil (best)	40 pounds.
Tallow oil	30 "
Cocoa-nut oil	10 "
Cotton-seed oil	20 "
	100 "

Manipulate as for the white soap, with 50 pounds of the mixed lyes at 36°—5 or 6 pounds of it being potash lye—and color with about an ounce of anatto dissolved in a pint of weak lye. This soap, if carefully made of good material, will be of a clear orange-yellow color, and can be used for the marsh-mallow and other yellow soaps, or in combination with the white or cocoa-nut oil soaps, to make a variety.

For a soap of second quality, notably the honey and glycerine, the manufacturer can make a soap that may be called half-palm soap with rosin, which latter material will cause a little more trouble in its manipulation by the cold process. For, as I have remarked, rosin is not saponifiable with alkali, and is, in fact, an adulteration, though of a nature to improve it for some purposes, causing a more copious lather, and making the soap that contains it more soluble.

For a half-palm soap with rosin, take

Tallow or suet	40 pounds.
Palm oil	30 "
Cotton-seed oil	20 "
Rosin	10 "

100 pounds in all. Soda lye, 36°, 50 pounds.

Take out about 6 pounds of the lye to dissolve with the rosin separately, which is not to be added until the soap by its thickness and evenness shows it is nearly complete; when if on adding the rosin it thickens too soon, a little warm water is added, say about a quart at a time, to facilitate complete combination.

This soap, if properly made, is of a pale yellow or fawn color, of a plastic consistence, which it will retain for a long time, and is exceedingly useful to use in conjunction with the other soaps. I have given various styles, colors, and perfumes under as many different names.

Of the cocoa-nut oil soap, I have, in my last chapter, given the proper formula with suitable instructions, remarking that, if made like the boiled soaps given, it would be apt to retain too much of the salt of separation; so I advise a sort of modified cold process, where the lye is somewhat weaker, admitting sufficient water to allow a slight boiling to form a better combination of its parts. This soap should also be kept in stock with the others given, and will be sufficient for all practical purposes; and, by the aid of remelting or with the mill, nearly all kinds can be made.

CHAPTER XXI.

CASTILE SOAP FROM COTTON-SEED OIL.

In our Southern States, where cotton is grown in the greatest quantity and of the best quality in the world, the seed has long been known to have an abundance of oil, the extraction of which was very difficult on account of the adhering fibre. From this cause the seed was allowed to rot, and was used for manure. When, however, machinery was invented for hulling the seed, the oil could be extracted with facility. The large amount of hull and adhering fibre these seeds possess will be understood when it is known that it sometimes takes five bushels of seed to make one bushel ready for the mill. The hull and fibre are used for paper stock, and are, of course, very valuable.

When they were able to remove the hull and make the oil, another difficulty arose in the large amount of objectionable color the crude oil contained, and which was due to dark resinous spots, contained in the seed; the color, however, has been overcome, for it is now refined by means of chemicals, caustic lye, etc., and bleached with sulphuric acid, and pressed to remove a large amount of stearine it contains, and which, with the oils, is used for a great many purposes, this latter being sometimes sold and bottled as salad oil from its sweet nutty taste when fresh and pure.

Cotton-seed oil, when well refined, is a bland, bright yellowish oil, very similar to almond oil, though it has some of the properties of a drying oil, but taking a very long time to dry. This drying property does not seem to deter the maker of cheap perfumery from bottling large quantities for common hair oil, or from buying it for that purpose under the name of salad oil, often not knowing from what source it is obtained.

To the soap-maker it possesses very valuable properties, for nothing has yet been discovered that is so good and economical a substitute for olive oil; and when a portion of lard and bleached palm oil is mixed with it, for making Marseilles or Castile soap, it is difficult to distinguish the imitation from the genuine soap. The importance of this oil in the manufacture of soap is, to me, so great that I deem it necessary to devote some space to its description, and particularly as few soap-makers have as yet availed themselves of its benefits, and to try and give them some hints for its manufacture into a soap that may be called castile soap, from its close resemblance.

In saponifying cotton-seed oil, there is no peculiar difficulty more than in making a good castile soap from olive oil, though the soap is made somewhat sooner if the stearine is left in it, which stearine is generally pressed out to permit the oleine to remain fluid in our coldest weather.

To make a white castile soap, take

Cotton-seed oil	80 pounds.
Lard, good quality	10 "
Olive oil	10 "

And prepare the lye by close calculation in this manner: 50 pounds to mark 15° Baumé, 50 pounds at 21°, and 50 pounds at 27°, making 150 pounds for this quantity of grease. The lye to be made of the English caustic soda, and rendered clear and caustic with one-fourth of lime.

To the melted grease in the kettle pour the first 50 pounds of lye at 15°, keeping it stirred as the heat is raised to boiling, and as it froths beating it down quickly to prevent its overflowing; boil for three or four hours, when add by degrees the 50 pounds of lye at 21°, and boil for five or six hours longer, keeping up the stirring, and, when it becomes a perfectly smooth mass, turn off the heat and let it rest for the lye to separate. After some hours' rest the spent lye is drawn off, the heat is raised, and the last 50 pounds of lye at 27° are poured in, and allowed to boil briskly for four or five hours, when the soap ought to grain and appear flakey when pressed between the fingers; when again turn off the heat and allow the lye to separate, and draw off after some hours' rest.

In finishing or fitting a lye of carbonate of potash of 6° or 8°, say 25 pounds are stirred in with a gentle heat until the soap presents a perfectly homogeneous syrupy mass, when it can be left to divide—the scum to the top and the gray soap to the bottom, with the fine soap between, which is dipped into the frames, and the scum and dark soap kept to make the mottled soap.

The result should be about 150 pounds of the best soap having a fine white appearance, and 30 to 40 pounds of inferior soaps that can be mixed with the mottled castile soap.

To make a mottled castile soap, take of

Cotton-seed oil	80 pounds.
Lard, good	10 "
Palm oil, bleached . . .	10 "

The bleached palm improves the odor, causing a greater resemblance to the Marseilles soap, and is cheaper than the olive oil. Sulphuretted soda lyes are preferred by the French soap-makers for their mottled soap; but, as we are using the English soft lye or artificial lyes, we will have to adopt a modified process. The sulphuretted crude soda forms the colored mottling, the sulphur combines with the iron of the kettle and other impurities, and forms the oxide giving the blue color, which turns red on all those parts exposed to the air.

To make this soap, proceed very much as for the white soap. To the melted grease pour on the 50 pounds of the weaker lye at 15°, gently raising the heat while they are mixing, which should be done by gently stirring, and keeping down the froth by beating, and regulating the heat to prevent too rapid boiling. After three or four hours, pour in the 50 pounds of lye at 21°, and continue the stirring, and as the froth subsides bring to a more rapid ebullition, and when it granulates shut off the heat and let it rest for four or five hours. Now draw off the lyes and proceed to the enlargage or coction, by putting into the melted soap the third 50 pounds of lye at 27°, which is added while constantly beating and stirring. Stir in also about 5 pounds of common salt, and continue the boiling for six or eight hours, as may be required, or until the grains separate, as can be seen by taking out a portion with a knife or pressing between the fingers, when a little experience will show a flakey scale free from the lye; let the heat be stopped and the soap allowed to settle until next day, when after drawing off the salted lye it can be finished. The soap is finished with weak sal-soda lye, or, if the soap is neutral, with water having a little salt in solution, for if it needs water the grains will appear hard and dry, when the soap will have to be boiled until it forms a smooth mass. The soap is again allowed to rest, and the next day again thoroughly stirred and put in the frame, when it is ready for the mottling. This is done by putting into a small watering-pot with a rose-spout about 4 ounces of sulphate of iron, dissolved in a pint of warm water, and pouring it from the rose on the top of the soap in the frame, while the crutch is plunged up and down to give the streaky marbled appearance. Of course this requires some practice, as it should present a uniformity throughout the entire mass, but is not difficult to accomplish with a little experience.

If this soap is carefully made, it will be as good as most of the mottled castile soaps we import, and should be made so economically as to yield a good profit while being sold at a less price than the imported article.

I devote some space to the description of the manufacture of these soaps from the cotton-seed oil, believing that the cheapness and other advantages of the raw material will induce soap-makers to give it the consideration it seems to deserve for making a good and cheap soap, and that they may see a source of profit in its manufacture. While it is not supposed that the perfumer or toilet soap-maker can give much time to this class of soaps, I yet deem the subject of sufficient importance to endeavor to draw the attention thereto of those engaged in the manufacture of soaps alone.

CHAPTER XXII.

COMPOUNDING TOILET SOAPS.

By compounding soaps I mean the making of toilet soaps of different names, colors, and perfumes from the different kinds of soap, boiled or cold, for making which I have given the many details. Thus we suppose the maker of toilet soap has in stock white soap, palm soap, yellow or half palm and cocoanut oil soap, and with them he can proceed to make any kind needed. We have shown how the almond soap is made from the white cold soap by perfuming in the pan with the oil of bitter almonds or oil of mirbane.

Honey soap can be made also of the half palm soap with rosin, by putting in the pan just before turning into the frame 8 ounces of citronella oil and 2 ounces of lemon-grass oil to each 100 pounds.

Glycerine soap can be perfumed in the same way; for each 100 pounds take—

Oil of	cassia	2 ounces.
"	caraway	1 "
"	lavender	4 "
"	mirbane	1 "

Let both of these soaps be a bright yellow, the last of a somewhat darker shade to distinguish it.

Marsh-mallow soap can be made by an admixture of the palm and the half palm soap, and perfumed to each 100 pounds—

Oil of	lavender	6 ounces.
"	lemon grass	4 "
"	peppermint	½ "
"	petit-grain	½ "

To make a good rose soap take equal parts of the white and cocoa-nut oil soap, and color 100 pounds with 12 ounces of French vermilion, and perfume with—

Oil of	rose geranium	4 ounces.
"	rose	1 "
"	cinnamon	1 "
"	bergamot	2 "

White Windsor Soap.

To 50 pounds each of the white soap and cocoa-nut oil soap, mix in the mill this perfume—

Oil of lavender	 4	ounces.
" rosemary	 4	"
" thyme	 2	"
" cloves	 1	"
" caraway	 1	"

Brown Windsor Soap.

This popular soap, when properly prepared, is made in the following manner: Take of boiled palm soap and half-palm soap each 50 pounds; put in the stripper, and make into thin shavings, and spread upon sheets of strong paper to dry; when dry, melt in a marine bath with a small portion of an aromatic water, and when it is again hard enough proceed to cut it up and mill it as before, drying it again and remelting and adding caramel to color; and after the third operation add the following perfume to the 100 pounds:—

Oil of bergamot	 4	ounces.
" caraway	 2	"
" cassia	 2	"
" lavender	 8	"
" cloves	 1	"
" petit-grain	. . . 1	"

Mould or cut into small square cakes, and wrap them in a neat paper wrapper.

Brown Windsor soap owes its fine emollient properties to the amount of labor employed in its manufacture, for it is almost needless to say that the more soap is worked and handled, and melted and remelted, the better it becomes. This soap is, in large establishments, often made of the scraps of all other kinds of soaps that accumulate from moulding and manipulating, but it is better to color and mould them from good soap, for the toilet soap-maker should endeavor to keep up the standard excellence of the well-known old Brown Windsor Soap.

To the good taste and good judgment, and to the enterprise of the toilet soap manufacturer, I must leave the formulas for the numerous soaps to be found in all the markets; with his stock and colors and perfumes he cannot have any trouble in making any or all of them.

I will now give the formulas for making some of the superfine soaps by the cold process, for about 75 pounds of soap.

Benzoin Soap. (Savon au Benzoin.)

Hard body with benzoin	30	pounds.
Cocoa-nut oil	9	"
Cotton-seed oil	10	"
Yellow wax	1	"
Mixed caustic lye, 36°	25	"

Saponify in the manner directed for the soap by the cold process, and add of perfume—

Flowers of benzoin	4	ounces.
Oil of bergamot	3	"
" lavender	2	"
" geranium	1	"
Tincture of benzoin	8	"
Gum tragacanth (in mucilage)	2	"

The mucilage of tragacanth is made by dissolving the 2 ounces of gum in 2 pints of water by maceration for about twenty-four hours, stirring and straining, and is added to the soap after all the alkali is in.

It helps to make the soap more soluble, adds to its emolliency, and is softening to the skin, and should be used in all superfine soaps. The benzoin soap should be colored a light brown to resemble the gum.

Ambergris or Ambrosial Soap.

(Savon d'Ambré Surfin.)

Hard body with ambergris	15 pounds.
" " musk	5 "
" " ambrette	10 "
Jasmine pomade, No. 24	10 "
Rose " "	10 "
Beeswax	½ "
Gum tragacanth	2 ounces.
Caustic lye of soda, 36°	25 pounds.

Saponify in the usnal manner for cold soaps, taking care to keep the heat under 150° F., and when finished perfume with—

Oil of lavender	2 ounces.
Tincture of ambergris	8 "

Color lilac or light purple.

Bouquet Soap. (Savon au Bouquet.)

Soft body	30 pounds.
Cotton-seed oil	10 "
Cocoa-nut oil	9 "
White wax	1 "
Gum tragacanth	1½ ounces.
Caustic lye, 10 per cent. of potash	25 pounds.

Make this soap as directed for cold soap, and perfume with—

Oil of bergamot . . .	4 ounces.
" cedrat	4 "
" cloves	2 "
" thyme	1 "
" neroli	1 "

Color a light yellow.

Lettuce Soap. (Savon au Suc de Laitue.)

Lard with lettuce-juice . .	30 pounds.
Spermaceti	1 "
Cocoa-nut oil	10 "
Cotton-seed oil	9 "
Gum tragacanth, dissolved in lettuce-juice	2 ounces.
Caustic lye, 36°	25 pounds.

Saponify and perfume with—

Oil of bitter almond . . .	1½ ounces.
" bergamot . . .	4 "
" cloves	1 "
Powdered orris root . . .	4 "

Color light green.

Musk Soap. (Savon au Musc.)

Hard body of musk . . .	15 pounds.
Rose pomade, No. 24 . . .	5 "
Cotton-seed oil	20 "
Cocoa-nut oil	10 "
Gum tragacanth . . .	2 ounces.
Caustic lye, 36°	25 pounds.

Saponify and color brown, and perfume with—

Oil of bergamot . . .	4 ounces.
" rose	¼ "
" cloves	½ "
Tincture of musk . . .	2 "

Millefleur Soap. (Superfine.)

Hard body of ambrette . .	10 pounds.
" " vanilla . . .	10 "
Cassie pomade, No. 24 . .	5 "
Rose " " . .	5 "
Cocoa-nut oil	15 "
Cocoa butter	4 "
Yellow wax	1 "
Caustic lye, mixed, 36° . .	25 "
Gum tragacanth . . .	2 ounces.

Color light brown, saponify, and perfume with—

Oil of lavender	1 ounce.
" bergamot . . .	2 "
" geranium . . .	½ "
" cloves	½ "
Tincture of musk . . .	2 "
" ambergris . .	1 "

Violet Soap. (Superfine.)

Violet pomade, No. 24 . .	10 pounds.
Oil of jasmine, " . .	10 "
" cassie, " . .	10 "
Palm oil (bleached) . . .	20 "
Wax	1 "
Gum tragacanth . . .	2 ounces.
Caustic soda lye, 36° . .	25 pounds.

Saponify by the cold process, and perfume with—

Extract of violet, No. 2	. .	8 ounces.
" rose, "	. .	8 "
Tincture of ambrette	. .	8 "

Color yellowish-green.

In this manner can the maker of toilet soaps make all the known varieties of superfine soaps, and it would be unnecessary to give further recipes.

CHAPTER XXIII.

MISCELLANEOUS SOAPS.

In this chapter I must give some details of other varieties of soap that may be demanded to make a proper assortment, or be required to meet the current demands of the trade. Soft soaps, as I have said, are made with potash lye, and, owing to the limited quantity sold, they are usually made in a small way by the cold process, as described in making the hard soda soaps. The old formulas for making the soft white soap, or shaving cream, directed it to be made with lard, which does not by itself make a satisfactory soap, as it does not produce a sufficiently copious lather, so necessary for shaving.

Shaving Cream. (White potash soap.)

Veal suet	. . . . .	60 pounds.
Lard	. . . . . .	20 "
Cocoa-nut oil	. . . .	20 "
Potash lye, 36°	. . . .	50 "

Melt the grease in a pan, of the kind described before and illustrated by Fig. 38, or by means of a steam jacket, as seen by Fig. 39; divide the alkali into two parts, and dilute one with water to make it mark about 21°, and place it so that it will run gently into the melted grease. When the grease is about 112° F. turn on the lye; keep stirring and regulate the temperature below 200°; in about two hours the soap will begin to form and will separate in grains; then add the other portion of lye at 36°, and continue the constant stirring until it becomes too stiff to work, when remove the fire, and beat it, while cooling, into as smooth a mass as possible, when cover the pan or remove into any suitable wooden vessel. The pearly appearance has yet to be given by means of beating in small portions in a marble mortar, or by running it rapidly through the stone rollers of the mill. To make almond cream, perfume with oil of bitter almonds and a little bergamot. To make the rose shaving cream, color with fine French vermilion, of the proportion of a drachm to the pound of cream, and perfume with oil of rose and rhodium. To make ambrosial, color with tincture of archil and perfume with tinctures of ambergris and musk, oils of cloves and bergamot. The colors and perfumes are mixed at the time of milling or rubbing in the mortar.

Floating Soaps.

These soaps have many admirers, and when made of the proper materials are excellent, as the particles of air with which they are filled cause them to lather freely. They should only be made of vegetable oil soaps, as soap with tallow or lard will not float. To prepare

Nymph Floating Soap,

Take Palm oil soap . . . . 30 pounds.
Cocoa-nut oil soap . . . 20 "

Let them be stripped or milled and put in a marine bath with a gallon of water, and when perfectly dissolved let it be rapidly stirred with a churn-like contrivance to about twice its capacity, when it can be turned into shallow frames. The accompanying figure will give an idea of a suitable apparatus.

Fig. 46.

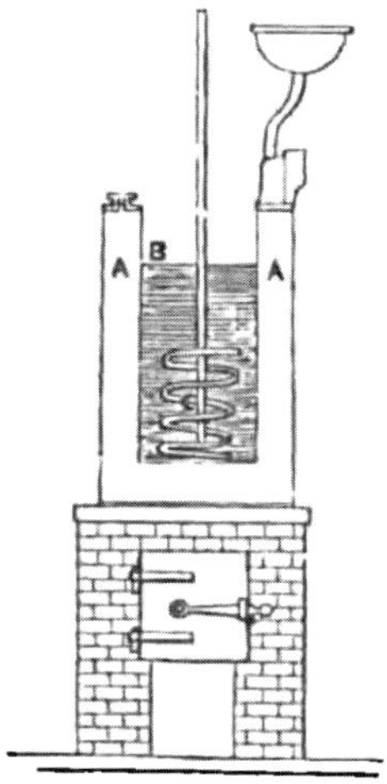

Kettle for floating soaps.

Powdered Soaps

Are a very convenient form for using soap for shaving or lavatory purposes, and are when well made very neutral. To make them—

Take the best boiled white soap, and, having milled it into strips, put it on sheets of clean, strong paper, in a warm, dry place, free from dust, and when perfectly hard and dry grind it in the mill to an impalpable powder, using a drum sieve to make it uniform. If the soap is to remain white, perfume it with oil of bitter almonds. If red, color with a drachm of fine vermilion to each pound of powder, and perfume like rose soap. If yellow, color with powdered gamboge, and perfume as desired. As a rule, the color should be added before sieving.

Sapophane or Oleophane.

This transparent soft soap is much patronized by some people, and is usually made from good soaps dissolved in strong alcohol.

Take of soap of tallow and rosin	6 pounds.
Alcohol, 95°	8 pints.

The soap is to be well milled and dried and put into a water-bath with the alcohol; stirred until all is dissolved; colored with tincture of saffron; and perfumed with

Oil of cinnamon	¼ ounce.
" cloves	¼ "
" lavender	1 "
Tincture of styrax . . .	1 "

And immediately put into the bottle intended for vending.

Soap Essences

Are made by the solution of soap in alcohol; and to make them, soaps made with vegetable oils must only be used, as all others would solidify or become opaque on cooling. Take

White castile soap . . .	12 ounces.
Alcohol, 85°	4 pints.
Liquor potassa, U. S. P. . .	½ ounce.

Let the soap be cut up into fine shavings and dissolved in a water-bath with the alcohol and liquor potassa, and when it is dissolved perfume and put into bottles.

Alcohol of 85° is about the proper strength, and the alkali is added to keep it liquid. The usual perfume is

Oil of geranium	. . . .	3 drachms.
" lemon grass	. . .	4 "
" cloves	. . . .	1 "

This essence will retain a little glycerine in solution, and is a delightful and convenient article for shaving, cleaning the teeth, etc.; and I would suggest to the perfumer that he could prepare many other similar preparations that would be pleasant to use and might become popular.

Transparent Soaps.

These salable soaps are made with alcohol and curd soap; the curd soap must be a soap made of tallow or suet, as there have not been discovered any others that will remain transparent. The soap is stripped and milled and dried perfectly dry; and the alcohol should be 95°, or the process may fail.

The curd soap is reduced to shavings and perfectly dried and mixed with twice its weight of alcohol of 95°, and put into an alembic, Fig. 47, fitted with a stirrer, when after a day's rest it is put into a water-bath, and, by means of a condenser, the most of the alcohol is distilled off and recovered to use again, or for something else; when but little comes over, stop the heat, and when it has become somewhat cool pour it into moulds, which are usually spherical and much larger than the soap is intended to be, Fig. 42, as it requires some drying and exposure to the air to make it transparent, when it is turned into balls or pressed into cakes in moulds. The perfume is added just previous to pouring from the still. Color red with tincture of archil; yellow with tincture of saffron.

There is a recipe for making a transparent soap by the cold process, which results in a great saving of time over the old method. Take

Tallow or suet (refined) . .	20 pounds.
Caustic lye, 36°, 10 per cent. of potash	10 "
Alcohol, 95°	2 gallons.

Saponify the tallow with 5 pounds of the lye (in the manner described for cold soaps), stirring for about two hours; add the other 5 pounds to the alcohol, with the heat under 140° F., and add very gradually, still stirring; and when the soap begins to thicken, and is thoroughly mixed, turn into a frame, which should be surrounded with a cotton cloth to keep the heat in, and cool as gradually as possible. This soap attains its transparency by about a week's exposure to the air. The color and perfume should be put in previously to pouring into the frame.

A cheaper kind of transparent soap is made with tallow and rosin soap dissolved in alcohol, and can be made in two ways: first, by the process already given for transparent soap, by distillation of the excess of alcohol; second, by having the soap of tallow and rosin; which should be a boiled soap, cut, milled and dried, and to each pound, put into a vessel with cover and insert into a water-bath, adding 1 pint of strong alcohol, and when dissolved put into a frame and allow to remain for a few days to harden.

Fig. 47.

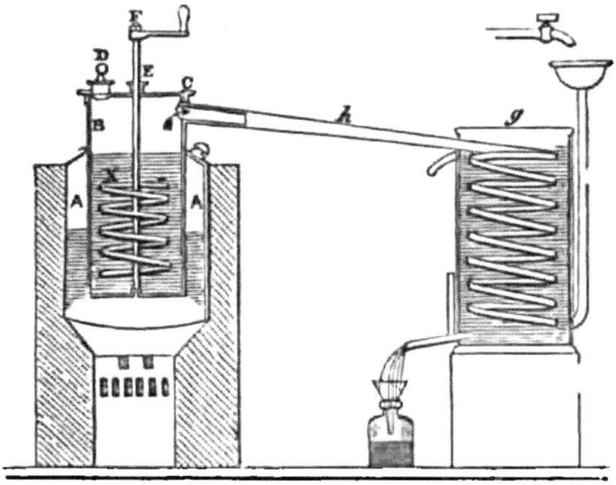

Still and water-bath for transparent soaps.

Wash Balls or Savonettes.

These spherical lumps of soap have been long in use, and have had a large sale, and are still in demand. Nearly all the second quality soaps of which we have given the formulas can be moulded into that form, though they are usually made from the mottled or marbled or the transparent soap. They are made by a very simple instrument of glass or metal, being a cup of suitable size, with sharp cutting rim, which, being held in the right hand, while the lump of soap is in the palm of the left, is passed over the surface of the lump, cutting the uneven surface in all directions, leaving a perfectly round lump in the hand. Of course it may require some practice to be expert at it, for they have to be of uniform size, but the process is simple and soon acquired.

The variegated or marbled soap in red and blue veins has the handsomest appearance in these globes of soap, and these veins are usually given to the soap while in the frame, as previously described, red being made with vermilion and blue with ultramarine. The perfume is generally a mixture of sassafras, thyme, and cloves, though, of course, the toilet soap-maker can have them of any color and perfume he desires; but fine soaps are seldom seen in this form.

CHAPTER XXIV.

MILLING AND MOULDING TOILET SOAPS.

Toilet soaps are much improved by the amount of labor bestowed upon their manufacture, and to this is due much of the superiority they have over the common soaps, the ingredients being much the same; and as I have remarked of the old brown Windsor, so generally admired, its good qualities lie in the frequency of its melting and drying, and the labor in its manufacture; so that when the maker of toilet soaps has supplied himself with a stock of white, palm, half-palm, and cocoa-nut oil soaps, he may produce by means of labor, color, and perfume any soap he requires.

Besides the machinery and implements already given, it will be necessary to have a stripper to shave up the soap into thin shreds, and a mill to grind it and thoroughly mix all the colors and perfumes.

Fig. 48.

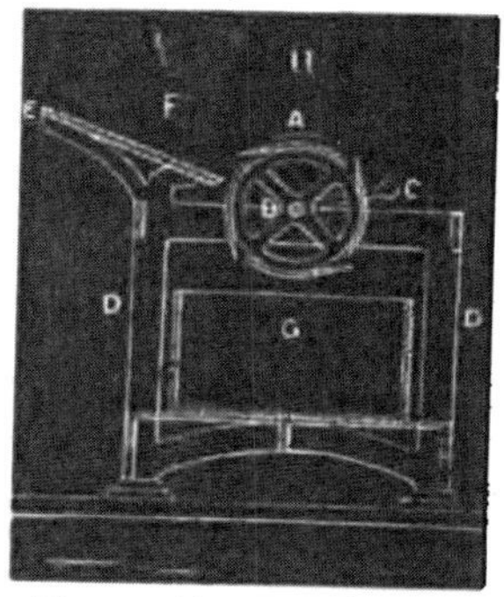

Soap cutter or stripper.

A stripping machine (Fig. 48) consists of—

A. The cutter.

B. Iron shaft which traverses the centre of the cutter, with a handle, C, to give it motion.

D D. Frame upon which the cutter rests.

E. Inclined plane of wood on which the bar of soap, F, is slid towards the cutter.

G. Box to receive the cut soap.

The bar of soap, being put upon the inclined plane, as the cutter revolves, is shaved into small shavings and falls into the box below, and being mixed with the color or perfume is put into the hopper of the mill to be thoroughly combined.

A milling machine (Fig. 49) consists of—

A A. Frame of iron which supports the machine.

B B B. Cylinders of granite or iron to grind the soap.

C. Crank and fly-wheel, to give motion to the machine; with power, a pulley is put in its stead.

D. A scraper formed of a large blade of steel, and fixed against the last cylinder to scrape the soap from it.

Fig. 49.

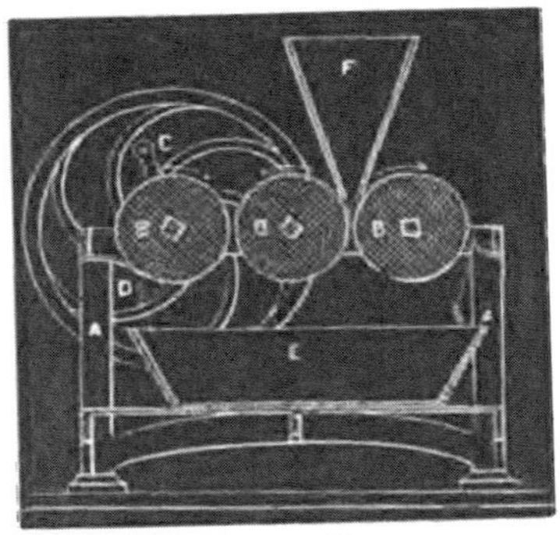

Soap mill.

E. Large wooden box (zinc lined) to receive the crushed soap.

F. Hopper to receive the shavings of soap and give them to the cylinders.

These machines save a great deal of labor, as before their use it was customary to shave up the soap with a plane or knife, and remelt it with the colors and perfumes to effect a combination of the ingredients.

The soap, being shaved up and ground in the proportions required of white soap, palm soap, half-palm soap, or cocoa-nut oil soap, as the formula calls for, can, when in the boxes, be mixed with the suitable color and perfume, and put into the hopper of the mill and run through a sufficient number of times to form a perfectly homogeneous paste.

When the soap is made to suit, it is next formed into rough pieces of suitable weight for the mould, and of somewhat similar form to the intended cake. This is usually done by hand, and is called plotting, and in large laboratories it is usual to have a machine for the purpose. These plotting machines are of various forms, and are used for pushing out the soap through an orifice of suitable size and cutting off the cake of soap as it exudes, which falling on an endless belt is carried into a receiver. When the cakes are plotted into some shape suitable for the mould, and weighing about 20 per cent. more to allow for drying, they are placed on the racks to dry; these racks are made of strips of poplar or beachwood, and so arranged that the air can reach all parts of the soap. Fig. 37 gives an idea of a suitable rack.

After the pieces of soap have dried a few days they can be moulded, which is done in several kinds of forms. Figure 34 shows a lever press which, for small cakes, is the most expeditious. Figure 50 shows a screw press that has great power, and is suitable for moulding the largest cakes.

Fig. 50.

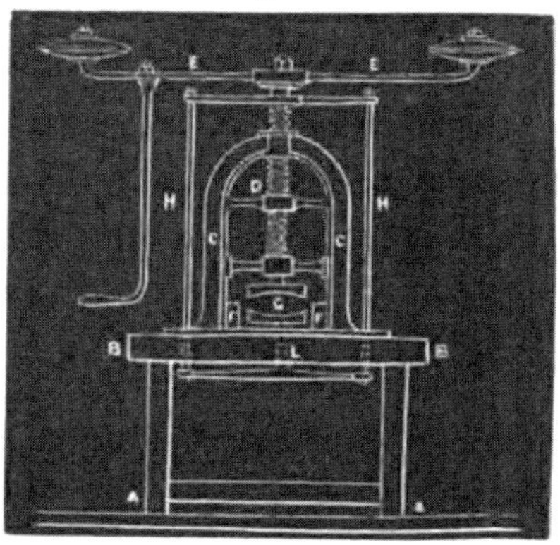

Screw press for toilet soaps.

A A. Platform to support the press.
B B. Strong oak board used to receive the press.
C C. Frame of the press.

D. Screw provided with groove to receive the upper shell of the mould.

E E is the fly, surmounted with balls at each end.

F F. Cast-iron matrix to receive the two dies.

G. Brass mould of two pieces.

H H. Rods adapted by means of screws to a horizontal bar below E E, which passes under the matrix and raises the rod L after each pressure, and raises the lower shell of the mould, when the cake can be taken from the mould and another substituted to be pressed into form.

There are still other implements needed to complete the list, as: A pair or two of scales to weigh the soap in bulk and in small cakes of different sizes. Several tables to hold the different tools and to work upon. A marble mortar of good capacity. Two or three other mortars of wedgwood and glass. Sieves, pallet-knives, trays to hold the moulded soap, graduated measures for measuring liquids, etc. etc.

In moulding the plotted cakes into the required form, they are taken after they have become sufficiently dry, and with the hands dipped into alcohol and rubbed to take off the white spots and clean them for the mould, and prevent their sticking to the dies; and if the cakes are too soft, salt and water are used to prevent their sticking in the moulds.

If the soap is of fine quality it may still be necessary to let it dry a few days more after moulding, when it is again rubbed with a piece of soft rag and alcohol, and put into neat boxes or into wrappers.

The soaps that can be made by this process of milling are innumerable, and it would be impossible to give them all, so I shall only give the most popular and best known, as—

Bouquet Soap.

White soap	50 pounds.
Half-palm soap . . .	50 "

10 ounces of powdered gamboge to color, and add to perfume it—

Oil of bergamot	8 ounces.
" cloves	2 "
" thyme	4 "
" rosemary	4 "
" neroli	2 "

The soap is first stripped, then milled, and then the color and perfume are mixed in the box, when it is run through the mill several times until perfectly uniform in color, when it is plotted, dried, and moulded as directed; and these directions apply to all the following formulas:—

Rose Soap.

White soap (cold or boiled) .	50 pounds.
Cacoa-nut oil	50 "

To color take 12 ounces of French vermilion. To perfume take—

Oil of rose	3 ounces.
" bergamot	4 "
" cloves	1 "
" neroli	1 "
" cinnamon (true) . .	1 "

Marshmallow Soap.

Palm soap (boiled or cold soap) .	50 pounds.
White " " " .	50 "

Color with tincture of annotto. Perfume with—

Oil of lavender	4	ounces.
" lemon	2	"
" lemon-grass	2	"
" peppermint	2	"
" petit-grain	2	"

Elder Flower Soap.

Half-palm soap	100 pounds.
Color with tincture of annotto and ultramarine	q. s.

Perfume with—

Oil of bergamot	4	ounces.
" cassia	1½	"
" lavender	3½	"
" petit-grain	1	"
" almonds	1	"

It is quite common now to add to soap an emollient substance, such as rice-flour, corn-meal, or oatmeal, from the softness these meals give to the skin, and especially to the hands.

Oatmeal Soap.

White soap	50	pounds.
Half-palm soap	20	"
Cocoa-nut oil soap	13	"
Oatmeal (coarse ground)	12	"

After stripping the soap the meal is sieved in and moistened with water, to allow for the dryness of the meal.

For cleaning the dirt from the hands of mechanics and others, sand is incorporated into soap; also powdered pumice-stone, making poncine soap; and also sawdust, etc. etc. These ingredients are best added to the melted soap, for they would be likely to injure the mill. They can be added to the finished soap in the frame, sufficient water being added to give a proper consistency to it.

Erasive Soap, for removing Grease Spots from Clothes.

Cocoa-nut oil soap . . . 20 pounds.

Melt and add 1 quart of water to make it fluid, when 10 pounds of dried and powdered fuller's earth are stirred in, and when mixed allowed to cool in the frame. Add perfume if desired, such as oil of sassafras, cloves, lavender, or thyme.

The honey and glycerine soaps are, as I have before said, usually made solid in the frame.

SOAPS BY PATENT PROCESSES.

New processes for making soaps are being constantly invented, involving the use of new patented machinery; the products being more or less perfect. That of Messrs. Hodgson and Holden is very ingenious, and causes a combination of the materials by means of steam injected into a cylinder of iron, the steam-pipe passing through its centre, which is perforated with holes for the escape of the steam while the cylinder revolves. The action of the steam during the revolution of the cylinder produces a complete combination and saponification of the materials, and is said to produce a very satisfactory result; though I cannot see how the degree of moisture injected with the steam can be regulated, and the soap made with this apparatus must, therefore, be of a very uncertain consistence.

A much better invention is that of Messrs. Bennet and Gibbs, in which carbonated alkali is made to combine with the oils or greases in a similar iron cylinder under the influence of heat and high steam pressure, with agitation to cause a thorough mixture of the ingredients, and produces a very fair soap, containing all the glycerine. The oils or greases, in the proportion of 100 pounds to about 34 pounds of carbonate of soda or soda ash, and 100 pounds of water, are put into an iron cylinder of great strength, and the heat is raised sufficiently to cause a pressure of 350 to 400 pounds to the square inch. A revolving shaft like that of a churn is kept in motion for about an hour, the heat being kept as regular as possible, or at least the pressure uniform. By this means the combination will be very complete; and in the preparation of toilet soaps, when the proportion of alkali, oils, and water is very accurately calculated, this mode of manipulation should be very effective, and, like the soap made by the cold process, would contain all the glycerine.

This apparatus might also be effectively used in making soaps to simulate Marseilles soaps from the cotton-seed oil, as shown in Chapter XXI.

APPENDIX.

SECTION I.

SYRUPS, JELLIES, CANDIES—THEIR FLAVORS AND COLORS.

WITH our rapid march in the arts of civilization and wealth we naturally look for all our surroundings to improve in an equal ratio. While in our earlier days we may have been satisfied with the ordinary kinds of candies and confectionery, not knowing there were better to be had, or finer qualities made, but when in going abroad we see and taste the products of other countries; we naturally ask why our own people, having equal advantages, do not endeavor to improve their productions, and if not excel at least rival the Europeans in this useful business? For while we have access to all the different ingredients they use, it would seem to be nothing but carelessness or indifference, or a dread of innovation upon established methods to prevent this necessary improvement in this art or trade, as in almost all others we endeavor to rival and often do excel our foreign instructors.

In the matter of color for candies, bon-bons, and other confections, the makers are often criminally careless, as there are some who are unprincipled enough, or perhaps through ignorance, use many colors that are mineral and often very deleterious. Many a mother grieves over a sick child, wondering at the cause of its nausea and fever, and its disgust of wholesome food, when a little observation would discover the evil to originate in the apparently innocent stick of candy given it the day before; which candy may have had lead, tin, mercury, or even arsenic or copper in the handsome color that attracted her at the time of purchasing it.

It is not my desire to cause needless alarm, but to call the proper attention of intelligent people to a subject that has called forth much attention in England and on the continent, where penal laws have been enacted to prohibit the use of poisonous ingredients in candies, and other articles used as food and drink, as we often read of alum and other drugs being put in bread, and litharge, sugar of lead, and red precipitate in wine, arsenic and nux vomica in beer, etc. It is certainly criminal to sell poison to the innocent purchaser who thinks he is getting wholesome food, and it is but just that a proper punishment should be meted out to the offender.

This offence in the confectioner is particularly criminal, as in coloring and flavoring his candies he can procure all the colors that he needs, and generally of vegetable origin, and entirely free from any deleterious influence whatever, and which would cost but little more than his pernicious ingredients.

Confining myself to a limited space in treating this subject, I will not be able to give full details for any one to manufacture these colors, for it requires a knowledge of chemistry, and costly apparatus to do so, but knowing from my own experiments the perfect feasibility of making all necessary colors from harmless substances, I have thought it proper to comment upon it here, and more particularly as I perceive that Mr. Otto Luthy, an experienced chemist of Philadelphia, is now manufacturing a complete line of these vegetable colors and carmines especially prepared for the use of confectioners, liquor dealers, etc., which are submitted to full analytical test to prove them perfectly harmless.

Although I think this subject of such importance, I cannot dwell longer upon it, but shall take every opportunity to call the attention of my readers and the public to the abuse referred to, and also to secure if possible proper legislation upon it.

The object of this chapter is to give formulas for syrups and jellies and fruit flavors, and I am digressing in occupying so much space on the colors, but my readers will see the occasion for it.

The artificial fruit flavors for syrups and candies I do not consider dangerous or unwholsome, for they have been used for twenty odd years in candy and syrup without ever having any ill effects. Although they are not so pleasant as the natural fruit, yet they can be used where the fruit could not be obtained, and are an excellent substitute, and are often identically analogous in their chemical constituents, although compounded from such divers substances.

I do not suppose the perfumer or apothecary will care to make these artificial flavors, as they are made much better and cheaper by the manufacturing chemist; therefore, it is unnecessary to give the formulas for their preparation, for they are intricate, and they require appropriate chemical apparatus.

Apple essence is chemically the solution of valerianate of ethyloxide.

Quince essence is a spiritous solution of the pelarginate of ethyloxide.

Pear oil is the alcoholic solution of the acetate of amyloxide.

Pineapple oil is the spiritous solution of the butyrate of ethyloxide.

All of these so-called oils are merely ethers derived from organic substances by the chemical action of acids and salts, and to give instructions for their manufacture would occupy much space, nor do I think it would be profitable to make them in a small way, and it would be more economical to purchase the assortment properly prepared for the purposes of the maker of syrups and flavors.

There are also prepared by many chemists what are called pure fruit juices, but which are seldom genuine, and when pure, have undergone some process by heat or otherwise that impairs their pleasantness of flavor; so whenever the pharmacist has the opportunity of procuring the fresh fruit it is immeasurably superior in delicacy of taste to any artificial or so-called pure fruit juices which are often only a dilute syrup artificially flavored, with a little glycerine added to preserve them from spoiling.

Therefore let him make genuine fruit syrups from the fresh fruits, which can be prepared in concentrated form in this manner, say—

Strawberry Syrup.

Fresh strawberries . . .	12 quarts.
Sugar (crushed) . . .	20 pounds.
Water	4 pints.

Put the strawberries in some convenient earthen vessel in layers with 10 pounds of the sugar; let them rest until the next day, when they will be found melted by the absorption of their juice by the sugar; stir well and strain through a coarse strong cloth, reserving the mark, into which stir the 4 pints of water and strain again; mix the liquids; put into a kettle, and as the mixture becomes warm add the remaining 10 pounds of sugar, when boil gently, take off the scum that rises and strain through a fine cloth. This will make about a gallon of concentrated syrup, which will bear diluting with an equal measure of simple syrup, made in the proportion of 2 pounds of crushed sugar to a pint of water.

In this manner can be made all other needed fruit syrups, such as—

Blackberry syrup.
Cherry syrup.
Pineapple syrup.
Peach syrup.
Raspberry syrup, etc. etc.

The syrup of banana will have to be made with the artificial flavor similar to that given with the flavoring extracts.

Simple syrup	1 gallon.
Extract of banana . . .	1 ounce.
Citric acid	½ "

Lemon Syrup.

Extract of lemon . . .	1½ ounce.
Citric acid	2 "
Simple syrup	1 gallon.

Orange Syrup.

Extract of orange . . .	2 ounces.
Citric acid	1 "
Tincture of saffron . . .	½ "
Simple syrup	1 gallon.

Catawba Syrup.

Catawba wine	1 quart.
Citric acid	1 ounce.
Simple syrup	1 gallon.

Coffee Syrup.

Extract of coffee . . .	4 ounces.
Simple syrup	1 gallon.

Rose Syrup.

Extract of rose	2 ounces.
Liq. carmine	q. s.
Simple syrup	1 gallon.

Orgeat Syrup.

Blanched sweet almonds . .	2 pounds.
Crushed sugar	2 "
Water	1½ pint.
Simple syrup	6½ "
Extract of bitter almonds . .	½ ounce.
Orange-flower water . . .	2 "

Beat the almonds to a pulp with the water; strain the milk thus made, and add the other ingredients, and strain.

Sarsaparilla Syrup.

Simple syrup	1 gallon.
Oil of sassafras	1 drachm.
" aniseed	½ "
" gaultheria . . .	1 "
Caramel to color . . .	q. s.
Syrup of gum Arabic to make it froth	q. s.

The sarsaparilla syrups for drinking and soda waters are so only in name and flavor, none of the medicine entering into them; though if the syrup slightly medicated be needed, it may be made as follows:—

Sarsaparilla Syrup.

Sarsaparilla root, bruised . .	1 pound.
Liquorice " " . .	1 "
Sassafras bark, " . .	½ "
Water	2 gallons.
Sugar	20 pounds.

Boil gently and strain off 12 pints, and make into syrup, when flavor with

Oil of sassafras	½ ounce.
" aniseed	¼ "
" gaultheria . . .	¼ "

Sherbet Syrup.

Banana essence or extract . .	1 ounce.
Sherry wine	1 pint.
Simple syrup	6 "

Vanilla Syrup.

Extract of vanilla . . .	3 ounces.
Simple syrup	1 gallon.

Cream Syrup

Can be made of fresh cream, in the proportion of 1½ pounds of sugar to 1 pint of cream; or, if the cream cannot be had, a syrup can be made of the almond milk, as directed in orgeat syrup.

The bottlers of soda-water cannot well afford syrups so concentrated. They are accustomed to use a syrup with less sugar, say 12 pounds of sugar to 1 gallon of water; and the three most used are lemon, ginger, and sarsaparilla.

Lemon Syrup. (For bottlers of soda-water.)

Essence of lemon . . .	1 pint.
Tartaric acid	1 pound.
Simple syrup	15 gallons.

Ginger Syrup. (For bottlers of soda-water.)

Essence of ginger . . .	1 pint.
Simple syrup	10 gallons.

Sarsaparilla Syrup. (For bottlers of soda-water.)

Syrup	10 gallons.
Caramel	1 pint.
Oil of sassafras	1 ounce.
" aniseed	½ "
" gaultheria . . .	½ "

Raspberry Syrup. (For bottlers)

Extract of raspberry (artificial)	1 pint.
Tartaric acid	1 pound.
Syrup	25 gallons.
Liq. carmine to color . .	q. s.

And in this manner can the bottler of soda-water make any artificial fruit syrups, or any other syrup, from the formulas given.

Raspberry Vinegar.

Fresh raspberries . . .	12 quarts.
Acetic acid (from sugar) . .	10 ounces.
Water	10 pints.
Crushed sugar	25 pounds.

Mix the acetic acid with the water and stir with the fruit; let it rest for twenty-four hours; strain through hair sieve or coarse cloth, and boil with the sugar; skim and strain; let it boil gently. This process yields a very superior article, which will keep well and retain its natural flavor. For an ordinary syrup for the soda fountain, add a pint of white wine vinegar to a gallon of raspberry syrup, natural or artificial.

Fruit Jellies.

The making of jelly from fruit has some peculiarities that may well be mentioned, as in unskilful hands the product is not very good, either to the palate or the eye, from the fact of the improper boiling of the fruit juices with sugar, as a chemical change often takes place in the conversion of cane sugar into grape sugar by contact with the acid and the aid of heat. In making, as an example,

Currant Jelly,

Let the juice be extracted from the fruit by pressure, and to each pint of juice add two pounds of crushed sugar; and when the sugar is dissolved, and it has come to a gentle boil, it is finished, and can be strained through flannel and put up in jars or glasses.

And so with nearly all fruits of an acid nature, long boiling or insufficient sugar will injure them and alter their flavor. There are now many of these jellies used for medicinal purposes, and they call for the attention of the pharmacist.

In making the fruit jellies from the artificial flavors it is necessary for the manufacturer to have recourse to gelatine, to supply the mucilage usual in all fruits. Therefore, to each quart of jelly, an ounce of Cooper's or other good gelatine is first dissolved in the water and strained, and then the sugar added in the proportion of 2 pounds to the pint of liquid, when the flavor and required color can be added. For instance—

Quince Jelly.

Sugar	8 pounds.
Quince essence	1 ounce.
Water	4 pints.
Gelatine	2 ounces.
Liq. carmine	$\frac{1}{2}$ "
Citric acid	1 "

To the 4 pints of water add the gelatine; let it stand twelve hours, then heat to dissolve, and strain; boil the sugar with the water to see if perfectly clear, when remove from the fire, and as it cools dissolve the acid in it and put in the quince essence, and color, when it can be put up in jars. In coloring be careful to give one appropriate to the name of the jelly.

Fruit Acid.

Citric acid	8 ounces.
Pure water	8 "

In frequent use for flavoring and for syrups.

Kissengen Water.

Chloride of sodium . . .	8 ounces.
Bicarbonate of soda . . .	2 drachms.
Sulphate of soda . . .	2 "
Phosphate of soda . . .	15 grains.
Muriate of ammonia . . .	5 "
Carbonate of magnesia . .	½ ounce.
Sulphate of magnesia . . .	2 "
Water	2½ pints.

½ pint to 10 gallons C. A. water.

Vichy Water.

Sulphate of potash . . .	3 drachms.
Chloride of soda . . .	7 "
Sulphate "	2 "
Carbonate "	4 ounces.
Phosphate "	½ drachm.
Carbonate of ammonia . .	10 grains.
Water	3 pints.

½ pint to 10 gallons C. A. water.

Seidlitz Water.

Chloride of soda . . .	3 ounces.
Carbonate "	1 "
Sulphate "	2 "
Chloride of lime	1 drachm.
Water	2 pints.

½ pint in 10 gallons C. A. water.

Spa Water.

Chloride of soda . . .	2 ounces.
Carbonate " . . .	1 "
Sulphate of magnesia . .	2 "
Sulphate of iron . . .	30 grains.
Water	2 pints.

½ pint to 10 gallons C. A. water.

Saratoga Water.

Chloride of soda . . .	4 ounces.
Bicarbonate " . . .	1 "
Iodide " . . .	20 grains.
Bromide of potash . . .	10 "
Carbonate of magnesia . .	2 ounces.
Carbonate of iron . . .	30 grains.
Water	2½ pints.

½ pint to 10 gallons C. A. water.

These imitations of the spring waters are usually put into a 10-gallon fountain, and charged in the usual manner with the carbonic acid gas.

SECTION II.

LIQUORS, CORDIALS, DOMESTIC WINES, ETC.

THIS subject should be treated scientifically, and to some extent must be to enable a practical person to understand the nature of the ingredients needed to manipulate the many pleasant and useful articles in the catalogue of a complete apothecary store; articles now looked for and generally kept in all well-conducted establishments, and they should be of better quality and character than those found among the lower class of liquor dealers.

On the subject of fermentation and distillation a large volume might be written without exhausting it, for it has occupied the minds of men for many centuries. Osiris among the Egyptians, Bacchus among the Greeks, and Noah among the Jews, according to tradition, taught man the art of cultivating the grape, and the making of wine, but they knew nothing of the science or the causes of alcoholic fermentation, for it is scarcely more than a century since chemistry discovered its true causes under the genius and labor of Lavoisier, who was the first to establish the fact that sugar, or substances capable of being formed into sugar, were alone capable of entering into spiritous fermentation.

If sugar be dissolved in an excess of water, and excluded from the air, it will remain without change, but if air be admitted it is decomposed, becoming brown and sour as aceteous fermentation ensues. If, however, any organic substance be brought into contact with it, being in a state of change, the sugar will participate in the process: blood, glue, white of egg, or flesh that has begun to putrefy, will excite fermentation, but yeast is the most remarkable; vegetable albumen, gluten, liquorice, and substances that exist in all fruits, contain large quantities of nitrogen. Thus, when fruit is crushed, the sugar of the juice in contact with the albumen or gluten and exposed to the air absorbs oxygen rapidly, and the sugar passes into fermentation actively, and alcohol is formed.

Oxygen is necessary at the commencement of the decomposition, which, once begun, extends throughout the mass without requiring any further action from the air. This is what may be called a natural fermentation. The fermentation of yeast may be called an artificial fermentation. The starch of the grain is converted into sugar by the action of heat and moisture, and the malt thus made is infused in water, and allowed to ferment, when the yeast is precipited, and if purified will be found to be a grayish-yellow granular substance without taste or smell, insoluble in water or alcohol, though the former when warm takes up about $\frac{1}{400}$th of it.

A solution of pure sugar which has been made to ferment by the addition of yeast furnishes no new yeast, but there remains, after the process, a portion of that originally mixed in an altered inoperative condition, should the quantity be exactly adequate to the decomposition of the sugar, or in an operative state should the quantity have been originally excessive.

But if the fermentative liquor contain vegetable albumen or gluten or both, as is usually the case with the sweet juices of fruits, these substances become changed into ferments in the course of the fermentation induced by the yeast, and being superfluous, so to speak, they remain entire at the end, and can be collected and used in another operation.

On this principle is founded the increased production of yeast, which can be done artificially in this manner: Take two parts of barley malt and one of wheat flour, and stir into six parts of water until thoroughly mixed, put upon a slow fire until the temperature is at 160° Fahr., when sugar will form, then pour into a flat dish, and when cooled down to 60° Fahr. stir in a gill of good beer yeast, which will soon cause brisk fermentation. This makes a good yeast for bakers' or family use, and which, if kept in a cool place, will keep good and active for ten days or more.

There are so many fruits grown in our country, which are frequently abundant and cheap, and nearly all of which will make good wines if properly gathered and manipulated, that it is very desirable to know something about the processes for making them. I have made most excellent wines from blackberries, strawberries, raspberries, currants, elderberries, pie-plant or rhubarb, and many native grapes of different kinds. It would occupy too much space to give the processes for all of them, but when I describe one it will serve as a guide to all.

Blackberry Wine.

To each quart of blackberries put a half pound of pure sugar, and let it stand a day, when strain through a hair sieve, and for each pint of juice take a pint of warm water, and pour over the marc from the first straining, when strain again to get all the substance of the berries; mix the juices and put into a barrel or keg, and when it begins to ferment, put into the cellar for equality of temperature, which should be about 66° Fahr. Let the keg be nearly full, so that the froth may run from the bung, which will carry off a great deal of the impurities; let it also be kept perfectly quiet. If there be any tendency to become sour, add a little strong syrup. When the fermentation has ceased, bung it up tight, or if possible rack it off from the lees into another keg, and stop it perfectly tight, and keep it until mid-winter, when it can be bottled or drunk as desired.

Should the wine be sound and of good flavor, it is advisable to put into each bottle an ounce of syrup, unless it be already sweet.

When grapes are used let them be gathered when perfectly ripe, and in clear weather, and all the unripe and imperfect berries be picked from them. Press out the juice, and put into a keg or barrel completely full, and keep in a cool, quiet place with the bung out, so that as the fermentation proceeds the froth will exude, and can be kept full by adding syrup or more juice when the fermentation ceases, and if the wine be not sour bung it up, and keep it some months before bottling. It is always best to rack it off if it be convenient, and in bottling to add a little syrup to each bottle.

Raisin Wine.

A very good wine can be made of raisins, and in England much of the port that they so much affect is made of them, flavored with elderberries and colored to suit. To 50 pounds of good raisins cleaned from stalks and dirt, cut or crushed, but not washed, put about 12 gallons of soft water, keep it about the temperature of 70° Fahr.; in about two weeks let the wine be separated by straining into a keg with 1 gallon of syrup, and half a pound of cream of tartar. After a month's rest let it be racked off and put in the cellar. If wanted to imitate port wine put into it about 4 pints of elderberry or prune juice.

Should it not ferment promptly, add a gill of good

yeast, and should there be a tendency to sour add some rectified spirit. Raisins also make a good

London Sherry.

Raisins	50 pounds.
Water	10 gallons.
Cider	5 "
Syrup	½ "
Argols	½ pound.
Wild-cherry bark	½ "
Rectified spirit	1 pint.

The process is much the same as above given for raisin wine.

Champagne Wine.

Cider (sound and good)	10 gallons.
Sugar	5 pounds.
Argols, white	¼ "
Tincture of orris	¼ "
Rectified spirit	4 pints.
Yeast	¼ "
Acetic ether	1 ounce.

This is bottled before fermentation ceases with an ounce of simple syrup to each bottle, and well corked and tied with wire.

To imitate—

Burgundy Wine.

Raisins, crushed (good)	5 pounds.
Cider	10 gallons.
Red tartar	¼ pound.
Tincture of rhatany	¼ "
Sugar	3 "

Let it fill the keg and be kept at a moderate temperature of about 70° with a rag over the bung hole to keep out insects. When the fermentation has ceased let it be racked off, bunged up, and add one ounce of essence of bitter almonds, and put away for some weeks or months if convenient.

To imitate—

Malaga Wine.

Good raisins (crushed) . .	10 pounds.
Cider (good)	10 gallons.
Rectified spirit	½ "
Syrup	½ "
Elder flowers	½ pound.
Acetic ether	1 ounce.

Proceed as for Burgundy, and color with a little caramel.

To imitate—

Claret Wine.

Cider (good and sound) . .	10 gallons.
Rectified spirit	1 "
Tincture of rhatany . . .	½ pint.
" orris root . .	½ "
Tartaric acid	2 ounces.

Proceed as for the Burgundy wine.

Champagne Cider.

Cider, good and sound . .	10 gallons.
Syrup	½ "
Rectified spirit	2 pints.
Argols	2 ounces.

Let it stand twenty-four hours, and bottle, adding to each bottle a drachm of bicarbonate of potash; cork well and wire.

To imitate—

Cider.

Apple essence	2 ounces.
Sugar	6 pounds.
Water	10 gallons.
Yeast	1 gill.

Put into a keg with bung out, and in a warm place. Do not put the bung in till fermentation ceases.

Ginger Ale.

Syrup	2 gallons.
Extract of Jamaica ginger .	8 ounces.
Water	4 gallons.
Tartaric acid	4 ounces.
Yeast	1 gill.

Let it ferment a few days, and bottle after fermentation ceases.

Spruce Beer.

Molasses	1 gallon.
Water	5 "
Essence of spruce (heavy) .	4 ounces.
Yeast	1 gill.

Let it ferment a little before bottling.

Root Beer.

Lignum root (bruised) . .	2 pounds.
Sassafras bark	1 "
Molasses	1 gallon.
Water	5 "
Yeast	1 gill.

Boil the root and bark in the water, strain, and add the molasses; let it ferment, and add a little oil of wintergreen.

Mead.

Honey	½ gallon.
Light-brown sugar . . .	4 pounds.
Water	6 gallons.
Essence of lemon . . .	½ ounce.
Essence of almonds . . .	½ "
Yeast	1 gill.

Let the flavors be rubbed up with a portion of the sugar, when mix and ferment as for the spruce beer.

Pineapple Cider

Can be made like the imitation cider, using the pineapple essence instead of the apple.

To make an imitation of—

Cognac Brandy.

Rectified spirits (proof) . .	10 gallons.
French oil of cognac . . .	1 drachm.
Tincture of orris . . .	4 ounces.
Acetic ether	2 "
Tincture of vanilla . . .	1 "
Caramel, to color . . .	q. s.

Let the spirit be pure and thoroughly rectified, and the oil of cognac dissolved in a little strong alcohol before mixing with the spirit. Let the whole stand a month before using.

To imitate—

Apple Brandy.

Rectified spirits	10 gallons.
Glycerine	4 ounces.
Tartaric acid	2 "
Apple essence	1 "
Syrup	1 pint.

To imitate—

Holland Gin.

Rectified spirits	10 gallons.
Spirit	2 pints.
Glycerine	½ "
Spirits of nitrous ether . .	¼ "
Oil of juniper (fresh and pure) .	1 ounce.
Alcohol	1 pint.

Dissolve the oil in the alcohol, and add it to the other mixed ingredients; let it rest a month before using.

To imitate—

Jamaica Rum.

Rum essence (ether) . . .	1 ounce.
Glycerine	8 "
Rectified spirits	10 gallons.
Caramel, to color . . .	q. s.

Baume de Vie. (Balsam of Life.)

Rhubarb root	2 ounces.
Aloes	1 "
Gentian	1 "
Saffron	½ "
Agaric	1 "
Zedory	1 "
Rectified spirit	2 gallons.

Let the ingredients be bruised, and macerate with the spirit two or three weeks, when filter. An excellent tonic aperient, given in a dose of a wineglassful.

To make a good—

Wine Bitters.

Bruised gentian root	8 ounces.
" orange-peel	4 "
" cardamom seed	1 "
" grains of paradise	1 "
" cinnamon	1 "
" sp. saffron	1 "
" cloves	1 "
Rectified spirits	5 gallons.
Simple syrup	½ "

Macerate the spirits with the ingredients for two or three weeks, filter, and add the syrup.

Aromatic Herb Bitters.

Lemon-peel	4 ounces.
Orange-peel	2 "
Angelica-peel	½ "
Orris-peel	½ "
Aniseed	½ "
Cardamom seed	½ "
Allspice	½ "
Cloves	½ "
Cinnamon	½ "
Sage	½ "
Marjoram	½ "
Ger. camomile	½ "
Caramel, to color	q. s.
Rectified spirits	4½ gallons.
Syrup	½ "

Let the whole macerate together for a month, when filter.

LIQUORS AND CORDIALS.

Essence d'Absinthe.

Wormwood herb . . .	1 pound.
Oil of wormwood . . .	½ ounce.
Simple syrup	½ gallon.
Rectified spirits	2½ "

Put the finely divided herb with the spirits for two weeks, filter, and add the oil dissolved in ½ pint of alcohol; add the syrup, and color green with a few currant leaves.

Aniseed Cordial. (Huile d'Anisette.)

Oil of star aniseed . . .	½ ounce.
Syrup	1 gallon.
Rectified spirits . . .	2 "
Tr. saffron	1 drachm.

Cinnamon Cordial. (Huile de Cannella.)

Oil of Ceylon cinnamon . .	35 drops.
Extract of rose	½ ounce.
Syrup	1 gallon.
Rectified spirits	2 "
Caramel, to color . . .	q. s.

Clove Cordial. (Huile d' Œilett.)

Oil of cloves	20 drops.
" Ceylon cinnamon . .	5 "
Syrup	3 quarts.
Rectified spirits	2 "
Caramel, to color . . .	q. s.

Curaçoa Cordial.

Oil of bitter orange	½ ounce.
" neroli	½ drachm.
" Ceylon cinnamon	5 drops.
Syrup	1 gallon.
Rectified spirits	2 "
Tincture of saffron	½ ounce.

Ginger Cordial.

Extract of ginger	2 ounces.
Syrup	½ gallon.
Rectified spirits	1½ "
Caramel, to color	q. s.

Mint Cordial. (Huile de Minthe.)

Oil of peppermint	½ ounce.
Alcohol	1 pint.
Syrup	5 "
Rectified spirits	10 "

Color light-green.

Orange-Flower Cordial.

Oil of neroli petals	1 drachm.
" bitter orange	1 "
Alcohol	1 pint.
Syrup	1 gallon.
Tincture of saffron	½ ounce.
Rectified spirits	1½ gallons.

Perfect Love Cordial.

Extract of cloves	½ ounce.
" lemon	2 "
" rose	¼ "
" nutmegs	¼ "
Syrup	1 gallon.
Rectified spirits	1½ "

Noyau Cordial. (Huile de Noyau.)

Oil of bitter almonds	1 drachm.
" neroli petals	½ "
" bitter orange	½ "
Alcohol	1 pint.
Syrup	1 gallon.
Rectified spirits	1½ "

Pineapple Cordial.

Pineapple, extract	2 ounces.
Extract of lemon	½ "
Syrup	1 gallon.
Rectified spirits	1½ "

Rose Cordial.

Extract of rose	2 ounces.
Syrup	1 gallon.
Rectified spirits	1½ "

Color with liquid carmine light red.

Strawberry Cordial. (Ratafia de Frambois.)

Juice of fresh strawberries	1 pint.
Syrup	½ gallon.
Rectified spirits	½ "
Color with liquid carmine	q. s.

Vanilla Cordial.

Extract of vanilla . . .	2 ounces.
Syrup	1 gallon.
Rectified spirits	1½ "
Color with caramel . . .	q. s.

Usquebaugh. (Aromatic cordial.)

Oil of cloves	2 drachms.
" aniseed	1 "
" coriander	1 "
Extract of ginger . . .	1 ounce.
Alcohol	1 pint.
Rectified spirits	1½ gallon.
Syrup	1 "
Caramel to color.	q. s.

Rum Shrub.

Extract of orange . . .	1 ounce.
" lemon . . .	1 "
Citric acid	1 "
Syrup	1 quart.
Jamaica rum	2½ gallons.
Caramel to color . . .	q. s.

Vinegar.

Vinegar can be made from so many things that economy can be practised in having a simple apparatus to make it. In a keg or barrel arrange a false bottom with a number of holes bored in it. Place it three or four inches from the bottom, tapping it at that part for spigot. Break up charcoal about the size of walnuts, fill the keg or barrel half full, bore small holes of about a quarter of an inch all around the sides above and within a few inches of the false bottom, slanting them downwards. Break up more charcoal about the size of peas, and nearly fill the vessel, then place a perforated board upon it and a piece of canvas over that so that the liquid can pass slowly and evenly through the charcoal; lastly fit on a cover over the top.

First pass through the barrel a few gallons of good, strong vinegar, then mix 1 pint of whiskey with 12 pints of water, and pass it slowly through, and it will be converted into vinegar by the time it reaches the bottom. The juice of fruit, cider, tomatoes, etc. etc., can all be used for the purpose.

The action of the air upon the liquid finely divided by the porous substance, and in a warm atmosphere will soon convert the liquid into vinegar; the temperature should be about 100 Fahr.

Sugar and water, the settlings of molasses barrels, diluted with water, can be used to make this vinegar. Let them stand a few hours, adding a little yeast for fermentation, when pass through your percolater or generator, and they will make excellent vinegar.

SECTION III.

FLAVORS AND PERFUMES FOR SEGARS AND TOBACCO.

TOBACCO, so universally used by savage and civilized, from the time of Sir Walter Raleigh, in the sixteenth century, is said to have been introduced into Great Britain by him on his return from Virginia. Since that time it seems to have rapidly increased in use, for at the present time it is one of the greatest articles of commerce, as the United States and the West Indies produce annually nearly 500,000,000 of pounds, and it is estimated that the consumption of that amount of vegetable material by combustion would produce 5,000,000,000 pounds of carbonic acid gas; a large contribution to the constant demand upon the atmosphere for that valuable gas by the vegetation of the world.

In the analysis of tobacco leaves there are found nicotine, gum, malic acid, resin, albumen, malate of ammonia, sulphate of potassa, chloride of potassa, phosphate of lime, starch, silica, etc. Nicotine is the peculiar active principle, and is an exceedingly powerful substance, only one part being in a thousand parts of the leaf, but that one part gives the quality to tobacco that causes so much pleasure in its use.

Segars, snuffs, and tobacco are generally perfumed and flavored, and particularly the tobaccos that are grown in our Southern States that have a strong narcotic flavor when smoked or chewed. The tobacconist uses a number of perfumes for his flavoring, the most prominent are—

Ambergris,	Calamus root,
Ambrette,	Orris root,
Benzoin,	Tonquin beans,
Cedar-wood,	Valerian root,
Rhodium wood,	Cascarilla bark,
Santal wood,	Vanilla beans,
Musk,	Tolu,
Civet,	Storax,
Oil of bergamot,	Oil of roses,
" lemon,	" cassie,

Oil of lavender,	Oil of cloves,
" verbena,	" rhodium,
" nutmeg,	" rose geranium, etc.

The perfumes for snuffs vary according to taste, and are usually a combination of several of these ingredients, either in powder, in tincture, or the essential oil. In perfuming a quantity of snuff the perfumes are generally mixed with a small portion of the snuff, and then incorporated into the mass by sieving or other means. The tinctures I have given of almost all of these drugs can be used for this purpose, and are about a suitable strength. Many tobacconists keep a supply of mixed essences to perfume their snuffs to the taste of their customers. Some of them are made by the following formulas:—

Oil of lemon	1 ounce.
" cloves	½ "
" nutmegs	¼ "
Tincture of Tonquin	1 pint.

Or—

Oil of bergamot	2 ounces.
" lavender	1 "
" cloves	½ "
Tincture of orris	1 pint.

Or—

Oil of bergamot	1 ounce.
" cassia	1 drachm.
" rose geranium	½ ounce.
Tincture of Tolu	1 pint.

Or—

Oil of calamus	¼ ounce.
" cinnamon	¼ "
Tincture of Tonquin	1 pint.

Or—

Oil of rose	½ ounce.
Tincture of musk	2 "
" ambergris	2 "
" ambrette	10 "
" Tonquin	2 "

A few drops of any of these essences will perfume a pound of snuff, and from the ingredients given can also be made a powder that can be used in the same manner, though I do not think it so desirable, as it adulterates the snuff more or less.

For segars and smoking-tobacco many of these ingredients can be used, and usually in the form of essence. But when the desire is to improve the flavor of a strong tobacco, and that is the usual object of a perfume, some other preparation may be useful.

As Virginia tobacco and tobacco classed with it contain the most nicotine, and are on that account very strong, it is advisable to steam them by injecting steam into a barrel containing the loosely packed leaves. Or it is soaked over night in salted water to extract some of the rank flavor and dark color, and when dry enough to make into segars it can be perfumed with an essence something like this:—

Tincture of cascarilla	6 ounces.
" Tonquin	4 "
" Tolu	2 "
" orris	2 "
" valerian	2 "
Oil of nutmegs	½ "
" cloves	¼ "
" rhodium	1 drachm.

There are a number of flavors sold called Yara, Havana, or Spanish flavors, that are generally made by procuring the tobacco of fine quality, and making a strong fluid extract or tincture with diluted alcohol, and perfuming with some of the odors I have enumerated.

For chewing-tobacco the use of perfumes is very limited, as many that would be pleasant to the nose and to the palate when burned, are not agreeable in the mouth; so that the flavor has to be such as is of pleasant taste, such as liquorice and other pleasant drugs. Of the manner of curing and manufacturing tobacco for chewing, I cannot pretend to give particulars, as they vary with each manufacturer; each endeavoring to make it of a flavor original or peculiar to himself, or he has a variety, each with its particular name and flavor, by mixing different growths of tobacco and varying the flavor.

And here I cannot forbear giving my strong disapproval of the use of this narcotic herb in any and every form, for although the practice of smoking has become so general among all nations, it really does great harm. Some seek in tobacco-smoke an agreeable narcotism, others imagine it beneficial to their health; but to most people smoking is merely a dreamy recourse against *ennui*, which ere long becomes an indispensable stimulant. The filthiness of the habit, the offensive odor which persons under its influence emit from their mouths and clothes, the stupor it often occasions, as well as the sallow complexions, black and carious teeth, and impaired digestion, all prove the great consumption of tobacco to have a most evil influence upon mankind, akin to the dreadful evil of the excessive use of ardent spirits.

SECTION IV.

WEIGHTS AND MEASURES.

FOR measuring liquids, an instrument called an hydrometer is used, which is usually a graduated glass tube, having a hollow bulb towards its lower end, terminating in a smaller bulb weighted with mercury; the instrument sinks or rises according as the fluid is heavier or lighter than distilled water, which is marked 0 as a standard.

That for alkalies has been frequently referred to, and illustrated elsewhere, and gives the approximate strength of the solution of alkalies at the standard temperature of 60° Fahrenheit, and is generally sufficiently correct.

The alcoholometer, or hydrometer for spirits, is very much the same, except that alcohol, being much lighter than water, the instrument sinks the deeper as the spirit increases in strength.

Spirits in the United States are sold by the proof gallon, which contains 50 per cent. of alcohol, and the proof is reckoned from that point, but called 100, but which is really double the strength. Thus, alcohol marked 95° is 90° over proof. The 90 is added to the 100, making 190, and divided in half makes the 95 per cent.

There are other and more correct instruments for ascertaining the strength of spirits than the glass hydrometer, but which are much more expensive. That of Gender's is made of silver, and has an accompanying thermometer, graduated with three scales, and graded from the standard of 60° Fahr., showing, as the temperature of the liquid rises or falls from that point, how much to add or to subtract from the degree marked on the hydrometer.

For example, suppose the spirit to mark 32° with the hydrometer, and the temperature to mark by the thermometer 6° above the 60° or standard, then the 6° is to be deducted from the 32° indicated by the hydrometer, and shows the spirit to be 26° above proof. If, on the other hand, the thermometer shows 6° below the 60°, then the 6° is added to the 32°, and the spirit will be 38° above proof.

Thus, in the formulas of this work, spirits and alcohol have been given the degrees mentioned as thus above proof, according to these calculations; and when rectified spirits are called for, proof spirit is intended, and if not at hand can be made of 95° alcohol, in the proportion of 9 parts of alcohol to 7 parts of pure water, using the rectified or Cologne spirits.

The terms used for dry measure or weights allude to those used by the apothecary, or a modified Troy weight, as per table.

APOTHECARIES' WEIGHT.

Pounds.	Ounces.	Drachms.	Scruples.	Grains.
℔	℥	ʒ	℈	gr.
1	12	96	288	5760
	1	8	24	480
		1	3	60
			1	20

APOTHECARIES' MEASURE.

Gallon.	Pint.	Fluidounce.	Fluidrachm.	Minim.
Cong.	O	f℥	fʒ	♏
1	8	128	1024	61440
	1	16	128	7680
		1	8	480
			1	60

FRENCH DECIMAL WEIGHTS.

Names.	Equivalent in grammes.	Equivalent in Apothecaries' Weight.			
		lb.	oz.	dr.	gr.
Milligramme . . .	.001				
Centigramme . . .	.01				
Decigramme . . .	.1				1.5
Gramme	1.				15.4
Decagramme . . .	10.			2	34.
Hectogramme . . .	100.		3	1	43.
Kilogramme, or Kilo .	1000.	2	3	1	14.
Myriagramme . . .	10000.	26	9	4	20.

FRENCH DECIMAL MEASURES.

Names.	Equivalent in litres.	Equivalent in Apothecaries' Measure.
Millilitre	.001	16.2318 minims.
Centilitre	.01	2.7053 fluidounces.
Decilitre	.1	3.3813 fluidrachms.
Litre	1.	2.1135 pints.
Decalitre	10.	2.6419 gallons.
Hectolitre	100.	
Kilolitre	1000.	
Myrialitre. . . .	10000.	

In all cases in this work, when the drop or drops are ordered, the minim or measured drop is intended, or the 60th part of a fluidrachm. The actual drop of oils or fluids is very uncertain, and varies between 60 and 120 in the fluidrachm.

SECTION V.

MISCELLANEOUS FORMULAS.

As a secondary part of this work it may be useful to give the recipes, formulas, and character of many articles for the pharmacist or perfumer; that though they may not be actually essential, may yet prove very useful.

In this department it is not intended to give general recipes, but only such as are likely to be of service in his business and applicable to the numerous uses contingent thereto.

Almond Powder for the Hands.

Almonds (blanched and powdered)	1 pound.
White Castile soap (dried and powdered)	8 ounces.
Orris root (powdered) . .	2 "
Pumice stone (fine powdered) .	6 "
Essential oil of almonds . .	2 drachms.

Sieved all together into a fine powder.

Useful for cleansing, softening, and whitening the hands.

Alum Soap. (Detersive Toilet Soap.)

White soap (by cold process) .	5 pounds.
Powdered alum	½ "
Olive oil	2 ounces.

This soap is cut into shavings and dissolved by

heat, and the oil and powdered alum stirred in. Perfume to suit. It has the property of whitening the skin.

Aromatic Candles for Perfuming Apartments.

Melt camphor and balsam of Peru with the stearine or with whatever material the candles may be made; or impregnate the wicks with perfume, by steeping them in some aromatic tincture and drying them.

Antiseptic Soap for Preserving Birds, Animals, Anatomical Preparations, etc.

Curd Soap	2 pounds.
Carbonate of potash . . .	¼ "
Arsenic	½ "
Camphor	¼ "

Dissolve the soap with a small portion of water in a marine bath, when add the other ingredients previously powdered and mixed together.

Areca Nut Tooth Paste.

Charcoal of the betel nut . .	8 ounces.
Powdered cloves . . .	1 "
" cinnamon . . .	1 "
" orris	2 "

Made into a paste with honey.

This paste has fine properties as a whitener of the teeth.

Ambergris Wine.

10 drops of tincture of ambergris added to 1 gallon of claret or Burgundy wine improves the bouquet very much.

Arrack (Imitation).

An half drachm of benzoic acid added to a quart of New England Rum, of good age, will imitate this favorite tipple.

Annealing Glass Vessels.

In order to guard against any imperfection in the annealing of glass retorts and other apparatus used by the perfumer and chemist, it were well to put them in a vessel with oil, and raise the heat to the boiling point, when, after being boiled for a quarter of an hour, and suffered to cool very gradually, they will be found well tempered.

Augia Sinensis. (Chinese Varnish.)

This very useful balsam, of a greenish, turpentine-like consistence, used by the Chinese as a varnish or lacker, is perhaps one of the best and most durable known, and might be imported and used in this country with great advantage, as it can be colored any color, and is susceptible of a very fine polish.

Japan Lacker.

The lacker or varnish used by the Japanese is procured from the rhus vernix or swamp sumach, cultivated in Japan and growing wild in this country. The trunk of the tree is wounded, when the juice which flows soon blackens in the air; when purified and colored it affords this celebrated varnish.

Amalgams for Filling Teeth.

One part of grain gold or silver is treated in a crucible with two parts of mercury, and stirred with an iron rod until combined. When cold enough to handle, the excess of mercury can be pressed out by straining through a piece of chamois leather. These are a durable stopping for cavities in teeth.

Anotta Coloring for Butter.

Roco seed	1 pound.
Carbonate of potash . . .	2 ounces.
Water	2 pints.

Let the seed be ground to a coarse powder, and boiled with the water for half an hour; add the salt of tartar; when strain and bottle. Owing to the impurities of the anotta of commerce, this article can be made of much better quality by using the seed.

AROMATIC AND MEDICATED BATHS.

Aromatic Bath.

Lavender, thyme, and rosemary, of each	8 ounces.
Cloves and peppermint, of each .	½ "

Macerate in warm water for two hours; strain and add to an ordinary bath.

Alkaline Bath.

Carbonate of soda (crystal) .	6 ounces.
Borax.	1 "

Dissolve in a quart of hot water.

This is the proper quantity for an ordinary bath of 30 gallons.

Sea-Water Bath.

Muriate of soda	2 pounds.
Sulphate of soda	1 "
Chloride of lime	½ "
" " magnesia . .	½ "

Dissolve in about 2 gallons of warm water, and add to an ordinary bath of 30 gallons.

Camphorated Bath.

Tincture of camphor	. . .	1 ounce.
" " benzoin	. . .	½ "
Cologne water	. . . .	2 "

Drop slowly into an ordinary bath, and it will be found very refreshing, as it is a fragrant tonic and cosmetic.

Emollient Bath.

Barley meal	. . . .	1 pound.
Bran	. . . . . .	2 "
Borax	. . . . .	1 ounce.

Dissolve in two quarts of warm water, and add to an ordinary bath. Well adapted to soften the skin.

Perfumed Bath.

Cologne water	. . . .	3 ounces.
Rose "	. . . . .	1 pint.
Tincture of vanilla	. . .	½ ounce.

Mix the Cologne and tincture, and add to the rose-water by degrees, and put into an ordinary bath.

Milk Bath.

Marshmallow flowers	. . .	½ pound.
Hyssop herb	. . . .	¼ "
Bran flour	. . . . .	4 "

This mixture added to an ordinary bath will be found a good substitute for a milk bath, which is very expensive.

Sulphuretted Bath.

Sulphuret of potash . . .	2 ounces.

Dissolved in a quart of warm water, and added to an ordinary bath.

Blonde Liquid for Bleaching the Hair.

Muriatic acid	2 ounces.
Aqua ammonia	½ "
Rose-water	1 pint.

This mixture applied to dark hair is said to change it to a flaxen hue, as will also a solution of sulphide of cadmium.

Blacking for Shoes (Liquid).

Ivory black	50 pounds.
Cod-liver oil	1 gallon.
Oil of vitriol	10 pounds.
Powdered gum senegal . .	1 "
Molasses	4 gallons.
Vinegar	15 "

Grind the ivory black and gum and oil with a portion of the vinegar; add the molasses, and pour in very slowly the oil of vitriol while stirring, and, when combined, add the balance of the vinegar.

Blacking for Shoes (Paste).

Ivory black	25 pounds.
Molasses	2 gallons.
Oil of vitriol	4 pounds.
Cod-liver oil	4 gallons.
Vinegar	6 "
Powdered gum Arabic . .	½ pound.

Let all the ingredients be mixed together (except the oil of vitriol) and ground into a paste, when the vitriol is slowly stirred in, and let it be stirred every day for a week before using or boxing, to insure a perfect combination.

Brushes of Root for the Teeth.

Root brushes for the teeth are prepared from liquorice root, selecting pieces of about half an inch in thickness, scraping off the outer bark and slitting one end, for about half or three-quarters of an inch, with repeated slits, to form a brush, and then immersing them in a solution of liquid carmine or a decoction of Brazil wood to color them.

Bronzing Liquid (for Iron).

Blue vitriol	1	ounce.
Spirits of nitre	½	"
Tincture of chloride of iron	½	"
Aqua fortis	¼	"
Water	1	"

Dissolve the blue vitriol in the water, and add the other ingredients separately.

In using, the iron articles should be made bright and clean, and this liquid should remain on them for about a day, and be then wiped off, and a coat of lacker put on them while warm; the appearance can be improved by a little color in the lacker.

Bougies and Catheters.

These useful surgical appliances are made of a cylindrical web of cotton and saturated several times with the following varnish, each time drying by moderate heat, when they can be polished with tripoli and oil.

India-rubber Varnish for Catheters.

Caoutchouc	8 ounces.
Amber	4 "
Linseed oil (boiled) . . .	12 "
Spirits of turpentine . . .	4 "

The India-rubber is cut into small pieces, and dissolved in the hot oil, adding the amber and turpentine while cooling.

Bunion and Corn Plasters.

These plasters are made of various substances, as leather, felt, amadou, etc.; the white felt being the most common. In preparing these the felt is stretched upon a frame or a partition, and first coated with a solution of dextrine, and when dry with four or five coats of fine isinglass in solution of 6 ounces to 1 quart of water.

Those of chamois leather or of amadou are prepared in the same manner. They are cut with a hole in the centre to allow the head of the corn or bunion to be free from the pressure of the shoe.

Hungarian Corn or Bunion Plaster.

Diachylon plaster . . .	4 ounces.
Beeswax	2 "
Gum galbanum	1 "
Olive oil	1 "
Verdigris, in powder . . .	1 "

The powdered verdigris is stirred into the other ingredients previously dissolved together by heat. This is usually formed into sticks, and applied to soft leather of proper size for the corn or bunion.

German Corn Plaster.

Galbanum plaster . . .	4 ounces.
Black pitch	2 "
Sal ammoniac	½ "

Stir the powdered sal ammoniac into the melted plaster; this is also used for warts.

Corn Solvent.

Salts of tartar (desiccated) .	1 ounce.
Bole Armenia	½ "
Resin ointment	1 "

This is spread upon kid, the exact size of the corn or bunion, and after some hours the feet are put into warm water, and the corn will be found soft enough to pick out with the fingers. Care must be taken to keep the solvent off the surrounding skin, as it is quite caustic.

Chilblain Lotion.

Alum	½ ounce.
Camphor	1 drachm.
Cucumber juice	2 ounces.

Chilblain Ointment.

Powdered galls	1 ounce.
Resin ointment	3 "

Another—

Spermaceti ointment . . .	2 ounces.
Sugar of lead	1 drachm.
Glycerine	½ ounce.

Lotion for Chapped Hands.

Borax	2 drachms.
Glycerine	2 "
Honey	2 "
Rose-water	4 ounces.

Cerate for Chapped Hands.

Spermaceti	2 ounces.
Glycerine	½ "
Sal ammoniac	1 drachm.

Calledermic Powder for Whitening the Skin.

Powdered marshmallow root .	2 ounces.
Carbonate of soda . . .	2 "
Barley meal	12 "

Used as a soap powder.

Lotion for Scurf on Infants' Heads.

Borax	¼ ounce.
Glycerine	½ "
Rose-water	3 "

Applied once a day it will soften the scurf, and it will come off, and also prevent its forming again.

Brilliantine for the Hair.

Veal fat	4 ounces.
Spermaceti	2 "
Castor oil	2 "
Oil of almonds	½ drachm.
" bergamot	2 "
" cloves	1 "

Ointment for Barber's Itch.

Spermaceti ointment . . .	2 ounces.
Lac sulphur	2 drachms.
Vermilion	1 "
Rose-water.	½ ounce.

Liquid for Bleaching Sponges.

Muriatic acid	2 ounces.
Sulphuric "	1 "
Water	2 pounds.

Let the sponges be well washed, and freed from sand and stones, and while wet put into this liquid, and after three or four hours taken out and washed in clean water until they are free from acid; lastly, dry in the shade. If not white enough the process can be repeated.

Cement for China, Glass, etc.

Isinglass (finest) . . .	2 ounces.
Gum ammoniac	½ "
" mastic	1 "
Alcohol	1 "

Let the isinglass swell in 8 ounces of water for about six hours; pour off the water, when apply heat to dissolve it. Rub up the gum ammoniac with the dissolved isinglass until mixed, then strain. Dissolve the gum mastic in the alcohol by aid of heat, strain, and mix the two liquids. To be kept in well-corked bottles. When wanted for use, warm the bottle of cement in hot water, and let the articles to be mended also be warmed.

Collodion Cement.

Powdered nitrate of potash .	2 drachms.
Concentrated sulphuric acid .	3 "
Carded cotton	10 grains.

Mix the nitrate of potash with the acid in a porcelain capsule, and gradually add the cotton, and stir for a few minutes; wash it thoroughly in water free from all acid, when pull it apart and dry by moderate heat, taking care not to come too near the fire, as it is a species of gun-cotton; dissolve it in a little rectified sulphuric ether and a portion of alcohol, and it will form a strong adhesive cement, perfectly transparent and colorless.

India-rubber Cement for Leather, etc.

India-rubber	2 drachms.
Chloroform	2 fl. ozs.
Gum mastic	½ ounce.

Shred the rubber and dissolve in the chloroform, when add the mastic in powder. Useful to join leather or rubber to leather, etc., and it will make leather water-proof.

Cement for Meerschaum, Marble, Alabaster, etc.

White of	4 eggs.
Quicklime	2 ounces.

Makes a useful luting when spread on muslin and applied to joints, etc.

Cement for Stone, etc.

White sand	4 ounces.
Litharge	½ "
Linseed oil	q. s.

Made into a soft putty, and put in the joints, soon becomes hard.

Cloux-Fumantis.

Under this name aromatics are made into small sticks, and burnt to perfume apartments.

Powdered benzoin	2 ounces.	
" santal	2	"
" olibanum	1½	"
" cascarilla	1	"
" charcoal	7	"
" nitre, cinnamon, and cloves, each	1	"

Made into three-inch sticks, with mucilage of gum tragacanth.

Carmine.

Cochineal (ground)	1 pound.	
Salts of tartar	½ ounce.	
Powdered alum	1¼	"
Fish glue	½	"
Water	8 gallons.	

Boil the cochineal with the salts of tartar for about twenty minutes, remove from the fire, and stir in the powdered alum. After standing about an hour, the clear liquor is decanted into another boiler, and the isinglass added after being dissolved in about a quart of warm water; and when it boils, and the carmine rises in coagulum, it is removed from the fire and stirred for about fifteen minutes, when the carmine will precipitate; when the liquor is decanted off, and the precipitate dried on a filter. The liquor still retains a good deal of color, and can be used to make rouge by coloring talc, or can be made into vinaigre rouge, and bottled.

Carthamus, or Rouge Vegetal.

Safflower, from which this fine rouge is obtained, contains two coloring principles. The yellow matter is first washed out by putting it into a bag and kneading it under water until no more color can be extracted. The flowers are then put into a cullender, and water in which carbonate of soda is dissolved poured slowly through them, until they become yellow. The liquor is then acidulated with citric acid, when the fine coloring matter is precipitated upon some finely levigated talc placed in the bottom of the copper. The color will be more or less brilliant according to the amount of talc used.

Crinogen, to promote the Growth of the Beard.

Veal fat	1 pound.
Tincture of cantharides . .	1 ounce.
" vanilla . . .	1 "
Oil of petit-grain . . .	½ drachm.

Chlorine Tooth-wash.

Chlorate of potash . . .	1 ounce.
Tincture of myrrh . . .	1 "
" aquilla bark . .	½ "
" orris . . .	1 "
Orange-flower water . . .	12 "

An excellent dentifrice and mouth-wash.

Castillian Tooth-paste.

White Castile soap (powdered) .	2 ounces.
Cuttle-fish bone " .	1 "
Precipitated chalk " .	5 "
Honey	q. s.

Perfume with oils of lavender and cloves, and color red with liquid carmine.

Crême Neige. (Snow Cream.)

Spermaceti	4 ounces.
White wax	2 "
Oil of benne	10 "
Rose-water	2 "
Glycerine	1 "
Extract of rose (No. 1) . .	1 drachm.

A very pleasant cosmetic cream for all irritations of the skin.

Capuchin Powder, to destroy Lice on Head or Body.

Powdered cevadilla seed . .	1 ounce.
" parsley " . .	1 "
" tobacco " . .	1 "
" starch " . .	1 "

Compound Chamomile Powder, to destroy Bedbugs.

Powdered Persian or red chamomile . . .	2 ounces.
" black pepper . .	1 "
Flowers of sulphur . . .	1 "

Detersive Lotion for Cleansing the Hair.

Borax	1 ounce.
Bicarbonate of soda . . .	½ "
Camphor	1 drachm.
Glycerine	½ ounce.
Rose-water	1 quart.
Alcohol	2 ounces.

Dissolve the camphor in the alcohol, and add to

the other ingredients previously mixed. A pleasant and useful wash for the hair.

Diamond Dust for the Hair.

White smalts are well washed and rubbed into a coarse powder in an iron mortar, and put into neat paper boxes holding about a quarter of an ounce.

Gold Dust for the Hair.

Florem leaf, such as is used in common gilding, is rubbed to a coarse powder in a Wedgwood mortar, and put into small paper boxes, and neatly labelled.

Silver Dust for the Hair.

White leaf or Dutch metal is rubbed in a mortar, and finely divided, and put up in neat boxes holding about a drachm.

Disinfecting Segars.

The tobacco with which the segars are filled, is saturated with an aromatic tincture similar to that given for perfuming and flavoring segars in a former chapter.

Liquid Drier for Varnish, Paints, etc.

Sulphate of zinc	4 ounces.
Black oxide of manganese . .	1 pound.
Linseed oil	3 quarts.
Spirits of turpentine . . .	1 gallon.

The first two ingredients are to be boiled with the oil for two hours, when the oil is poured off clear, and turpentine added.

Drier in Powder for Paint, etc.

Sulphate of zinc (desiccated)	.	4 ounces.
Sugar of lead "	. .	4 "
Litharge	. . . . .	2 pounds.

Mixed and ground into a fine powder, it dries and hardens paint very well.

Essence of Soap or Shaving Liquid.

White shaving cream	. . .	4 ounces.
Alcohol, 80°	. . . .	8 "
Liquor potassa, U.S.P.	. .	2 drachms.
Rose-water	. . . .	8 ounces.
Oil of cassia	. . . .	10 drops.
" bergamot	. . .	20 "

Dissolve the soap in the rose-water and potash lye, and add the alcohol in which the oils are dissolved.

Evaporating Lotion for Headache.

Solution of acetate of ammonia	.	1 ounce.
Sulphuric ether	. . . .	½ "
Cologne water	. . . .	1 "
Orange-flower water	. . .	1½ "

Another—

Aromatic vinegar	. . .	2 ounces.
Tincture of camphor	. . .	½ "
Sulphuric ether	. . . .	½ "
Rose-water	. . . . .	3 "

Elaidic Acid.

When oil or oleic acid is treated with hyponitric acid, a beautiful white crystalline substance is obtained; that being well washed to free it from all acid, it could be used by the perfumer in cerates, cold cream, cosmetics, etc., to great advantage.

Eye Paint, or Kohol.

When camphor is burnt, and the smoke condensed and collected, it can be formed into a paste, and used as the Eastern ladies do, by applying it to the eyelids to give a brilliant effect to the eyes.

Eye Salve.

Citrine ointment	1 drachm.
Spermaceti ointment . . .	2 ounces.

Used for all diseases of the eyelids.

Eye-water.

Acetate of zinc	20 grains.
Acetic acid	5 drops.
Camphor-water	2 ounces.
Rose-water	8 "

A useful wash for inflamed eyes, and in the ophthalmia of infants or adults.

Eau de Cologne. (Cheap.)

Oil of bergamot, lemon, orange, rosemary, of each . . .	1 ounce.
Oil of cloves	1 drachm.
Tincture of orris	4 ounces.
Alcohol	1 gallon.
Water	3 pints.

Elixir of Rose for the Teeth.

Tincture of rhatany . . .	2 drachms.
" camphor . . .	1 "
" cochineal . .	2 "
Otto of roses	10 drops.
Rose-water, triple . . .	6 ounces.

English Tooth Powder.

Prepared chalk	4 ounces.
Pumice, finely powdered . .	1 "
Camphor	½ "
Oil of spearmint . . .	½ drachm.

Ethereal Aromatic Tincture. (Stomachic and Anti-Spasmodic.)

Cinnamon, nutmegs, and cloves, of each	2 drachms.
Vanilla	1 "
Castor	½ "
Alcohol	12 ounces.
Sulphuric ether	4 "

Macerate for ten days. Dose, a teaspoonful.

Essential Salt of Lemons for Removing Fruit Stains, Iron-Mold, etc., from Linen.

Oxalic acid	½ ounce.
Cream of tartar	1 "

Powder separately and mix. To use, a small portion is dissolved in warm water and applied, and the part is well washed in pure water.

Freckle Wash.

Sal ammoniac	1 drachm.
Glycerine	1 ounce.
Rose-water	15 "

Apply night and morning with a fine sponge.

Fly-powder to Destroy Flies.

Cobalt, black pepper, and brown sugar, of each	1 ounce.

Fly-paper to Destroy Flies.

Coarse paper is saturated with a solution of cobalt and sugar, and dried.

Frankincense.

Gum olibanum	2 ounces.
" benzoin	½ "
" myrrh	½ "
Prepared charcoal . . .	5 "

Powdered together; this is the formula for that used in the churches.

Ferruginous Pomade for Darkening the Hair.

Veal fat	1 pound.
Yellow wax	4 ounces.
Oil of benne	8 "
Sulphate of iron . . .	6 drachms.
Pyrogallic acid	4 "
Rose-water	1 ounce.
Oil of cloves	2 drachms.
" lavender	4 "

Melt the fat, wax, and oil together, and rub up the sulphate of iron with a portion of the water and stir in; dissolve the pyrogallic acid with the rest of the water, and add lastly the perfumes.

Frigorific or Freezing Mixture. To Cool the Water of Receivers in Distillation, etc. etc.

Muriate of ammonia. Sulphate of soda.

These substances in coarse powder are kept separate, and when wanted equal parts are thrown separately into the refrigerator or upon the ice in the ice-cream freezer.

French Tooth Powder.

Sugar of milk	4 ounces.
Carbonate of magnesia . .	1 "
Powdered pumice . . .	½ "
Sulphate of quinine . . .	¼ "
Powdered orris-root . . .	2 "
Oil of peppermint . . .	1 drachm.
" cassia	½ "

Furniture Polish.

Gum shellac	1 ounce.
" copal	½ "
Wood naphtha	4 "
Strong alcohol	12 "

This is for light-colored woods. If wanted for dark woods add a drachm of dragon's blood; polish with an oiled rag.

Another for Varnished Furniture.

Beeswax	1 ounce.
Linseed oil	4 "
Alcohol	5 "

Dissolve the wax in the oil by aid of heat.

Furniture Oil.

Boiled linseed oil	4 ounces.
Oil of lavender	½ "
Acetic acid	2 "
Alcohol, 95°	1½ "

If wanted dark, color with alkanet root.

Another for Renewing Furniture.

Pale linseed oil	8 ounces.
Shellac varnish	4 "
Wood naphtha	4 "

Put on the furniture, and after an hour it is well rubbed to restore the polish, remove scratches, etc.

Furniture Cream.

Linseed oil (pale) . . .	4 ounces.
Strong vinegar	2 "
" alcohol	2 "

Gelée Cosmetique or Curling Fluid.

Carrageen moss	½ ounce.
Eau de Cologne	1 "
Extract of millefleur . . .	1 "
Water	1 pint.

The moss is swelled over night in the water, heated to dissolve, strained and perfumed, and colored red with liquid carmine, or yellow with tincture of saffron. A very good mixture for the hair.

Glycerine Jelly for Chapped Hands.

St. Vincent arrow-root . . .	2 drachms.
Water	½ ounce.
Glycerine	½ drachm.
Tincture of saffron . . .	½ "
Eau de Cologne	½ "

Let the arrow-root be mixed with the water clarified by heat, when stir in the glycerine, color and perfume. It should be transparent, and is a very pleasant form for using glycerine.

Glove Cleaner.

Rectified benzine	4 ounces.
Oil of lavender	¼ "

A pleasant and good cleaner.

Glove Cleaner. (French.)

Gum tragacanth . . .	½ ounce.
White Castile soap . . .	1 "
Rose-water	1 pint.
Tincture of musk . . .	10 drops.

Dissolve the soap in the water, put the gum in, and when swelled stir well to thoroughly mix, when strain and perfume. A valuable cleaner, as the gloves remain soft.

Ginger Beer.

Concentrated essence of Jamaica ginger . .	2 ounces.
The juice and rind of .	4 lemons.
White sugar . . .	2 pounds.
Water	1½ gallons.
Yeast	1 tablespoonful.

To be kept in a warm place for about two days, when it is strained and bottled if not wanted for present use.

Green or Elder-leaf Ointment.

Lard	2 pounds.
Suet	1 "
Fresh elder leaves . . .	2 "

Let the leaves be added to the melted grease, and stewed until they lose their color. Keep up the heat to evaporate the moisture, but do not let it boil. This is considered a cooling emollient for chafes, burns, etc.

Glue from Rice Flour.

Mix rice flour with cold water, and boil gently till clear, when it will be found a very useful cement for joining fine articles, pasting, etc.

Liquid Glue.

Good glue	4 ounces.
Muriatic acid	½ "
Sulphate of zinc . . .	½ "
Water	½ pint.

Break up the glue, put it in the water, let it swell for a few hours, heat to dissolve, when add the acid and sulphate of zinc; keep it hot for some hours, frequently stirring, and it will remain liquid when cold.

Mouth Glue.

Glue (best)	1 pound.
Sugar	¼ "

Let the glue swell in about a pint of water for some hours, pour off the excess of water, heat to dissolve, add the sugar, and when sufficiently evaporated pour on a marble slab and cut into squares. This is a very handy article, for it is dissolved in the mouth when wanted for use.

Gutta-percha Dressing.

Gutta-percha	1 drachm.
Chloroform	1 fl. ounce.

Spread upon muslin and applied to a wound it will form a water-proof dressing.

Gold-beater's Skin for Plaster.

The finest baudrouches are stretched upon a board, and one side coated with a solution of Russia isinglass, and when dry cut into squares, and enveloped.

Hand Powder, for Whitening the Hands.

White Castile soap (powdered)	.	4 ounces.
Cuttle-fish bone "	.	4 "
Blanched almonds "	.	8 "
Orris-root . . "	.	2 "
Oil of cloves . . .	.	½ drachm.
" lavender . . .	.	1 "

Used as a soap powder, it has a great detersive and softening effect.

Hair Powder.

Starch, in fine powder .	.	1 pound.
Orris-root	.	1 ounce.
Oil of rhodium . . .	.	10 drops.

Hair Cream. (Crême de Noisettes.)

Oil of hazelnuts	.	1 pound.
Spermaceti	.	4 ounces.
Jasmine oil from flowers .	.	1 "

Drying Hair Wash for Moist Hair.

Cologne or lavender water .	.	4 ounces.
Borax	.	½ "
Rose-water	.	3 "
Tincture of cochineal .	.	½ "

Horse-Radish Mouth Wash.

Horse-radish root . . .	1 ounce.
Boiling water	1 pint.
Tincture of rhatany . . .	2 drachms.

Horse-radish is said to be a valuable remedy for sore gums, toothache, etc.

Horse-Radish Lotion for the Skin, etc.

Horse-radish root . . .	1 ounce.
Boiling water	1 pint.
Borax	2 drachms.

In this form horse-radish can be used to advantage for freckles, tan, etc.

Herbs and Flowers (to Preserve).

Recent and fresh flowers and herbs, intended for distillation, can be preserved for a long time, by packing them in a tight keg or barrel, with about one-fourth their weight of salt (well dried), placing a heavy cover on them to exclude the air, and keeping them in the cellar or other cool place.

Honey Water.

Rectified spirit 70° . . .	5 pints.
Extract of rose No. 2 . .	1 "
" jasmine " . .	1 "
Oil of lavender	2 drachms.
" bergamot . . .	2 "
" rosemary . . .	1 "
" cloves	1 "
" thyme	1 "

Tincture of musk . . .	4 ounces.
" Peru balsam . .	2 "
" orris-root . .	8 "

A very fragrant toilet water or perfume for the handkerchief.

Honey of Roses. (Confection.)

Red-rose leaves (dried and powdered)	4 ounces.
Clarified honey	¾ pint.

Useful as a vehicle for many articles.

Honey Mouth Wash.

Red-rose leaves (dried) . .	2 ounces.
Rose-water	8 "
Clarified honey	6 "

Immerse the rose-leaves in the water, and heat gently for two hours, when strain and add the honey. A very pleasant and useful wash for the mouth, gargle for sore throat, etc.

Hungarian Hair Dye (in two Preparations).

No. 1, Mordant.

Hydrosulphate of ammonia .	10 fl. drachms.
Liquor of potassa, U. S. P. .	2 " "
Rose-water	12 " "

No. 2, Dye.

Nitrate of silver (crystals). .	2 drachms.
Aqua ammonia	q. s.
Rose-water	2½ ounces.

This is a valuable hair dye, and gives a reliable and natural black or brown color; if a brown color is wanted, dilute No. 2 one-half.

Hair Oil. (Cheap.)

Cotton-seed oil	1 gallon.
Oil of bergamot	4 drachms.
" lemon	2 "
" cloves	1 "
" thyme	1 "

In this manner most of the cheap hair oils are now made. This formula can be used for bear's oil or antique oil. Colored red with alkanet it can be called rose hair oil, making some change in the perfume.

Iodinated Oil for Scalp Sores, etc.

Iodine	1 drachm.
Benne oil	1 pint.
Oil of lemon	2 drachms.
" almonds	½ "
" fennel	½ "
Carbolic acid	5 grains.

This will be found a very healing preparation for all diseases of the scalp.

Iodine Lotion. (Cosmetic.)

Iodine	10 grains.
Iodide of potash	20 "
Rose-water (triple)	1 pint.

A very serviceable lotion for pimples, pustules, itch, etc. etc.

Itch Ointment.

Spermaceti ointment	2 ounces.
Almond oil	½ "
Lac sulphur	½ "
Salt	1 drachm.
Oil of lemon, oil of almonds, and oil of neroli, of each	10 drops.

A pleasant and effective remedy.

Isinglass Plaster. (Court Plaster.)

This very useful article is made out by water-proofing the silk on one side with a solution of India rubber, in chloroform and tincture of benzoin, and then coating the other side with a solution of the best isinglass, of two ounces to a pint of water; two or three coats of which are put on with a flat camel's-hair brush, letting each coat dry before the next is applied. The silk is of three colors—white, pink, and black.

Indelible Ink for Marking Linen.

Nitrate of silver (crystal)	1 drachm.
Gum Arabic	20 grains.
Pyrogallic acid	10 "
Indigo	5 "
Distilled water	2 ounces.

Another that will not corrode the pen—

Chloride of platinum	½ drachm.
Sugar	10 grains.
Gum	10 "
Salts of tartar	5 "
Distilled water	10 drachms.

Another—

Gluten of wheat	½ ounce.
Acetic acid	½ "
Indigo	5 grains.
Lamp black	10 "
Water	4 ounces.
Oil of cloves	10 drops.

Ink, English Black.

Aleppo galls (bruised)	8 ounces.
Sulphate of iron	4 "
Gum Arabic, powdered	2 "
Water	1 "
Creasote	10 drops.

Let the galls be steeped in the water for about a day before the iron and gum are added. This makes a reliable black ink that will not fade.

Ink, Blue-black Fluid.

Aleppo galls (good)	10 ounces.
Sulphate of iron	3 "
Gum senegal	2 "
Cloves (bruised)	½ "
Sulphate of indigo	1 drachm.
Sugar	1 ounce.
Water	1 gallon.

Put the bruised galls and cloves in the water, and stir frequently for two days, strain, and press out all the liquid, next put in the sulphate of iron, gum, and sugar, stir frequently until all is dissolved, strain again and add the sulphate of indigo. This is a good, permanent ink which will also copy well.

Invisible Ink.

Chloride of cobalt	5 grains.
" nickle	5 "
Distilled water	1 pint.

This solution written on white paper will not be visible, but when heated will turn green, and again disappear when cool.

Ink Powder.

Bruised galls	2 pounds.
Ground logwood	½ "
Copperas	1 "
White sugar	2 ounces.
Gum Arabic, powdered	4 "

Mix well together. Two ounces will make a pint of good ink.

Juniper Tar Pomade.

Juniper tar (limpid)	2 ounces.
Hard body	8 "
Pomade of Peru balsam	1 "
Oil of lavender	1 drachm.
" lemon grass	1 "
Tincture of musk	½ "

Juniper tar is a remedy for all eruptions, salt rheum, etc., of the scalp, and this is a pleasant mode of applying it.

Kalydor for the Skin.

Glycerine	1 ounce.
Borax	½ "
Orange-flower water	1½ pint.

Kaolin Cosmetic or White.

Kaolin	1 pound.
Corn starch	⅓ "
Honey-water	1 ounce.

The powder is made into a mass with water and moulded to suit the box intended for it, and when dry is smoothed off and packed with colored cotton.

Lavender Vinegar.

Oil of garden lavender (good) .	1 drachm.
Acetic acid (from sugar) . .	1 ounce.
Rose-water	1 pint.

Agitate the oil with the acid several times for about a day, gradually add the rose-water and filter. Thus can be made the vinegar of almost all perfumes.

Lime Juice Lotion.

Lemon juice (fresh) . . .	4 ounces.
Glycerine	2 "
Alcohol	2 "
Rose-water, triple . . .	1½ "

A very pleasant preparation for acne, freckles, itching, and irritation of the skin.

Lisbon Water.

Oil of Portugal	1 ounce.
" lemon	½ "
" rose	½ drachm.
" neroli, petale . . .	½ "
Alcohol, 80°	2 pints.

Once a very celebrated perfume, and it is exceedingly pleasant.

Extract of the Cedar of Lebanon.

Oil of cedar	½ ounce.
Alcohol	12 "
Tincture of vanilla . . .	2 "
Rose-water, triple . . .	4 "

Labdanum Pastils.

Gum labdanum	1 ounce.
" benzoin	½ "
Powdered charcoal . . .	2½ "

Made into cones with mucilage of gum tragacanth, dried and burnt to perfume apartments.

Lettuce Water. (Cosmetic.)

Lettuce leaves, fresh . . .	4 pounds.
Warm water	1 gallon.

Bruise the lettuce, and keep at a gentle heat for about three hours, when strain and add four ounces of alcohol to keep it. Used as a cosmetic and to allay irritation.

Lip Salve. (Italian.)

Butter of coco	2 ounces.
Oil of benne	1 "
White wax	½ "
Powdered alum	½ "
Vermilion	1 drachm.

Lycopodium Powder.

Lycopodium	1 ounce.
Oxide of zinc	½ "
Starch	3 "

For excoriations of the skin, to make new skin on sores, etc.

Lutes for Joints of Apparatuses, etc.

A useful lute for chemical apparatuses and distillation is made by mixing the white of egg with an equal quantity of water and thickening with slaked lime; it should be spread upon strips of muslin. It soon hardens, and will stand a great heat.

Another—
Liquid glue mixed with whiting and spread upon muslin is also a good luting for joints of stills, etc.

Another—
Linseed meal mixed with lime-water to the consistence of putty or thick paste is a useful lute.

May-dew Milk for the Complexion.

Red rose leaves	2 ounces.
Borax	½ "
Glycerine	1 "
Tincture of benzoin . . .	1 "
Rose-water, triple . . .	1½ pints.

Milk of Roses.

White soft soap	½ ounce.
Blanched almonds . . .	2 "
Rose-water, triple . . .	1 pint.
Liquid carmine	10 drops.

Mole Salve.

Diachylon plaster . . .	½ ounce.
Tartar emetic	1 drachm.
Croton oil	5 drops.

This plaster should be spread the exact size of the mole, and kept on until it suppurates, then remove and let heal; it may leave a slight scar.

Mosquito Lotion for Mosquito Bites, etc.

Aqua ammonia	1 ounce.
Glycerine	½ "
Rose-water	4 "

Musk Root or Sambul.

This root, which is imported from the East Indies, is often used as a perfume in essences and sachet powders; in the latter it is particularly useful, as it supplies bulk, and has the odor of musk in a great degree.

Mustard Essence.

Black mustard seed . . .	2 ounces.
Acetic acid	2 "
Spirits of camphor . . .	8 "
Oil of rosemary . . .	1 "

Let the seeds macerate with the acid for two or three days; strain and add the other ingredients. A useful embrocation in rheumatism, sprains, etc.

Myrrh Water. Mouth Wash.

Gum myrrh	2 drachms.
" Arabic	1 "
Alcohol	½ ounce.
Water	7½ "

A mouth wash and gargle.

Marine Cement, Water-proof.

India-rubber	1 ounce.
Shellac	2 "
Naphtha	4 "

Myrtle Pomade.

Lard (purified)	3 pounds.
Suet "	1 "
Oil of pimento	2 drachms.
" bergamot . . .	6 "
" neroli	2 "

Lacquer for Foil, Metal, etc.

Gum shellac	3 ounces.
" elemi	½ "
" sandarach	1 "
Alcohol, 90°	3 pints.

By having the alcoholic solutions of the different aniline colors, this lacquer can be colored any color desired. It is put on with a flat camel's hair brush, and the article warmed sufficiently to set it.

Palma-Rosa Pomade.

Lard (purified)	3 pounds.
Suet "	1 "
Oil of ginger grass . . .	½ ounce.
" lemon " . . .	2 drachms.
" geranium . . .	2 "
" cloves	2 "

Color light green.

Nipple Wash.

Nitrate of lead	½ drachm.
Nitrous ether	½ "
Glycerine	½ "
Tincture of rhatany	½ "
Rose-water	3½ "

Care should be taken to thoroughly wash off the nipples before nursing.

Peach Water.

Alcohol, 80°	2 pints.
Tincture of Tolu	2 ounces.
Extract of jasmine, No. 2 . .	4 "
" orange-flower, No. 2.	4 "
Oil of almonds (essential) . . .	1 drachm.

A very pleasant toilet water.

Pearls of Roses, or Perfumed Beads.

Red rose leaves, powdered . .	4 ounces.
Carmine	20 grains.
Tincture of musk . . .	1 drachm.
Mucilage of gum tragacanth .	q. s.

Made into spheres, perforated and dried, and strung as beads; when carefully made and polished they are pretty and of nice perfume; they can also be made of any other odor desired.

Polish for Shoes and Leather.

Gum tragacanth	2 ounces.
Isinglass	1 "
Beer	1 gallon.
Glycerine	1 pound.
Extract of logwood . . .	2 ounces.
Powdered galls	1 "
Copperas	2 "

Steep the logwood, galls, and copperas in the beer for some days; add the glycerine to prevent its getting too sour; strain and dissolve the gum and isinglass in the mixture, and if necessary strain again.

Perfume (cheap) for Pomade or Hair Oil.

Oil of bergamot	4	ounces.
" lemon	2	"
" cloves	1	"
" thyme	½	"

Another—

Oil of orange	4	ounces.
" rosemary	2	"
" pimento	1	"
" petit-grain	½	"

Another—

Oil of lemon	4	ounces.
" thyme	1	"
" lemon grass	2	"
" cloves	½	"

Another—

Oil of orange	4	ounces.
" caraway	1	"
" ginger grass	2	"
" cassia	½	"

Another—

Oil of bergamot	4	ounces.
" lavender	2	"
" cloves	1	"
" neroli	½	"

Populeum Pomade, or Ointment for Piles.

Poplar buds	4	ounces.
Lard	12	"
Honey	2	"
Suet	4	"
Powdered orris	1	"

Powder for Perspiring Feet.

Powdered alum	1 ounce.
" orris-root . . .	2 "
" rice	5 "

Powder for Fumigation.

Powdered olibanum, cascarilla, benzoin, cloves, cinnamon, of each	1 ounce.

Mixed together and burnt on stove or hot shovel to perfume apartments.

Parchment Paper.

Take heavy white printing paper and immerse a few seconds in a solution of sulphuric acid 6 ounces, water 1 ounce, and wash it in running water to free it from acid. Useful for tying over bottles and jars.

Preventive Lotion.

Carbonate of potash . . .	2 drachms.
Tannin	15 grains.
Rose-water	1 pint.
Liquid carmine	10 drops.

Phosphated Tooth Powder.

Phosphate of soda . . .	1 ounce.
Prepared chalk	12 "
Powdered orris	2 "
" myrrh . . .	½ "
" Bole Armenia . .	1½ "

Rhatany Tooth Paste.

Powdered rhatany . . .	2 ounces.
" myrrh . . .	½ "
" orris	½ "
Prepared chalk	3 "
Honey	q. s.

Razor Paste.

Levigated emery, jewellers' rouge, spermaceti ointment, of each . 1 ounce.

Rubbed into the leather of the strop.

Ratafia of Fruit.

Fruit syrup (any kind) . . .	2 pints.
Aromatic syrup	1 "
Rectified spirit	3 "

Color to suit.

Rasma, Turkish.

Orpiment	1 ounce.
Quicklime	8 "
Starch	4 "

A very quick depilatory but poisonous, and to be used with care.

Rancid Butter, to Remedy.

Knead it with fresh milk for some time, and then in cold water; butter is sometimes wanted as a vehicle for perfumes and drugs.

Sealing-wax, Red. No. 1.

Shellac	1 pound.
Venice turpentine (true) . .	8 ounces.
Vermilion	8 "

Another. Red, No. 2—

Rosin, fine yellow . . .	1 pound.
Shellac	½ "
Venice turpentine . . .	½ "
Vermilion	3 ounces.

Another. Black—

Colophony	4 ounces.
Venice turpentine . . .	1 pound.
Shellac	¾ "
Lampblack	q. s.

Shampoo Liquor.

Carbonate of ammonia . .	½ ounce.
" soda . . .	½ "
Rum	½ pint.
Water	1 "

Stye Lotion.

Camphor water	1 ounce.
Muriate of morphia . . .	2 grains.

Styptic to Stop the Bleeding of Wounds, etc.

Powdered alum, tannin, charcoal in fine powder, of each . . 1 ounce.

Tetter Ointment.

Citrine ointment	2 drachms.
Spermaceti ointment . . .	2 ounces.
Carbolic acid	5 grains.
Balsam of Peru	½ drachm.
Oil of lemon	10 drops.

Toothache Drops.

Hoffmann's anodyne . . .	½ ounce.
Oil of peppermint . . .	½ "
Sulphate of morphia . . .	10 grains.

Tricophalon Pomade.

Lard	1 pound.
Veal fat	2 "
White wax	4 ounces.
Oil of benne	4 "
" geranium	1 "
" verbena	1 "
" cloves	½ "

Varnish for Artists.

Gum mastic, in powder . .	4 ounces.
" copal (selected) . . .	2 "
Ground glass	4 "
Pale linseed oil	8 "
Rectified spirits of turpentine .	1½ pint.

The gums are put with the oil and glass in a glass flask or copper vessel, heated by sand-bath, and stirred till dissolved. The turpentine is added while cooling; the glass is used to facilitate the solution of the gums, and prevent them adhering to the bottom.

Varnish for Maps, Prints, etc.

Gum mastic	2½ ounces.
" sandrac	1 "
" camphor	½ "
Alcohol, 95°	8 "

Another for (ditto)—

Balsam of Canada	1 ounce.
Spirits of turpentine	2 "

The paper should be sized with a solution of isinglass, and dried before the varnish is applied.

Varnish or Lacquer for Gilt Wares.

Gum shellac	2 ounces.
" gamboge	1 "
Dragon's blood	1 "
Saffron	1 drachm.
Alcohol	1 pint.

Varnish for Waxed Tables, etc.

Beeswax	2 ounces.
Colophony	¼ "
Gum demar	1 "
Spirits of turpentine	1 pint.

This takes a fine polish with rubbing.

To facilitate the solution of gum copal it can be melted before a hot fire in a cullender, and suffered to drop into water, whence it is so finely divided that it will easily dissolve in turpentine, etc.

Gum shellac will also dissolve in spirits much easier if suffered to swell in ether a few hours.

Wart Pomade.

Soap cerate	1 ounce.
Powdered savin	1 drachm.
" verdigris . . .	1 "

Spread on leather the size of the wart, and keep on over night, and repeated if necessary.

Wig Paste to Fasten the Wig to the Head.

Isinglass	1 ounce.
Rose-water	8 "
Tincture of benzoin : . .	2 "
White turpentine . . .	2 "
Alcohol	4 "

The isinglass is dissolved in the rose-water, the turpentine in the alcohol and tincture, when the two solutions are mixed.

Vegetable Tincture for Darkening the Hair.

Green walnut hulls . . .	4 ounces.
Claret wine	8 "

This tincture has been long in use as a dye for the hair, and, if carefully used, it is good.

Omitted on page 77:—

Tincture of Orris.

Orris root in coarse powder .	2 pounds.
Alcohol	7 pints.
Water	1 "

Put the root with the water and two pints alcohol in a displacer, and pour in by degrees the balance of the alcohol.

INDEX.